חצי נחמה

STUDIES IN THE WEEKLY PARASHAH

Based on the Lessons of
Nehama Leibowitz

חצי נחמה

STUDIES IN THE WEEKLY PARASHAH

Based on the Lessons of
Nehama Leibowitz

MOSHE SOKOLOW

URIM PUBLICATIONS
Jerusalem • New York

Studies in the Weekly Parashah Based on the Lessons of Nehama Leibowitz

By Moshe Sokolow

Copyright © 2008 by Moshe Sokolow

Layout design by Satya Levine

Printed at Hemed Press, Israel. First Edition.

ISBN-13: 978-965-524-004-7

ISBN-10: 965-524-004-5

Urim Publications

P.O. Box 52287, Jerusalem 91521 Israel

Lambda Publishers Inc.

3709 13th Avenue Brooklyn, New York 11218 U.S.A.

Tel: 718-972-5449 Fax: 718-972-6307, mh@ejudaica.com

www.UrimPublications.com

Contents

Acknowledgements   9

Bereishit

Bereishit: Telling *Peshat* from *Derash*   15
Rashi's exegetical program

Noah: After You; No, After You   20
Dealing with changes in sequence

Lekh Lekha: Have No Fear!   24
An "orientation"

Va-Yeira: Meet Lot   28
In comparison with Avraham

Hayyei Sarah: The Grave Consequences of Speech   33
Negotiating for the Makhpelah Cave

Tol'dot: Eating One's Words   40
Man of field vs. man of tents

Va-Yetze': It's Quite "Natural" (Or Is It?)   45
Peshat vs. *derash* of Yaakov's dream

Va-Yishlah: Requiting Good Deeds   51
Derekh ketzarah: The way of ellipsis

Va-Yeshev: No Trivial Pursuit   57
When a man is an "angel"

Mikeitz: Ups and Downs   62
Rashi on ascending and descending

Va-Yigash: Life and Death are in the Hands of Language   67
Resolving ambiguities

Va-Yehi: Who Said What to Whom?   72
Anonymity, ellipsis and repetition in the Bible

Shemot

Shemot: *Peshat, Derash* and *Mashma'*   79
Rashi's exegetical terminology

Va-'era: It's Hard to Say   85
Moshe's speech difficulty

Bo: The Prerequisite to Ge'ulah   90
Dealing with contradictions

Beshallah: Filling in the "Gaps"   96
Peshat, derash and the missing links

Yitro: When Two Are One   103
Rashi's proficiency in Hebrew grammar

Mishpatim: Rashbam – More than Meets the Eye   108
Rashi vs. Rashbam: plumbing the depths of *peshat*

Terumah: It's Ibn Ezra's Turn   114
Ibn Ezra's exegetical program: *kabbalah* vs. *sevarah*

Tetzaveh: Rashi Was French, After All   118
Lexicography and French "glosses" (*le'azim*)

Ki Tissa': The Sin of the Golden Calf – A Biblical Whodunit
The major exegetes on Aharon's complicity   123

Va-Yak'heil: Who Turned Off the Lights?   127
Introducing the Karaites

**Pekudei: The Enterprise of the Mishkan and the Labor of Cosmic
Creation**   134
Melakhah vs. *avodah*; man as creator

Va-Yikra

Va-Yikra: Saying You're Sorry   143
Sefer ha-Hinukh: actions and intent

Tzav: It's *Deja Vu* All Over Again!   148
Comparing the *korbanot*

Shemini: You Are What You Eat: A Look at Kashrut   152
Yitzhak Arama and David Tzvi Hoffman

Tazria': Purity and Impurity, *Niddah* and Catharsis   157
Nehama and Yeshayahu Leibowitz and Joseph B. Soloveitchik

Metzora': "Beware of the Affliction"   162
Midrash vs. Maimonides; *tzara'at* as metaphor

Aharei Mot: Straying from the *Peshat*   167
Rashi's use of *al tikrei, gematria* and *notarikon*

Kedoshim: The "Body" of Torah   172
Gufei Torah and *Nekamah,* Malbim and Kant

Emor: Of Cows and Calves   177
Midrash, Maimonides, *Sefer ha-Hinukh* and Shadal

Behar: Finding Freedom in Servitude   181
Nehama on the search for truth

Behukotay: *Tokhehah;* Constructive Criticism   185
Sefer ha-Hinukh and *Keli Yakar* on rebuke

Bemidbar

Bemidbar: It's the Order That "Counts"   191
Rashi vs. Rashbam: Charting the order of march

Naso: What Does One Thing Have to Do with the Next?   196
Cassuto on connecting the textual "dots"

Beha'alotekha: Freedom from Responsibility?   200
Nehama and Shadal on "grumbling" and "hankering"

Shelah Lekha: "Man is Led on the Path He Wishes to Follow"
Nehama's *ahavat ha-aretz* and the calumny of the *meraglim*   204

Korah: The One versus the Many   208
Malbim and Nehama on *Korah va-'adato*

Hukkat: Fighting Fiery with Fiery   212
Peshat and *derash* and the *nehash ha-nehoshet*

Balak: Prophets and Sorcerers; Curses, Blessings and Discrepancies
A close look at Bil'am and a close reading of his text   217

Pinhas: The Danger Inherent in Zealotry   222
Rav Kook and the Netziv on vigilantism

Mattot: The First Halutzim   226
Moshe and the two-and-one-half tribes negotiate

Mas'ei: From Words to Sentences to Shakespeare   229
Nehama cites *Hamlet* to explain the sequence

Devarim

Devarim: Tough Words   237

    Rashi's Inclination to Indictment

Va-Et'hanan: Answering a "Wise Guy"   241
    Nehama and the *arba'ah banim*

Ekev: The Land of Israel: A Mixed Blessing   245
    Rashi's use of *mashal*; explaining the *shema'*

Re'eh: Rashi and Halakhah   249
    Hermeneutics and Targum Onkelos

Shof'tim: When Justice is Blind or Otherwise Doesn't See   254
    Rashi on repetition and redundancy

Ki-Tetze': Propinquity; Supplying the Missing Links   258
    Semikhut parashiyot

Ki-Tavo': Rashi and Philosophy   262
    Some thoughts on crime and punishment

Nitzavim: It's the *Tippehah* That Counts   266
    Rashi and *ta'amei ha-mikra*

Va-Yelekh: Elementary, My Dear Rashi   271
    Diagramming a *kal va-homer*

Ha'azinu: A Truly "Super" Commentary   276
    Keli Yakar on life and death

Ve-Zot ha-Berakhah: Changing the Lineup   280
    The order of blessing for Yaakov and Moshe

An Afterword   285

ACKNOWLEDGEMENTS

Nehama Leibowitz expressed her own view on the use and appreciation of Bible commentaries as follows:

> The use of commentaries must be very diversified.
>
> In some cases, the commentary stimulates us to recognize a problem in the text, which the student neither saw nor was sensitive to at all (and perhaps even the teacher would not have noticed it had he not read the commentary!). That is because the student is not accustomed to careful, critical reading: a close reading of the text that is sensitive to every syntactical puzzle, every linguistic anomaly, and every conceptual surprise.
>
> At other times, the commentary comes to provide an answer after the students attempted to resolve the problem by their own efforts – successfully or unsuccessfully.
>
> Sometimes, the commentary serves the teacher as a synopsis of a discussion that was held in class, in which case the students will not read it at all; rather the teacher will read it to the class or relate its content in words better understood by the students than those of the actual commentary.
>
> At other times, two different interpretations of the same issue will be placed before the students in order to educate them to weigh and distinguish the advantages and disadvantages of each commentary or in order to view the same issue from different perspectives.[1]

Although Nehama was eminently capable of novel interpretations of the Torah, she regularly eschewed them in favor of clarifying the existing, traditional ones. This was largely due to her innate modesty. She lived in a small and sparsely furnished apartment, sleeping in an alcove and working in a living room in which the most prominent furnishings were the metal shelves that housed multiple copies of her *gilyonot* (study sheets), which appeared weekly for thirty years (1941–1971) and for which she was awarded the prestigious Israel Prize in 1957.

---

[1] Nehama Leibowitz, *"Ha-meraglim."* In *Tokhniyot u-tekhanim be-hinukh u-vehora'ah,* edited by Hayyim Hamiel, 61. Jerusalem: 1983.

A study of these *gilyonot* (later adapted into the popular *Iyyunim* in the weekly portion, translated into English as *Studies in the Weekly Sidrah*) reveals citations from Mishnah, the Babylonian and Jerusalem Talmuds, Midrash, Maimonides, the exegetes of France, Spain, Provence, and Italy, Mendelssohn, Luzzato, Hirsch, Cassuto, Buber, and Kook, as well as Shakespeare, Gandhi, Steinbeck and Hayyim Nahman Bialik.

Nehama would pose questions about the Torah text and selected commentaries, and students from all parts of the world and all walks of life would respond. No correspondence course ever had so many diligent participants over so long a period of time; no other teacher could have sustained such interest for so long. Nearly twenty years after the *gilyonot* ceased to be formally circulated, her "students" would send in their replies to her questions and Nehama, red pen in hand, would read them, assess them, and return them.

For three generations of Torah students in Israel and the Diaspora, Nehama was *morateinu*, our teacher, par excellence. As noted, she brought to this daunting task a vast erudition in Jewish and secular classics, which she honed through regular forays into the stacks of the Hebrew University library, and a talent for pedagogy, which she refined through repeated expeditions into every corner of the country. Her energies and such resources as she had, which were devoted to her studies and to her students, remain her legacy. The quintessence of her pedagogic philosophy can be summed up in her own words:

> The most important thing is that the students should study Torah from all angles; search it out, and choose or reject interpretations – all providing that they engage in Torah out of love.[2]

■ ■ ■ ■

The Hebrew title of this book is a word play on the Talmudic adage *tzarat rabbim hatzi nehamah* (shared distress is a partial consolation). It simultaneously acknowledges my indebtedness to Nehama and underscores my independence from her. While I have chosen to replicate the methodology that she pioneered and used to great effect over many years, I have parted company with her in at least one significant way: unlike Nehama

---

[2] Nehama Leibowitz, *Torah Insights*. Jerusalem: 1995, 161.

in her *gilyonot*, I have sought to provide answers to the questions I have raised.

I was selective in the substance of these studies as well. First of all, I decided not to utilize the *Iyyunim/Studies* or the original *gilyonot*. What Nehama had already written needed neither repetition nor approbation. However, I used several of her lesser-known publications, particularly those that have never appeared in English. Foremost among these sources is the book of studies on Rashi that Nehama coauthored with Moshe Ahrend: *Perush Rashi la-torah: iyyunim be-shittato*, published by the Open University (1990). Second is *Limmud parshanei ha-torah u-derakhim le-hora'atam*, her systematic study of exegesis to the Book of Genesis, published by the World Zionist Organization (1975). All references to these and other works are annotated in the course of the book.

During the first year following Nehama's death, I published these studies weekly in her memory. I am indebted to Dr. Nahum Amsel, a veteran and distinguished student of Nehama, who accommodated this project on his website and who frequently supplemented these lessons with insights of his own.

I put a down payment on my personal debt of gratitude to Nehama in 1985, when I presented her with the manuscript of the index I had prepared (and later published)[3] to her *gilyonot*. Her reaction was typical: "Oh, my! Anyone reading this would think that I actually know something."

May this volume add to the collective gratitude of Nehama's myriad students who continue to benefit from all she knew and worked so hard to convey – with love.

יהי זכרה ברוך.

In taking note of blessed memories, I hasten to add that of my father, יוסף מרדכי בן אלתר נחמיה, Joseph Sokolow, Yeshiva College '42 and lifelong Mizrachist, who died on 26 Adar 5767, shortly after the final revision of this book was submitted. May my mother, my sisters and our entire family find some "nehamah," some consolation, in appreciating how much my father's love of Medinat Yisrael and of the Hebrew language sustained me in my study of Tanakh.

---

[3] *Mafteah ha-gilyonot*. New York: 1993.

I am indebted to Keren Keshet, long-time devotee of Nehama, for its support in bringing this book to publication. I am likewise grateful to Tzvi Mauer and the staff of Urim Publications for transforming an abstract idea into this handsome book.

My thanks, finally, to my wife, Judy, and to my son, Shalom, who read the entire manuscript with constructively critical eyes.

טוב עין יבורך.

Bereishit

BEREISHIT

Telling *Peshat* From *Derash*

RASHI'S EXEGETICAL PROGRAM

ഇ PREFACE

One of the most trying of all exegetical challenges is maintaining the distinction between *peshat*, the simple, straightforward meaning of the text, and *derash*, the meaning ascribed to the text in Midrash and Aggadah. The precise definitions of these two protean terms have generated most of the light – and a good deal of the heat – that has been shed on *parshanut ha-mikra* (Biblical exegesis). We will visit Rashi's most explicit statement on the subject, which occurs in his commentary to this week's *sidrah*, and analyze several instances of his consistency to his own principles.

Note: Nehama studied Rashi's use of Aggadic sources in minute detail in an essay that appears, in Hebrew, as an appendix to *Iyyunim hadashim be-sefer Shemot* (Jerusalem: 1978; 497–524), and in English as "Rashi's Criteria for Citing Midrashim" in *Torah Insights* (Jerusalem: 1995; 101–142).[1] We are certain to return to this subject often.

ഇ PART ONE: RASHI ON GENESIS 3:8

On this verse, Rashi supplements his commentary with the following "programmatic" statement, a declaration of his exegetical intent:

> There are many Aggadic midrashim that our Sages have already arranged, appropriately, in *Bereishit Rabbah* and other Midrashic anthologies. I have come only to [explain] the *peshat* of the text and

---

[1] Two critical studies, available in both English and Hebrew, on the use of the terms *peshat* and *derash* by Rashi, were written by Sarah Kamin and Benjamin Gelles.

those *aggadot* that resolve the language of Scripture, as "a word fitly spoken."

The phrase, "a word fitly spoken," originates in Mishlei 25:11, where it is the second half of a verse that begins, "Golden apples on a silver platter...." How does this citation denote Rashi's attitude towards the role of Aggadah? By way of analogy. Just as the value of golden apples – already great – can be enhanced further by placing them in silver settings, so can the value of good ideas, or good words, be enhanced by articulating them in a suitable context.

Rashi implies that Aggadic *midrashim* are like golden apples. Their intrinsic value, however great, can be enhanced even further if they are used in a suitable context: i.e., to resolve problems in the Biblical text.

As Nehama writes:

> The bibliographical note: "Our Sages have already arranged them in appropriate anthologies," shows that Rashi did not intend in this commentary to provide "an assortment of *midrashim*" or a rabbinic anthology. It is as though he were saying: Whoever is interested in studying *midrashim* for their own sake, let him not search in this commentary of mine, but let him go to the midrashic anthologies and look there. I, however (the *vav* being one of opposition), have come only to resolve repetitions and to answer questions rather than to adorn, beautify, or supplement Scripture (*Torah Insights*, 109).

We shall use Rashi's commentary to two verses in this week's *sidrah* in order to see this exegetical principle in action: What constitutes a problem in Scriptural language (difficulties can be linguistic, grammatical, logical, or philosophical), and what kind of Aggadah contributes to its resolution?

ഇ PART TWO: RASHI ON BEREISHIT 1:16

Rashi addresses himself here to a logical difficulty. The verse initially describes both luminaries [*ha-me'orot*] as *ha-gedolim* (large) and then proceeds, casually, to refer to one as *ha-gadol* (the large) and to the other as *ha-katan* (the small). Are both large or only one?

This very question is raised in the Talmud (*Hullin* 60b):

> Rabbi Shimon ben Pazi highlighted the contradiction: The verse says, "The two large luminaries;" how can it then say "the large and

16

small luminaries"? The moon said to God: Master of the universe, can two kings share one crown? He replied: Then go and diminish yourself. She replied: Master of the universe, shall I diminish myself for having spoken the truth? He replied: You may rule by day and by night.

This Aggadah attempts to resolve the difficulty in the Torah text by positing that the two luminaries were originally equal in size, but one of them – the moon – was subsequently diminished. In the process, it also explains a natural phenomenon, namely why the moon – unlike the sun – is visible both by day and by night.

An additional difficulty is perceived by the following Aggadah (cited in the anthology *Bet Midrash*). The verse specifically mentions "two luminaries," yet it names three: the sun, the moon, and the stars.

When God rebuked the moon and demoted it, some sparks fell off her onto the horizon and became the stars. Because the moon's light was diminished, it remained dark and even the stars did not shine as brightly as before – which is why they are called (in Hebrew): *kokhavim*, deriving from the word *le-khabot*, which means to extinguish.

According to this Midrash, the verse implies a common origin for all the luminaries, whereas Rashi appears to deny their common origin. According to Rashi (later in the same verse), the stars were appointed to console the moon over its diminished size.

The original difficulty in the text (two large luminaries, or one large and one small) could have been resolved by means of *peshat*, without resort to the Aggadah, by assuming that the first half of the verse designates the sun and the moon as the two largest luminaries, while the second half of the verse merely indicates that while larger than other luminaries (the stars) they were not necessarily of equal size to one another.

Indeed, the crux of the dilemma addressed by Nehama (in the aforementioned essay) is why Rashi utilizes *derash* when *peshat* explanations are readily available. Nehama explains that there are two schools of thought among the commentators on Rashi regarding this methodological quandary. One school stipulates that Rashi utilized *derash* only when he found the *peshat* lacking, while the other school says that Rashi was not beyond citing a *derash* "to magnify Torah and adorn it," i.e., for purely homiletic reasons, without thereby negating the *peshat*. We will seek to clarify this disagreement in the coming lessons.

✌ PART THREE: RASHI ON BEREISHIT 1:21: "THE TWO GREAT *TANINM*"

In this verse, we may discern two difficulties: one textual and the other contextual. The textual difficulty relates to the spelling of the word *taninm*; it is actually spelled *taninm* – without the *yod* that usually precedes the final *mem* of a plural noun. The contextual problem is that no other species is mentioned by name in this chapter; both land animals and birds are mentioned only as a genus. Why are the *taninm* different? To resolve these difficulties, Rashi uses the following Aggadah:

> Rabbi Yehudah said in the name of Rav: Whatever God created in His world, He created male and female. Even the straight Leviathan serpent and the crooked Leviathan serpent (cf. Isaiah 27:1) were created male and female. But if they had been able to procreate, they would have destroyed the entire world. What did God do? He castrated the male and froze [alt: salted] the female, preserving it for the righteous in the world to come (*Bava Batra* 74b).

This Aggadah accounts for the textual anomaly as follows: Since they were originally created male and female, they are entitled to a grammatically plural form; since only one of the species survived, however, the missing *yod* hints at the missing female. It also explains the contextual problem: The *taninm* warranted special mention because of their exceptional size and dangerous potential.

✌ EPILOGUE

Scholars have observed that in neither commentary does Rashi quote his Aggadic source verbatim. Indeed, Rashi's judicious editing of his sources (itself a significant exegetical consideration!) has often made their identification problematic. At times, scholars will differ on whether a particular comment is original to Rashi or borrowed from an earlier source. A most interesting example consists of his opening comment to the first verse of the Torah, which begins, "Rabbi Isaac said..." Until relatively recently, the aforementioned Rabbi Isaac was thought to have been Rashi's own father, and Rashi was praised for the filial piety he displays in starting his Torah commentary with his father's words. Today we know the words to be those of an older Rabbi Isaac, cited in a version of the Midrash *Tanhuma* whose text was first discovered in the nineteenth century.

NOAH

After You; No, After You

DEALING WITH CHANGES IN SEQUENCE

✍ PREFACE

Rashi is exceptionally sensitive to Biblical literary style and regularly comments on apparent deviations from convention. One such deviation concerns a series of related words (such as names of persons, places or things) that recurs within the Torah with a change in their sequence. Even though the discrepancies often appear to be insignificant – even trivial – Rashi assumes that they reflect profound truths.

✍ PART ONE: IN AND OUT OF THE "ARK"

If we compare the two verses that describe the entrance of Noah's family into the ark (6:18 and 7:7) with the two verses that describe their exit (8:16, 18), we will note the following discrepancy: The order in which they are instructed to enter – and in which they actually enter – is: Noah, his sons, his wife, his daughters-in-law. The order of departure, however, differs from instruction to practice: They are told to exit as Noah, his wife, his sons, and their wives, but they actually exit in the same order in which they entered.

Nehama explains their groupings by reference to Bereishit 2:24: "Let each man leave his parents and cleave to his wife," which she takes to mean that the normal disposition of a family groups couples together. That being the case, how do we account for the fact that fully three times (vs. 16 being the sole exception) they are grouped separately, by gender? Following the lead of the Midrash (both *Tanhuma* and *Bereishit Rabbah*), Rashi first states (6:18): "Men and women apart [because] they were forbidden to procreate," and later (7:7) adds: "They were forbidden to procreate because the world was in distress." After the threat had passed, however, they were instructed to exit husbands together with their wives, "since procreation was again permissible" (8:16).

As Nehama writes in explanation:

> Noah and his family were worthy to be spared from the disaster. It is prohibited, however, for an individual to tend to his personal concerns and live his own private life during a time that his community is confronting catastrophe. As our Sages have said (*Ta'anit* 11a): "While a community is in distress, let no one say, 'I will go home, eat and drink, and be tranquil.'" Therefore Noah and his family were forbidden to have sexual relations during the catastrophe. When they exited, though, they were permitted (*Rashi's Commentary on the Torah,* edited by Nehama Leibowitz and Moshe Ahrend, 223. Tel Aviv: Open University, 1990).

This explanation still leaves us wondering: If they were permitted to resume normal relations once the danger had passed, why did they still exit separately (8:18)? According to Rashi (9:9), their separate exits indicate their reluctance to procreate, lest a subsequent flood prove their new progeny to have been born in vain. Only when they secured a divine guarantee against a recurrence of the destruction (i.e., the rainbow) were they satisfied on that count.

How does Rashi presume to know when their reluctance was overcome? God's repetition of the imperative: "Be fruitful and multiply" (in 9:1, 7), along with His explicit promise to uphold His covenant with their descendants (9:9), imply that their future was now secure.

Rashi's explanation also illustrates how we may derive Biblical characters' motives from the text's description of their actions.

As Nehama has written:

> Changes in emphasis, approval and disapproval, and shades of meaning, are not imparted in the Torah through long-winded psychological explanations or verbose analysis, but through a subtle syntactical device or seemingly insignificant – but definitely unusual – turn of phrase, combination, order or choice of words (*Studies in the Book of Genesis,* Jerusalem: 1972, 121).

■ ■ ■ ■

Note: An ark [*teivah*] also features prominently in the story of Moshe.[1]

What distinction between the two arks does the Torah record in Bereishit 6:14 and Shemot 2:3?

Noah's ark was coated with pitch (tar) inside and out. Moshe's ark, however, was coated with pitch and clay. According to Rashi, Moshe's ark was coated with pitch on the outside and clay on the inside in order to spare him the malodor.[2]

❧ PART TWO: A BRIEF LOOK BACK

The *sidrah* of Ve-Zot ha-Berakhah gets short liturgical shrift. Not even allocated a Shabbat of its own, it is read (sometimes *ad infinitum!*) on *Simhat Torah*, often to the detriment of its content. We have an opportunity here to return, briefly, to that *sidrah* in order to pursue further the point we have been addressing thus far: Rashi's reactions to changes in sequence.

Both Yaakov (Bereishit 49:1–27) and Moshe (Devarim 33:1–29), before their deaths, blessed the Children of Israel. On both occasions, Zevulun received his blessing out of the chronological order of his birth. According to Rashi (Devarim 33:18), Zevulun, although born after Yissakhar, deserved priority because it was only by virtue of his labor that Yissakhar was able to study Torah. Hence, he is always blessed first.

Significantly, Rashi does not take note of this change in Bereishit, because the sequence there is uneven throughout, with Gad and Asher interrupting Dan and Naftali as well. Rashi in Devarim may also be influenced by the combination of Zevulun with Yissakhar in one blessing, which implies a specific connection between them.[3]

---

[1] By its rectangular dimensions (300x50x30) – as well as by its description as a *teivah* – Noah's ark was clearly a box, rather than a nautically designed vessel with a hull and keel. In the Mesopotamian "flood story" (the *Epic of Gilgamesh*), however, the hero, Utnapishtim, hires craftsmen who build a boat and sailors who navigate it. These distinctions underscore the fact that Noah survived the flood on account of his righteousness, not superior seamanship, and that his rescue was divinely engineered.

[2] The motif of sparing a righteous person a noxious odor is repeated by Rashi in the story of Yosef. Cf. Va-Yeshev, Part One.

[3] See our study of Ve-Zot ha-Berakhah for a more detailed analysis of this very point.

✃ PART THREE: ANOTHER ILLUSTRATION

Three verses list the names of the five daughters of Tzelafhad. In two of them (Bemidbar 26:33 and 27:1), the list is: Mahlah, Noah, Haglah, Milkah, Tirtzah. In the third (Bemidbar 36:11), however, the order varies: Mahlah, Tirtzah, Noah, Haglah, Milkah.

Why is the third list different? Abraham Ibn Ezra suggests that the discrepancy is due to the different contexts. The first two lists (along with Yehoshua 17:3) enumerate the women in order of their birth, while the third specifically relates to their marriages and therefore lists them in the order in which they were wed.

Rashi, too, attributes the discrepancy to different contexts, but arrives at a totally different conclusion. Unlike Ibn Ezra, Rashi believes that the third verse marks their order by age and that the sequence which appears in the other two verses is dictated by the order of "their wisdom."[4]

---

[4] While it is difficult to know for certain, it is likely that Rashi's association of the sequence with something other than marriage was influenced by the Talmudic prescription to marry off daughters in order of their birth (*Bava Batra* 120a).

For a Shakespearean perspective on the question, see our unit on Mas'ei (Part Four).

LEKH-LEKHA

Have No Fear!

AN "ORIENTATION"

❧ PREFACE

Let us begin with the cardinal directions in Biblical Hebrew. Logically, the easiest directions to follow are: in front of you, behind you, to your left, and to your right. The only prerequisite is which way do you face to begin? The Bible utilizes this logic, stipulating that the prime direction is east – a reasonable assumption given the prominence and importance of the sun. East, then, is *kedem* – literally, facing you, and the remaining cardinal directions are relative to that starting point: *ahor* – behind you (is west), *semol* – to your left (is north), and *yamin* – to your right (is south).

When Avraham and Lot separate from one another "to the left and to the right" (13:9), we have no need to speculate on where they stood and which way they were facing: they parted on a north-south axis. (Compare the translation, here, of *Targum Onkelos*, who renders "left and right" as *tzipona* – "north" – and *daroma* – "south.")

When Avraham chases after the four Mesopotamian kings who kidnapped Lot, the Torah says: "He pursued them to Hovah which is *semol* to Damascus" (14:15). Based on the explanation we have just provided, we understand that Hovah was to its north (without, as it were, having to rotate a map).

Indeed, the caption we utilized for the preface to this unit is an intentional pun. The verb "orient" ("to locate or place in a particular relation to the points of the compass") derives from the noun "Orient" (East), just as the cardinal Biblical directions are relative to the East.

✌ PART ONE: EAST IS EAST… OR IS IT?

In Bereishit 11:2, the Torah states that the builders of the Tower of Babel traveled "from *kedem*" to settle in a valley in the Land of Shin'ar. In Gen. 13:1, Lot is similarly described as traveling "from *kedem*" upon his separation from Avraham. The Midrash (*Bereishit Rabbah*) treats *kedem* in both cases as a metaphor:

- They traveled from *kedem*: Did they travel from the east to go east (cf. 10:30)? Rabbi Eliezer said in Rabbi Shimon's name: They betook themselves from the primordial One (*kadmon*) of the universe, saying: We desire neither Him nor His divinity.

- Lot traveled from *kedem*: He betook himself from the primordial One (*kadmon*) of the universe, saying: I desire neither Avraham nor his God.

Nehama explains:

> The similarity between the two *midrashim* is blatant. In both places, the Sages treat the word *kedem* homiletically, seeing in it an allusion that the ones who traveled – the Generation of Dispersion in the first case and Lot in the second – had distanced themselves, "betaken" themselves, from the Primordial One, i.e., the Creator. The [tower builders] could no longer bear His dominion so they rebelled against His divinity and His sovereignty. Lot, too, could no longer bear the lifestyle of Avraham who went about praying to God and building altars to His name (*Rashi's Commentary on the Torah*, 369).

Curiously, Rashi cites this interpretation to Lot's travels but not to those of the Generation of the Dispersion. If we refer back to the principle we first enunciated in Bereishit (and reviewed in Noah) regarding Rashi's relationship to his Aggadic sources, we will understand why.

Rashi claims to utilize Aggadah only to resolve a difficulty in the text that resists straightforward *peshat* interpretation. In the case of the tower builders, east is indeed the direction from which they came so there is no need to interpret *kedem* otherwise. In the case of Lot, however, we would have expected the Torah to say either that he traveled from Avraham or that he traveled from Beit-El (to the north), where we know they were then situated.

The appearance of *kedem* here is inconsistent with its literal rendition as east and, thus, an Aggadic interpretation is provided as well.

ଽ PART TWO: WHO'S AFRAID OF WHAT?

Each of three patriarchs was addressed by the words, *al-tira'* (fear not): Avraham in 15:1; Yitzhak in 26:24; and Yaakov in 46:3. The address to Avraham, however, is problematic. He has just won a resounding victory over a vastly superior force, been blessed by a priestly king, and spurned an offer of the wealth of Sodom. Thus, he would appear to have no fear that would need to be allayed.

Three explanations are offered by the Aggadah (*Bereishit Rabbah* 44:5):

> Rabbi Levi offered two [interpretations] and the Sages one. Rabbi Levi said: Avraham was afraid that there was even one righteous, God-fearing man amongst his victims…. God assured him that was not the case. Rabbi Levi also said: Avraham feared that a descendant of one of the kings he killed would gather an army and come to take revenge on him…. God said to him: "Do not fear, I will shield you." Just as a shield can withstand numerous swords, I can protect you from numerous attacks.
>
> According to the Sages, Avraham said: I was rescued from the blazing furnace, I was rescued from the attacking kings, perhaps I have exhausted my merit in this world and have none left for the world to come? God replied: "Do not fear, I will shield you." All that I did for you in this world is gratis; your true reward will be in the world to come….

Nehama, who recommends charts as useful pedagogical tools, would have us summarize these positions as follows:

Verse	Rabbi Levi I	R. Levi II	The Sages
Do not fear	lest I kill righteous	revenge	used up merit
shield you	from punishment	from enemies	gratis
great reward	—	—	in World to Come

Nehama was also particularly fond of soliciting from her audience one-word or two-word answers (which often are more revealing than longwinded explanations). She would challenge us here to succinctly characterize each of these three opinions. We might do so as follows:

- Rabbi Levi I: Avraham experienced a pang of conscience.

- Rabbi Levi II: Avraham experienced a natural fear of revenge.

- The Sages: Avraham's fear was spiritual in nature.

Let us compare the interpretations with that of Rashi and determine to which of them he subscribes.

Rashi comments (15:1):

> After these events: After the miracle of defeating the kings occurred, he expressed his concern saying: Perhaps I have been compensated for all my righteousness?
> Do not fear. I shall shield you: from punishment; you will not be punished for all those lives you took. Furthermore, regarding your concern over your reward, "Your reward is truly great."

Rashi appears to follow the opinion of the Sages in interpreting both "do not fear" and "great reward," while his interpretation of "shield you" inclines towards Rabbi Levi I.

The acknowledgment of Rashi's preferences highlights the questions: Why did he not follow the Sages' interpretation in its entirety, rather than mix in R. Levi I? Also, why did he ignore R. Levi II completely?

Rashi apparently feels that the Sages' interpretation of *magen* (shield) stretches the sense of the text too far since it seems to be based more on the Aramaic usage of the word [*magan*=gratis] than on its plain Hebrew meaning. There also appear to be two acceptable reasons for his rejection of R. Levi II: One, it does not address the end of the verse ("your reward is great"); and two, it belies the selfless initiative that Avraham took. As Nehama reminds us, Avraham is a *yerei elo-him*; he fears God, but no man.

VA-YEIRA

Meet Lot

IN COMPARISON WITH AVRAHAM

ဢ PREFACE

We first encounter Lot in the closing verses of the *sidrah* of Noah. He is the orphaned son of Avraham's brother Haran (with a *heh*), who died, prematurely, before the family left Ur Kasdim for Haran (with a *het*). When Avraham and his wife Sarah later depart for Canaan, Lot accompanies them (12:4). He drops out of sight while Avraham tours Canaan and sojourns in Egypt, reappearing at Avraham's side upon his return to Beit-El (13:5).

Lot possesses a wealth of livestock matching that of his uncle but their combined wealth is too great for their continued collective settlement. They agree to a geographical reapportionment and part amicably (13:11). Avraham continues to reside in the Land of Canaan, proper, while Lot takes up residence in the Cities of the Plain, particularly Sedom, which is pointedly described as "exceedingly evil and sinful before God" (13:13).

Lot's residence in Sedom is interrupted briefly by his capture by Mesopotamian marauders. After Avraham secures his freedom, he disappears back into Sedom to emerge again in our *sidrah* (19:1) on the eve of the city's destruction.

ဢ PART ONE: LOT'S HOSPITALITY: HOW DOES IT MATCH UP TO AVRAHAM'S?

Following another of Nehama's methodological techniques (she called them *trickim*), let us chart a comparison of Avraham's reception of his visitors (18:1 ff.) with Lot's (19:1ff.):

Avraham	Lot
1. seated at entrance to tent	**1.** seated at entrance to Sedom
2. looked up, spotted them, ran towards them, bowed low before them.	**2.** spotted them, rose to greet them bowed low before them.
3. He said: Sirs, if I please you please do not pass me by.	**3.** He said: Sirs, please turn into my house spend the night
4. We will bring water to wash your feet and rest beneath the tree.	**4.** wash your feet arise
5. I will bring bread to feed you then you will continue on your way, They said: Yes; Do as you say.	**5.** and continue your journey. They said: No; we'll sleep in the street.

Let us first note the several factual differences between the two receptions:

- Lot saw his visitors approach, whereas Avraham searched for his ("looked up").

- Lot "rose" to greet his visitors; Avraham "ran" towards his.

- Lot does not match Avraham's offer of food, initially, but after he pesters his guests into accepting his hospitality, he prepares food and drink.

Let us next consider the conclusion to which these facts point: They indicate that Lot's practice of hospitality appears to have been patterned after that of Avraham (Rashi: "He learned in Avraham's house how to seek after guests"), except that Avraham practiced it with greater alacrity and enthusiasm.

Another salient point can be inferred from the sequence in which Avraham and Lot offered their respective guests an opportunity to wash their feet: Avraham bade them wash their feet before they rested; Lot invited them to rest before washing their feet. Based upon this distinction, Rashi, in his commentary on "wash your feet" (18:4), offers us a qualitative assessment about Avraham vs. Lot. Since the dust on one's feet is presumed [by the Aggadah] to have idolatrous associations, Avraham was clearly more concerned about his guests' spiritual comportment than was Lot.

Upon closer examination, however, this implied criticism of Lot is not necessarily warranted. Avraham received his guests at high noon (*ke-hom hayom*) when relief from the heat – in the form of washing – is a more urgent need than rest. Lot, however, received his visitors in the evening (*ba-erev*) when lodging is a more timely need than personal hygiene.

ò PART TWO: LOT AND HIS DAUGHTERS: BRAVERY OR BRAVADO?

Our next glimpse of Lot's personality comes when the entire populace of Sedom surrounds his house and demands that he turn his visitors over to them for a purpose they designate as: *ve-nede'a otam* (19:4); literally, "that we shall know them." Rashi and Ibn Ezra assume it to be a euphemism for homosexuality, while Radak takes it to mean murder.

Lot's refusal to surrender his guests is met by Ramban with studied ambivalence.

> **Ramban:** We see this man's [Lot] praise and infamy simultaneously. He was very concerned over saving his guests because they were enjoying his hospitality, but pandering to the townspeople by surrendering his daughters is a sign of wickedness.

R. Hananel (Kairouan, eleventh century), on the other hand, interprets his actions heroically:

> **R. Hananel:** [God] forbid that he would surrender his daughters [to licentiousness]! Rather, this is as though one said to another, "My house is wide open; take what you please." Or as one might throw oneself over an intended murder victim saying, "Kill me," while knowing that it won't happen.

While Ramban strikes an evenhanded pose, his overall assessment appears to be critical. R. Hananel, on the other hand, gives Lot the benefit of the doubt. If we may venture our own opinion, there appears to be a textual proof. At the conclusion of v. 6, as Lot steps out of doors, we read: "He closed the door behind him" (*ve-hadelet sagar aharav*). This is not the action of a craven sinner ready to sacrifice his own daughters – and his own neck (see v. 9: "We'll do worse harm to you") – but a stalwart guardian of his home and family who bravely locks the door behind himself and turns, alone, to confront the mob.

✍ Part Three: Who Saved Lot?

At the outset, Avraham is visited by "three men" (18:2). In the continuation of the narrative, however, the Torah states: "The two angels (mal'akhim) arrived in Sedom" (19:1). A well-known Midrash explains how three became two: The one who was charged with bringing Sarah the news of Yitzhak's impending birth had discharged his function and, presumably, returned to his point of origin. Whether they were men or angels, however, is addressed by Rashi.

> **Rashi:** Yet earlier (18:2, 16, 22) they were called "men" (anashim) When the shekhinah was with them they were called men. Or: When they were with Avraham – who had great [spiritual] power, and in whose company angels were as frequent as men – they were called men, whereas in the company of Lot they were called angels.

How does the presence – or absence – of the shekhinah affect the Torah's choice of language? Angels are considered superior to humans, and when only the two appear together the superiority is maintained. In the presence of God, however, even angels appear human in comparison. Alternatively, the superiority of angels over humans is relative to specific humans. The angels were greater than Lot, but not greater than Avraham.

■ ■ ■ ■

We will return again to the question of mal'akhim[1], but for the time being, consider the following:

- What is the root of the noun mal'akh? To what other, prominent, Biblical noun is it related etymologically?

- What is the etymology of the English word "angel"? What does that indicate about its use as a translation for mal'akh?

---

[1] See the sidrah of Va-Yeshev, Part Three.

- How does the Targum of Onkelos translate it? Can you spot a correlation between his different translations and the different appearances of *mal'akh* in the Torah?

✖ PART FOUR: THANKS TO WHOSE VIRTUE WAS LOT SAVED?

Lot's rescue from Sedom is attributed by the Torah to a combination of his own virtue and an act of divine grace. In verse 15, the angels urge Lot to hurry and get his family out, "lest you perish for the city's sin." This implies that Lot had an independent virtue which spared him from being "swept away" on account of the city's wickedness. In verse 19, on the other hand, Lot himself appears to regard his salvation as an act of grace. "I have pleased you," he says to his deliverers, "and now you have magnified the grace (*hesed*) you have shown me by sparing my life."

The Talmud (*Berakhot* 54b), however, implies that Lot had no intrinsic merit:

> [Whoever sees Lot and his wife] should recite two blessings. On his wife: "Blessed is the true judge;" and on Lot: "Blessed is He Who remembers the righteous." R. Yohanan said: Even in His anger, God remembers the righteous. To wit: "When God destroyed the cities of the plain He remembered Avraham and dispatched Lot from the destruction" (19:29).

The blessing over Lot cites "remembers the righteous" and, in the proof text, the object of the verb "remember" is Avraham. This would appear to indicate that the halakhic prescription sides with the view that Lot had no virtue of his own and was spared only on account of the virtue of his uncle.

Note: What can we infer from the fact that throughout Avraham's lengthy bargaining session with God over the fate of Sedom, he never once specifically mentions Lot? Was Lot's fate never in doubt and his life never in jeopardy, or was Lot one of the city's "righteous" over whom Avraham negotiated?

HAYYEI SARAH

The Grave Consequences of Speech

NEGOTIATING FOR THE MAKHPELAH CAVE

❧ PREFACE

The Torah describes how Avraham purchased a field and a cave in Hevron to serve as Sarah's final resting place. Uncharacteristically, the Torah dwells on even the slightest details of the sale, including verbatim transcripts of Avraham's conversations with the local population (the Hittites) and the owner of the field (Ephron).

Our opening question is the same as that of Malbim: *mah yoshi'enu sippur zeh le-torah u-le-te'udah?* – i.e., "Of what halakhic or other traditional significance is this entire story?"

❧ PART ONE: CONTRASTING DIALOGUE

In the previous unit (Va-Yeira), we noted Nehama's technique of comparing and contrasting passages. Let us analyze the entire course of Avraham's transaction by transcribing the dialogue in parallel columns: one – what Avraham said, and the other – how the Hittites, or Ephron, responded. Consider and evaluate the correspondences:

Avraham	Hittites/Ephron
v. 4	**v. 6**
I am a stranger and sojourner in your midst; give me a hereditary burial plot among you to bury my dead.	You are a divine prince among us; bury your dead in our choicest plot; none of us will prevent you....
v. 9	**v. 11**
Let [Ephron] give me the double cave... let him sell it to me for full value... to serve as a hereditary burial plot.	I have given you the field and the cave in its midst.... I have given them to you – bury your dead.

Note, in particular, Avraham's opening declaration: "I am a stranger and sojourner (*ger ve-toshav*) in your midst." [Note: Some translators prefer: "resident-alien."] Is this just an expression of humility (to which the Hittites respond by saying, "Oh, no! You're a prince of a man!"), or does it contain very specific legal implications? To answer this question, it will be necessary to compare this verse with Va-Yikra 25:23, which employs the identical idiom: "The Land may never be sold in perpetuity, for it belongs entirely to Me; you are only strangers and sojourners (*gerim ve-toshavim*) in it."

Avraham's status vis-à-vis the Hittites resembles the status we occupy before God. Just as we cannot own land forever (but only up to the Jubilee year) because we are only "strangers and sojourners" before Him, so Avraham could not own a hereditary cave-tomb in Hevron because, legally, he was only a "stranger and sojourner" (and not a full-fledged citizen) vis-à-vis the Hittites.

✑ PART TWO: NEGOTIATION THROUGH INDIRECTION

During the negotiations, Avraham asks the Hittites to intercede on his behalf with one of their number, Ephron (v. 8), who turns out to be one of the assembly that Avraham is already addressing (v. 10). That being the case, why didn't Avraham just speak to Ephron directly? What need did he have for the Hittites' mediation?

34

While this just might be Hittite protocol, the Hizkuni (Rabbi Manoah ben Hizkiyah, thirteenth-century France) suspects something more significant. He writes:

> Avraham needed them all. Even had Ephron sold him the field, he would not have been permitted to use it as a cemetery without public permission.

Actually, this notion was first advanced by Sa'adiah Gaon (Egypt and Baghdad; 882–942) who likened it to the Talmudic law of *bar-meitzra*, which prohibits the use of private property for purposes that might irritate adjoining neighbors, such as a tannery or, by analogy, a cemetery. Sa'adiah does not assume for a moment that the Hittites were conversant with the tractate *Bava Batra*; he considers this regulation one which any enlightened society would legislate, not something uniquely Jewish. Utilizing the philosophical terminology he introduced in his treatise *Emunot ve-De'ot* (Beliefs and Opinions), this constitutes a rational imperative (*mitzvah sikhlit*) rather than a revealed one (*mitzvah shim'it*).

Indeed, other actions of Avraham indicate his dependence upon the Hittites, such as bowing to them not just once, which protocol might have demanded, but twice.

௮ PART THREE: THE SIGNIFICANCE

In the Preface, we acknowledged the question that Malbim addresses at the beginning of this week's *sidrah*: "Of what halakhic or other traditional significance is this entire story?" It is time to cite two replies to that question. The first comes from the Midrash *Bereishit Rabbah*:

> R. Yudan ben R. Shimon said: This is one of the three places about which the nations of the world cannot taunt Israel, saying: You have stolen them! They are: *me'arat ha-makhpelah*, *beit ha-mikdash*, and *kever Yosef*.

Ibn Ezra, too, recognized that the Torah's attention to minute detail here (v. 17, for instance, even takes note of the presence of trees in the field!) reflects an extraordinary significance, and he explains (as though in answer to Malbim's question) that this episode was reported to inform us of the superiority of Eretz Yisrael above all other countries.

Sa'adiah Gaon, whose thoughts on the subject we cited above (see Part Two), might have replied to this same question by saying that Avraham's separate approach to the Hittites comes to teach us the Halakhah of *bar-meitzra* (somewhat similar to contemporary zoning ordinances).

🔊 PART FOUR: CORRELATING AN EVENT AND ITS REPORT

Recall the exercise we conducted apropos of the *sidrah* of Noah, in which we dealt with discrepancies among lists of things that occur in sequences. A similar type of literary challenge we face in reading Torah closely occurs when a character in a Biblical event relates what transpired after that very event has already been narrated. Often there appear to be discrepancies between the two accounts. How do we resolve them? The premier such instance in the Torah concerns the encounter between Avraham's servant and Rivkah (Chapter 23).

The plot is well-known: Avraham instructs his major domo (Rashi, basing himself upon Hazal, identifies him with Eliezer) to travel to his ancestral homeland in order to find a bride for Yitzhak. The servant conceives a particular scenario to identify the appropriate woman, and no sooner does he arrive at his destination in Haran then the scenario unfolds – exactly as he envisioned it!

Let us focus on one detail: the gifts he bestows upon her. Compare the following verses and note the discrepancy:

vv. 22–24 (the narrative)	v. 47 (the servant's reiteration)
When the camels had done drinking the man took a golden ring...	I asked her: Whose daughter are you?
and two bracelets upon her hands...	She replied: I am the daughter of Betuel...
He asked: Whose daughter are you...	so I placed the ring in her nose
She replied: I am the daughter of Betuel...	and the bracelets upon her hands.

The discrepancy, of course, is whether the servant first questioned her identity, or gave her gifts. A look at the commentaries of Rashi and his grandson, Rashbam (Rabbi Shemuel ben Meir), reveals that both alternatives are feasible.

Rashi (v. 47): He reversed the order; he [actually] bestowed [the gifts] before questioning [her] since he did not want to be tripped up by his own words lest they ask: How could you have given her gifts without knowing who she was?

Rashbam (v. 22): It seems that he gave her [the gifts] only after asking her who she was, just as he reports later on (v. 47), but in order not to interrupt their conversation [the Torah] narrates the gift-giving first.

Utilizing Nehama's technique of succinctness,[1] we can characterize the two responses as follows: Rashi dismisses the servant's changes as self-serving, while Rashbam explains the Torah's alterations as a literary device.

Whenever major exegetes disagree, Nehama would insist that their disagreement be understood in terms of their different methodologies. When challenged: "Which one is right?" she would demur, observing that both could be valid inferences from different vantage points. Bearing that caution in mind, can we either produce an irrefutable proof for one view, or devise a challenge to the other?

Since Rashi dismisses the servant's changes as self-serving, the challenge to Rashi's interpretation is: How could it have benefited the servant to alter the facts to preserve his credibility when Rivkah would still have known that he was lying? Unless you subscribe to a conspiracy theory (that the servant deliberately lied and Rivkah knowingly helped in the "cover-up"), it would appear that there is no *a priori* reason to reject the servant's report. Moreover, would Avraham have sent an unreliable servant on such a sensitive mission? In light of this reasoning, the "literary device" approach appears more valid than the "self-serving" approach.

❧ PART FIVE: A NOTE ON THE MODALITIES OF VERBS

Nehama used linguistics only sparingly, preferring to rest her case on evidence better understood by wider audiences. Her interest in linguistic affairs, however, is borne out by several chapters of the book she prepared – along with Prof. Moshe Arend – for the Open University as an Introduction

---

[1] See Lekh Lekha, Part Two.

to Rashi. Here, we shall deal with a subject that may appear abstruse; but if it pertains to Rashi's commentary, it is surely pertinent all the same.

Speakers of European languages are familiar with verbal forms that present an "aspect" (also called a "modality") of the designated action rather than a tense (or, time), such as: can come, will do, would say. The question before us is whether Biblical Hebrew uses such an aspect. The answer will come from the verses we have just studied (23:10–13).

The verb that recurs most frequently in the exchange between Avraham and Ephron derives from the root *n-t-n* (to give). It appears here in two different forms: *natati* and *netatiha*, each appearing two times. According to a literal rendition of v. 11, a logical difficulty arises. If Ephron already gave Avraham the field (*ha-sadeh natati lakh*), and Avraham already paid his money (*ha-kesef natati lakh*), what is left to negotiate? Yet, the context makes it abundantly clear that these remarks were uttered *before* the deal was concluded.

While the response of modern linguists is to designate this use of the verb as "immediate future," which should be translated as: "I am giving," or, "I am about to give," any indication of the future would surely be better served by the imperfect form of the verb [i.e., *eten lakh, etnenah lakh*]. Compare Bereishit 30:25–33; 34:9–15; 38:16–18; 42:14–20. In all these cases, which also consist of negotiations, any action which has not yet transpired is indicated by the use of a future (imperfect) verbal form, not the past (perfect).

In light of the preceding discussion, we shall compare the following commentaries of Rashi:

> *natati lakh* (v. 11): It is as though it were given to you.
> *natati* (v. 13): In French, "*dones.*" I have prepared it and I wish it were already given.

Note that in neither case does Rashi assume that the designated action has actually been completed. Moreover, by paying close attention to the subjects of the respective verbs (Avraham and Ephron), we can see that Rashi gives two interpretations of the same word. The difference between them is in his perception of their respective motives. Avraham, of whose sincerity we have no doubt, treats his payment as though it were already made. Ephron, whose motives are dubious, seems to be saying that while he will accept payment for the field, it is only "as though" he will relinquish it, implying that in reality he might not.

More objectively, perhaps, the distinction may be born of another difference: Ephron is talking about real estate, while Avraham addresses chattel. Since land is not literally transferable, Ephron correctly addresses it "as though it were given." Avraham, on the other hand, is speaking about money about which he can legitimately say, "I have prepared it and I wish it were already given." Indeed, the legal term in Jewish law for property other than real estate is *mitaltelin,* which means, literally, "moveable."

Note: See the commentary of Rashi on Bereishit 15:18. How does he treat *natati* there?

TOL'DOT

Eating One's Words

MAN OF FIELD VS. MAN OF TENTS

❧ PREFACE: STAKING OUT THE ISSUES

In 25:27–28, the Torah describes the relationship between Yitzhak and his sons.

> The boys grew up; Esav became a man who knew the hunt (*yode'a tzayid*), a man of the field, while Yaakov was a simple man who dwells in tents (v. 27). Yitzhak loved Esav because prey was in his mouth (*ki tzayid be-fiv*), but Rivkah loved Yaakov (v. 28).

Several problems – literary and substantive – present themselves in these two verses. The first one we shall tackle is literary.

❧ PART ONE: AMBIGUOUS PRONOUN REFERENCE

"Reuven and Shimon got into *his* car." When you can't tell from the pronoun ("his") whose car they drove off in, you have a case of ambiguous pronoun reference. [If the subjects were Reuven and Rachel, however, the pronoun – being masculine – would be indicative.]

There is a similar ambiguity in verse 28: "Yitzhak loved Esav because prey was in *his* mouth." In whose mouth was the "prey" (*tzayid*) on account of which Yitzhak loved Esav? There are two possibilities: Either Yitzhak loved Esav because Esav placed prey in Yitzhak's mouth (i.e., he fed him), or Yitzhak loved him on account of something that was in Esav's mouth.

Rashi (25:28) notes both possibilities. He treats the first ("[Yitzhak] would eat of [Esav's] prey") as the *peshat*, and introduces the second one as a *derash*: "[the prey was] in Esav's mouth; he trapped and tricked him with his words." In the latter case, Rashi continues the exegetical line he started in the previous verse (27) where he commented on "who knew the hunt":

> To trap and trick his father with his mouth by asking, "Father, how does one tithe salt or straw?" His father imagined that he was punctilious in observing mitzvot.

A subsequent text in this *sidrah*, however, clearly upholds the *peshat* interpretation. Bereishit 27:1–4 reads: "As Yitzhak grew old… he summoned his son, Esav, and said: Now take your weapons, your quiver and bow, go out to the field and hunt me some prey (*tzayid*). Prepare me the victuals I like and bring them to me to eat…." Esav is actually directed to place prey in Yitzhak's mouth.

◈ Part Two: What's Wrong with the *Peshat?* An Insight into Ibn Ezra

Based upon the assumption (that we stipulated in the *sidrah* of Bereishit) that Rashi resorts to *derash* primarily when there is an inadequate *peshat*, what deficiency in the *peshat* prompts him to cite a *derash* here? Two answers recommend themselves: (1) In Hebrew syntax, ordinarily, pronouns refer to the nearest noun to which they correspond in number and gender. In this case, the noun nearest "his mouth" is Esav. (2) If it were Yitzhak's mouth, we would have expected a transitive verb in the clause, such as: "because he placed prey in his mouth" (*ki tzayid hevi be-fiv*).

The phrase *yodea' tzayid* recalls the earlier usage of *gibbor tzayid*, referring to Nimrod (10:9). A close look at Rashi and Ibn Ezra's interpretations of these similar phrases will prove enlightening.

With respect to Nimrod, Rashi says: "He trapped people's minds with his mouth," almost exactly as he interprets the phrase regarding Esav, while Ibn Ezra states: "[Nimrod] demonstrated the superiority of people over animals by being a brave hunter" (an interpretation that Ramban castigates as a "whitewash"). With regard to Esav, however, Ibn Ezra appears to concur in the Aggadic folk wisdom, saying that to "know the hunt" means: "Perpetually tricky, because it takes guile to catch a wild animal." Why doesn't Ibn Ezra treat hunting equally in both places?

His interpretation here is based upon a very close and sensitive reading of the text. Let us contrast what the Torah has to say about each of the twin brothers:

Esav	Yaakov
1. a man who knows the hunt	**1.** a simple man
2. a man of the field	**2.** who dwells in tents

Of these two pairs, the second offers a clear basis for comparison: the field and the tent are both places (of work or residence). The first pair, however, is problematic: What contrast is there between hunting, a profession, and simplicity, a trait of character? Ibn Ezra assumes that if the Torah grouped them together then they must contrast, so he interprets hunting, too, as a trait of character ("guile") rather than just as a profession.

✂ PART THREE: WHAT KIND OF MAN DWELLS IN TENTS?

While "field" and "tents" are intelligible, being "a man" of the one or the other is not as clear. Since Esav was a hunter, we assume that the field refers to the location of the animals he hunted; but what is the relationship between Yaakov's simple character and tents?

The Aggadah has a simple solution: Tents are places of Torah study, and the tents in which Yaakov resided were the "academies" of Shem and Ever. I should like to offer a *peshat* solution as well.

Recalling the earlier description of Yaval in 4:20 as: "the father of those who sit in tents and herd (*yoshev ohel u-mikneh*)," however, might the Torah be telling us that Yaakov, too, was a shepherd? Indeed, Hizkuni notes:

> According to the *peshat*, these are tents of shepherds.... Since the Torah will subsequently narrate that he tended Lavan's sheep, it advanced the explanation that he was a professional shepherd.

This identification opens up additional possibilities. If Yaakov was a shepherd, and Esav was "a man of the field," and if, additionally, a field is usually synonymous with agriculture, might Esav have been a farmer? Since the Torah explicitly designates him as a hunter that is unlikely. However, if he were a farmer, we would have a remarkable reprise of the relationship (and conflict) between Cain and Abel. Moreover, just as the shepherd came off best in that earlier encounter, so does the shepherd outdo the farmer in this contest, too.

Note: The early Israelites had a pronounced tendency towards shepherding. Yaakov-Yisrael is a shepherd, Yosef introduces his brothers to Pharaoh as shepherds, and Moshe and David are shepherds. In contrast, Noah is introduced as "a man of the soil" (*ish ha-adamah*) as the prelude to his intoxication. The Egyptians considered shepherding an abomination and both Egypt and Canaan were primarily agrarian societies.

✍ PART FOUR: RELATIVELY SPEAKING

Whenever the Torah uses an appositive phrase – a construction in which one noun or noun phrase is placed with another as an explanatory equivalent (e.g., Ibn Jannah, the medieval grammarian) – two questions occur:

1. Was it necessary to use the appositive as well as the proper noun?

2. In light of the appositive, was it necessary to use the proper noun, too?

Two verses in this week's *sidrah* employ appositives for Rivkah:

1. "Yitzhak was forty years old when he married Rivkah, daughter of Betuel, the Aramean, of Padan Aram, sister of Lavan, the Aramean" (25:20).

2. "Yitzhak dispatched Yaakov, who went to Padan Aram, to Lavan, son of Betuel, the Aramean, brother of Rivkah, mother of Yaakov and Esav" (28:5).

Considering all the attention the Torah lavished on Rivkah and her family in last week's *sidrah*, why is it necessary to reiterate her relationship to Betuel? The first verse in the *sidrah* (25:19) gives us a clue. It states: "This is the story of Yitzhak, son of Avraham; Avraham fathered Yitzhak." Why the redundancy? To emphasize Yitzhak's role as Avraham's successor, thereby fulfilling an earlier prophecy (21:12): "For through Yitzhak will your descendants be continued." Reference to Yitzhak's patriarchal lineage justifies the attention to Rivkah's.

But why is Rivkah's relationship to Yaakov and Esav repeated at the end of the *sidrah*?

Throughout most of the *sidrah*, she appears to have been the mother of Yaakov alone. She favors him (25:28), conspires with him (27:6), and offers to accept full responsibility should his masquerade be revealed (27:13). Only when Esav's anger becomes a palpable threat to Yaakov and she realizes how her one-sidedness has jeopardized them both does she acknowledge her love for them both: "Why should I be bereft of the two of you at the same time?" (27:45).

Having restored some measure of maternal equilibrium, she can now, perhaps for the first time since their conception, be called: "mother of Yaakov *and* Esav."

Note: Other examples of appositives in Bereishit include: "The woman whom you placed with me" (3:12); "Lot, who accompanied Avraham" (13:5); "Rachel, your younger daughter" (29:18); "Your brother, Esav" (32:7).

Note: Look at the commentary of Rashi on 28:5. On the words: "Rivkah, mother of Yaakov and Esav," he states: "I don't know what this teaches us." Ask yourself: If he knows of no purpose, why not simply be silent? Why advertise what he doesn't know?

VA-YETZE'

It's Quite "Natural" (Or Is It?)

PESHAT VS. *DERASH* OF YAAKOV'S DREAM

ଛଠ PART ONE: WHERE PARSHANIM DIFFER

Nehama regularly tackled the complex pedagogic issue of how to deal with differences of interpretation amongst *parshanim* (exegetes). Two different commentators render two disparate interpretations of the same word or verse. Why don't they see eye to eye, and in any case, which one should we follow? Her invariable answer was: Different exegetes exercised different methodologies, leading them to different conclusions. Providing their interpretations were arrived at through the proper use of their respective methodologies, Nehama argued, one could never say that one of them was right and the other wrong. Both are valid.

At the beginning of this week's *sidrah*, we have an opportunity to consider a striking difference between the respective interpretations of Rashi and Rashbam. Let us first review what we know of Rashi's approach to Aggadah, and contrast it to that of Rashbam.

Rashi

In our study of the *sidrah* of Bereishit, we cited Rashi's following comments to 3:8:

> There are many Aggadic *midrashim* which our Sages have appropriately arranged in *Bereishit Rabbah* and other Midrashic anthologies. I have come, however, only to [explain] the *peshat* of the text and those *aggadot* which resolve the language of Scripture, as "a word fitly spoken."

Rashbam

Rashbam's approach to the use of Aggadah is crystallized in his commentary to Bereishit 37:2 as follows:

> Our predecessors, on account of their piety, were preoccupied with [Halakhic] *derashot* – which are paramount – and, consequently, were not accustomed to plumb the depths of *peshat*.... Rabbi Shelomo, my maternal grandfather, who illuminated the eyes of the Diaspora and commented on the entire Tanakh, paid attention to the literal sense of Scripture (*peshuto shel mikra'*); I, Shemuel ben Meir, his grandson, however, argued with him – in person – and he admitted that if he only had the time he would have composed new interpretations in light of the daily discoveries in the realm of *peshat*.

In essence, then, while Rashi approves of using *aggadot* (*derash*) to resolve textual problems and anomalies, Rashbam believes that such problems can be resolved by the means of *peshat*.

✍ PART TWO: YAAKOV'S ODYSSEY

We shall place each consecutive element of this story in the left-hand margin, and place the respective commentaries of Rashi and Rashbam alongside them, in order to facilitate their comparison. The Aggadic interpretations of Rashi that we cite here appear after his commentary on v. 17.

Phrase	Rashi	Rashbam
1. Yaakov... went	He came to Haran	He went towards Haran

Rashi is troubled by the word *haranah* in the first verse. As he often notes, "placing a *heh* at the end of a word is the equivalent of putting [the preposition] *el* (to) before it." Since Yaakov appears to have gone directly from Beersheva to Haran, the story told here could only have happened subsequent to his arrival there.

Rashbam, however, is untroubled because "going to" someplace is not necessarily identical with "arriving" there.

Phrase	Rashi	Rashbam
2. He encountered	the mountain moved towards him	he came upon

The disagreement here is over *va-yifga* [he encountered], which Rashi interprets as "to strike," while Rashbam understands it to mean "come upon." The former presumes an unexpected, even violent, clash; the latter does not.

Phrase	Rashi	Rashbam
3. the place	Mount Moriah	somewhere outside Luz

The disagreement here is over the use of the definite article *ha-makom* (*the place*). Rashi assumes that implies a place that has previously achieved specificity and *the* place, *par excellence*, in the lives of the patriarchs would be Mt. Moriah. Rashbam says that whatever place one occupies at any given moment is specific enough to justify the definite article.

Phrase	Rashi	Rashbam
4. the sun set	prematurely, unseasonably	[at its usual time]

Here they disagree over the subtle word *ki*. Rashi prefers "because" and sees a causal relationship between the sun setting and Yaakov's bedding down for the night. Rashbam treats it as "when," seeing only a linkage in time, not a cause and effect.

Phrase	Rashi	Rashbam
5. he took from the stones	several	a single stone

The ambiguous phrase: *me-avnei ha-makom* engenders the next disagreement. Rashi says that since *avnei* is grammatically plural, it was plural in substance, too. If a later verse (28:18) uses the singular (*ha-even*), a miracle must have happened in the interim transforming the many into one. Rashbam says that if there was only one stone when he awoke (28:18), there was only one when he went to sleep.

Phrase	Rashi	Rashbam
6. going up and down	first up, then down	"common usage"

They next differ over the sequence of actions imputed to the "divine angels." Rashi presumes that the order in which an event is narrated in Scripture is, literally, the order in which it transpired. Rashbam says that Scripture often uses customary patterns of speech (*derekh 'eretz*) that need not be taken literally.

Phrase	Rashi	Rashbam
7. the land upon which you are lying	God folded all Israel beneath him	a small plot

Rashi says that if God promised Yaakov the land on which he slept, then he had to be sleeping on all of the Promised Land. Rashbam points out that the parcel of land he slept on was insignificant in itself, therefore God's promise continues: "And you will expand [in all directions]."

‰ PART THREE: SUMMARIZING AND CHARACTERIZING THE DIFFERENCES

Combining all the ingredients in Rashi's interpretation, we get the following composite narrative:

Yaakov, who had already reached Haran, was on his way back to Yerushalayim (to pray there) when God brought Har ha-Moriah to intercept him at Luz. In order to keep him there overnight, God caused the sun to set prematurely. Yaakov collected several stones which he placed about his head and went to sleep. In his dream, during which God compressed the entire Land of Israel beneath him, he saw angels first ascending and then descending a ladder. When he awoke, he discovered that God had fused the several stones together into one.

Recasting Rashbam's interpretation

Yaakov, on his way to Haran, stopped at an anonymous site outside Luz when he ran out of daylight for traveling. He went to sleep there on only as much ground as his body occupied. In his dream he saw angels going up and down a ladder in no significant sequence, and when he awakened, he took the single stone he had placed beneath his head the previous night and used it as a monument.

Utilizing Nehama's tactic that we have already labeled "succinctness,"[1] we can characterize each interpretation in a single word. Rashbam's is natural (or realistic), while Rashi's is supernatural (or miraculous). Rashi sees the elements in the narrative framework of the dream as divinely contrived to stick Yaakov in that place at that time. Rashbam, on the other hand, sees

---

[1] Cf. Lekh Lekha, Part Two.

only the casual, even random meandering of a man who gets stuck at a place not of his own choosing, where he cautiously beds down for the night.

Rashi sees Yaakov's dream as beginning with the sequential changing of the heavenly guard, continuing with the compression of the land on which he slept, and culminating with the fusion of the selected stones. Rashbam denies sequence, and, hence, significance to the movements of the angels, and declines to accommodate either the compression of the earth or that of the sundry stones.

Note: Implications

While Nehama is correct in stipulating that the differences between the interpretations of Rashi and Rashbam may not be characterized in terms of right and wrong, what significance should we attach to these very striking differences? As an educator, I make my remarks in the context of how I would present this material to students. The following remarks are mine and not Nehama's, and they reflect my own personal preferences and predilections – informed and influenced as they are by her example.[2]

If I were teaching the story of Yaakov's dream to a primary-school class, I would have them read Rashi's Aggadic interpretation only. At that stage, the most important educational goal is to impress them with the majesty of God and His miraculous providence (*hashgaha peratit*) – virtues that abound in the Aggadic rendition of the story. If the students raised no objection to it on their own, I would not feel constrained to raise it for them.

In a middle-school setting, I would have the students read both Rashi and Rashbam, and challenge them to come up with the characterizations of their approaches (just as we did, here, at the end of the previous section). At this stage, the "cognitive" goals of critical thinking and close reading assume the value accorded earlier to the "affective" religious goal of acknowledging miracles. Were the Aggadic interpretation to be challenged at this juncture, I would suggest that it depicts events from Yaakov's awestruck perspective.

In the upper school, I would use only the commentary of Rashi, but this time I would stimulate the students to offer their own challenges to the Aggadic interpretation: (a) linguistic challenges, emanating from grammatical

---

[2] See my article in *Pirkei Nehamah, Sefer Zikhron le-Nehamah Leibowitz* (Jerusalem, 2001). For additional insights on this topic by Nehama herself, see her book: *Limmud parshanei ha-mikra u-derakhim le-hora'atam* (Jerusalem: 1975), 297–306.

and syntactical analysis of the text; and: (b) logical challenges, based upon the incompatibility of the Aggadic version with known – or assumed – facts of nature. We would then proceed to compare their challenges with those that are explicit in the commentary of Rashbam (which we extrapolated, above, throughout Part Two).

At this stage – or at whatever stage this lesson occupies – I would emphasize the singular "affective" value of Rashbam's interpretation. According to Rashi, it is clear why Yaakov was so impressed by his experience; who wouldn't be inspired by moving mountains, unseasonable sunsets, and fusing stones? The usual challenge to religious life, however, is how to see God's providence in the absence of patent "miracles." It is a far greater spiritual accomplishment to remark, as Yaakov did after a fitful night's sleep in an ordinary place: "God truly exists in this place, and I did not know."

VA-YISHLAH

Requiting Good Deeds

DEREKH KETZARAH: THE WAY OF ELLIPSIS

ஐ PREFACE: THE MAN WHO CAME TO DINNER

One of the accepted norms of narrative art is that not all the details are required in every episode. Providing too many and unessential details can weary the reader. On the other hand, stimulating the reader to fill in some of the details through either the exercise of logic, or by reference to other texts, is a proven way of holding his/her interest in the narrative.

In the Torah commentary of Rav Sa'adiah Gaon, the story of Moshe in Midian serves as the paradigm of this literary norm. In Shemot 2:20, Yitro instructs his daughters to invite Moshe home for dinner. On one hand, the Torah doesn't say whether they invited him or whether he accepted; on the other hand, the next verse says that he married Zipporah. One may properly infer, Sa'adiah says, that if he remained in Midian and married one of Yitro's daughters then – at the very least – he stayed for dinner.

ஐ PART ONE: ELLIPSIS

The beginning of this week's *sidrah* (verses 4–7) contains another example of this phenomenon. The Torah records Yaakov's instructions to his messengers and it records their report to him; it does not explicitly say in between that they carried out their instructions. Rashi calls this phenomenon: *derekh ketzarah* (ellipsis), and utilizes it (*inter alia*) in his commentary on 2 Melakhim 4:26.[1] There, the prophet Elisha instructs his servant Gehazi to intercept the Shunamite woman and inquire of her health

---

[1] See, in greater detail, Va-Yehi, Part One.

and that of her husband and son. All Scripture adds thereupon is: "She said: All is well." Rashi comments: "This is elliptical. It should have said: He asked her and she said all is well."

Rashi's acquaintance with this literary phenomenon prompts us to ask: Why does he decline to point out the elliptical nature of the verses we noted at the beginning of our *sidrah*? It appears that in the case of Elisha, the continuation of the story depends upon the answer to the question he instructed his messenger to pose [i.e., how is the child?]. We might expect, therefore, the detailed recital of how the answer was obtained. In the case of Yaakov's messengers, however, the matter of consequence is Esav's menacing approach, not whether the message was delivered. As Ramban notes: "The messengers fulfilled their mission. Scripture doesn't report it, however, because that is unnecessary."

✌ PART TWO: NO [GOOD] DEED GOES UNREQUITED

Aggadah exhibits a pronounced tendency to identify otherwise anonymous Biblical characters. Rashi, for example, capitalized on this tendency by identifying the "survivor" who notified Avraham of Lot's capture (14:13) as Og, King of Bashan; the "elderly major domo" who carries out Avraham's instructions to find a proper bride for Yitzhak (24:2) as Eliezer; and the "man" who finds Yosef wandering about the outskirts of Shekhem (37:15) as the angel Gavriel.

In this week's *sidrah*, however, the Aggadah responds to an elliptical challenge by making a singular identification. Compare the following two verses:

32:7 – Esav is accompanied by four hundred men.

33:16 – Esav returned, that day, to Seir.

Conclusion: Esav appears to have returned home alone. Where were his four hundred men? Based on the literary principle of ellipsis, we could say that just as they accompanied him to Yaakov, so they must have accompanied him back home. The failure of Scripture to explicitly mention them is due to their insignificance relative to Esav, himself.

Read the following passages and try to answer the accompanying questions posed by Nehama.[2]

Bereishit Rabbah (79:19):

> Where were the four hundred men who accompanied him? One by one they dropped out and went their own ways, saying: Why should we be burned by Yaakov's glowing coal? When did God compensate them? Later on [detailing David's victory over Amalek]: "Not one escaped, save for four hundred young men who fled on camels" (1 Shemuel 30:17).

Rashi's commentary on Bereishit 33:16:

> Esav alone [returned], while the four hundred men who had accompanied him dropped out one at a time. Where did God compensate them? In David's time, to wit: "Save for four hundred young men who fled on camels" (1 Shemuel 30:17).

Rashi's commentary on 1 Shemuel 30:17:

> "[David smote them] on the morrow": The Amalekites experience being beaten on their morrow, to wit: "Tomorrow I [Moshe] will stand [atop the hill]" (Shemot 17:9). Therefore it says: "On the morrow."

Nehama treats these sources in her usual, methodical fashion, raising the following questions:

1. What concept is imbedded in the Aggadic notion that the same four hundred men are involved in both episodes?

2. The verse in 1 Shemuel states that the men escaped by riding on camels. Doesn't that contradict the Aggadah that says they escaped because they abandoned Esav?

3. Why does Rashi not cite the Aggadah in his commentary to Shemuel as he does here in Bereishit?

4. How does Rashi alter the text of the Aggadah in his commentary, and why does he do so?

---

[2] In a study of Rashi's adaptation of Aggadic *midrashim,* appearing in *Rashi's Commentary on the Torah,* 485.

5. What motivated Rashi in Shemuel to cite the Aggadah connecting Moshe's battle with Amalek to that of David?

6. Read Shemot 5:1 and Rashi's commentary there. What does it have in common with his commentary here?

While Nehama did not usually answer the questions she posed, in this case she did (*op. cit.,* 592):

1. Every good deed receives a reward, even if it takes some time for it to be paid out.

2. God's providence (*hashgahah*) works within nature. The provision of camels for their escape should be seen as providential.

3. In Bereishit, the citation solves a problem; in Shemuel it doesn't.

4. Rashi omits the line in the Aggadah which provides the 400 men's motivation for dropping out: "Why should we be burned by Yaakov's glowing coal?" A possible reason: In order for them to merit a reward for abandoning Esav – to Yaakov's decided advantage – there should be no appearance of an ulterior motive.

5. The odd phrasing: "on their morrow."

6. Rashi, there, describes the elders of Israel "dropping out" [from the company of Moshe and Aharon] and subsequently being punished. The concept is that just as every good deed [even if it was, essentially, passive in nature] is, ultimately, rewarded, every bad deed [even passive] is, ultimately, punished.

➣ PART THREE: WHAT IS THE PLURAL OF "GOD"? A POLEMICAL RESPONSE

The Hebrew word for god: *elohim* (as opposed to the particular name of God) is a homonym sharing several different meanings:[3]

1. God, as in: *bereishit bara' e-lohim* (Bereishit 1:1);

2. a deity, as in: *elohim aherim* (Shemot 20:3);

3. judges, as in: *asher yarshi'un elohim* (Shemot 22:7);

---

[3] Note: I have separated the letters *e-l* only when the word is clearly referring to God, Himself.

4. nobility, as in: *elohim lo tekallel* (Shemot 22:27);

5. an adjective meaning divine, as in: *tzelem elohim* (Bereishit 1:27).[4]

In spite of its plural appearance, the word is grammatically singular when applied to God (*bara'*), and plural only when referring to other deities (*aherim*), or to judges (*yarshi'un*). There are, however, exceptions to the rule. Here are two verses – one in this week's *sidrah* – in which the word, while referring to God, Himself, is grammatically plural. Let us look at the verses as well as Rashi's commentary thereupon.

1. Bereishit 20:13: It came about when *e-lohim* caused (*hit'u*) me to roam from my father's house....

   Rashi: "Caused" is plural. Do not be astonished, because divinity and sovereignty are often expressed in the plural... and every expression of mastery is plural, too....

2. Bereishit 35:7: There *e-lohim* appeared (*niglu*) to him....

   Rashi: Divinity and mastery are expressed in the plural on many occasions... likewise when it applies to a judge or overlord.

Rashi's "apology" for these exceptions must be understood in the context of Jewish-Christian polemics. The unity of God was a critical subject of debate in the Middle Ages. While Jews and Muslims were strict monotheists, there were still many polytheists in Europe and even the Christian trinity appeared suspicious to some Jewish and Muslim theologians. By addressing God in the plural, as it were, these Biblical citations could strengthen the hand of those who rejected the monotheistic God and His Torah and had to be carefully explained.

Note: In a similar vein, see the commentary of Rashi on Bereishit 1:26: "Let *us* make man" (*na'aseh adam*), and on 11:7: "Let *us* go down" (*havah neredah*). Taken together with the two commentaries just cited here, consider the following:

---

[4] *E-lohim* as a homonymous term is discussed by Rambam in *The Guide to the Perplexed*, Part One, Chapter 2. I have applied the discussion to *tzelem elohim* in "Discovering the Biblical Value of Human Life," *Ten Da'at* 10 (1997): 41–57.

- Can any of these expressions be explained as "the plural of majesty"? Perhaps the last two, although Rashi explains them otherwise.

- Why does Rashi not cite "expressions of mastery" in his commentary to 11:7, as he does to 20:13? In order to make the punishment fit the crime – *havah neredah* versus *havah nivneh* (see Rashi on 11:7).

VA-YESHEV

No Trivial Pursuit

WHEN A MAN IS AN "ANGEL"

৪১ PREFACE: THE INDIVIDUALITY OF READING

In an essay dealing specifically with the story of Yosef and his brothers
(Bereishit 42–43), Nehama says:

> It is not up to me to teach people how to read a chapter of Tanakh,
> as I have not been entrusted with the keys to that book... also
> because it is doubtful, in general, whether an individual can
> establish a reading process for the many. Should not each
> individual attempt to establish his own reading, a reading suitable
> to his spirit and soul? Just as his spirit and soul comprise a unique
> and one-time phenomenon in this world, so his reading of Tanakh,
> his understanding of the text, should be a one-time phenomenon –
> uniquely his – and not an imitation of something else which once
> was ("How to Read a Chapter of Tanakh," *Torah Insights*. Jerusalem:
> 1995, 163).

Nehama was not preaching hermeneutical anarchy; in the continuation
of her remarks she adds:

> I learned to read Tanakh from our great medieval commentators...
> and from their successors... [who] have something in common
> that I regard as very important to teach. This is the serious
> importance they attach to the written word; to every word, not only
> the major words that possess deep religious, philosophical, and
> ideological significance... but even to conjunctions (*vav ha-hibbur*)
> (*op. cit.,* 164).

✒ PART ONE: IT'S ALL IN THE DETAILS

One of the fundamental suppositions of Rashi is that there are not – nay, there cannot be – any unnecessary or trivial details in the Torah. Whenever such an ostensible detail appears in the Torah text, Rashi is quick to summon an Aggadah that attributes to it the significance it seemingly lacks. Here is an illustration from this week's *sidrah*:

> Bereishit 37:24–25: [Yosef's brothers] took him and cast him into a pit, an empty pit lacking water. They sat down to eat, looked up, and saw an Ishmaelite caravan approaching from Gilead, its camels laden with balm, balsam, and ladanum, which they were transporting to Egypt.

The reference to the "empty pit lacking water" appears to be – minimally – redundant, and – maximally – trivial. Rashi treats this classic redundancy by arguing that the Torah emphasizes the lack of water to indicate that it was only water that was absent in that pit, but other items – particularly snakes and scorpions – were present in it. In other words, Yosef's life was still in danger at this point in time.

The identification of the Ishmaelite cargo is equally "unnecessary." With Yosef's life hanging in the balance and his fate about to be determined between death and slavery, who cares what the Ishmaelite camels carried?

Rashi, nonetheless, attaches significance to these details, explaining that they remind us that God provides recompense for every deed.[1] Ishmaelite caravans ordinarily carried foul-smelling cargoes such as kerosene and tar; on account of Yosef's merit, however, this one's cargo was sweet-smelling. Considering the first point, however, we might add that Yosef has demerits as well, otherwise why emphasize, via the redundancy, that he was still in mortal jeopardy in the pit?

✒ PART TWO: WHERE THE DETAILS ARE

The relevant details of a story, however, are not always readily apparent. In the story of the sale of Yosef, for instance, some pertinent details are withheld from us for a while. Read the following verse from next week's *sidrah*:

---

[1] See our discussion of this principle in last week's *sidrah*, Part Two.

Bereishit 42:21: [The brothers] said one to another: We are guilty regarding our brother because we saw his mortal distress as he implored us, yet we did not listen. That is why this trouble has overtaken us.

In the earlier narrative (chapter 37), Yosef is not described as imploring his brothers. Why is that information "withheld" from us at that stage in the narrative? Ramban (42:21) provides three answers.

1. In chapter 37, Yosef as well as his brothers have their faults. Yosef tattles on and lords it over them, and they are too quick to condemn him. If the Torah were to take note of Yosef crying out, it would tip the affective balance entirely in his favor. In chapter 42, on the other hand, we are dealing with the brothers' remorse, not their earlier cruelty.

2. It would have been natural for Yosef to cry out in that predicament. Whatever is natural is also self-understood, and whatever is self-understood need not be explicitly mentioned.[2]

3. Abbreviating the event and elongating the account is an appropriate literary device. The detail of Yosef's crying out is cited in the account because there it affects the brothers, whereas it appears to have had no effect on them at the time of the event itself.

✌ PART THREE: WHO'S THAT MAN I SAW YOU WITH? THAT WAS NO MAN – THAT WAS....

When Yosef goes out to find his brothers in Shekhem, he suffers an initial setback: unbeknownst to him, they have moved on to Dotan. Yosef wanders about the outskirts of Shekhem searching for them until "a man" sets him straight.

A comparison between Rashi's commentary and those of Ibn Ezra and Ramban (all to 37:15) will be most illuminating.

A. Man or Angel?

Rashi: "It was [the archangel] Gavriel, as it is written (Daniel 9:11): "Gavriel, the man.""

---

[2] See the very first point we made in the *sidrah* of Va-Yishlah regarding ellipsis.

Ibn Ezra: "According to the *peshat*, a passerby."

Given Rashi's pronounced propensity towards straightforward interpretation, what compelled him to abandon the simple sense of the verse (*peshat*) – as stipulated by Ibn Ezra – and seek refuge in an Aggadah? Two considerations might have influenced his decision: the striking "coincidental" nature of their encounter, and the man's knowledge of the brothers' whereabouts.

How might Ibn Ezra respond to these considerations? Given the history of Yosef's brothers and the city of Shekhem (i.e., the rape of Dinah), it would have been more remarkable if anyone in the vicinity was not aware of their every move! In contemporary terms, we would venture that their photos adorned the walls of every post office in Shekhem, bearing the legend *Wanted: Dead.*

B. Is there "Coincidence?"

> **Ramban:** God summoned for him a guide – unawares – so he would fall into [his brothers'] hands. This is what our Sages meant when they referred to these persons as "angels." This episode is not narrated for naught, but to inform us that "God's counsel will triumph."

Ramban, as he indicates in his Prologue to the *humash*, is trying to synthesize the commentaries of his predecessors. In essence, he says, both are correct: Ibn Ezra is correct and the "man" was a mortal passerby; Rashi, however, is correct, too, since mortals who serve as divine agents are regarded, Aggadically, as "angels." Their appearance is due to Providence, not coincidence.

Note: The word "angel" derives from the Greek *angelos*, which means, literally, a messenger. In contemporary English, we usually reserve "angel" for divine messengers, although such expressions as "angel of mercy" for a nurse preserve the other usage. The Hebrew noun *mal'akh* is related to the noun *mela'khah*. Both derive from the verbal root *l-'-kh* (which never appears as a verb in the *Tanakh*). Since *melakhah* is defined as work or task, a *mal'akh* should be defined as one who performs the work or task.

Take several English translations of the Torah and see whether they translate all occurrences of *mal'akh* the same way. Compare them, if you wish, with the Aramaic *Targum* of *Onkelos*; sometimes he translates *mal'akh* as *izgeda* – a messenger – and other times as *mal'akha* – an angel. Can you detect a pattern to the different usages?[3]

C. Why Did Yosef Merit?

In the commentary of Rashi (to 37:25) that we cited in the opening passage, Yosef's merit earned him a trip to Egypt in a caravan bearing incense rather than one carrying the usual Ishmaelite cargo of tar and naphtha. While the merit appears to be the result of the respect he showed his father by following his instructions to report on the health of his brothers and their sheep, ordinary reverence for parents shouldn't entitle one to a special reward. Implicitly, then Yosef's reverence here was extraordinary.

As Rashbam notes (to 37:15):

> This [episode] was written to tell Yosef's praise, that he did not want to return to his father when he did not find [his brothers] in Shekhem. Instead, he searched for them until he found them. Even though he knew that they were jealous of him, he went and sought them out since his father had ordered him to "report to me."

Note: Bereishit 37:11 states explicitly, "His brothers envied him and his father kept it in mind." If Yaakov knew: (a) that Yosef's brothers harbored ill will toward him and (b) that Shekhem was dangerous territory for any son of Yaakov at any time (see 34:30), how could he have sent Yosef there alone?!

The Aggadah intimates that Yosef's mission was preordained and that Yaakov essentially had to dispatch him on it. Rashi even cites this Aggadah in his commentary (37:14):

> "He [Yaakov] dispatched him [Yosef] from the valley of Hevron." Isn't Hevron atop a mountain?… Rather [it means] he sent him on account of the profound advice of the venerable one who is buried in Hevron [Avraham], in fulfillment of that which was said to Avraham in the Covenant between the Pieces: "Your descendants will be strangers in a foreign land" (15:13).

---

[3] For more on *mal'akhim*, see Va-Yeira, Part Three.

MIKEITZ

Ups and Downs

RASHI ON ASCENDING AND DESCENDING

◌ PREFACE

In Va-Yeshev, we noted that Nehama wrote an essay devoted entirely to the story of Yosef and his brothers.[1] This week we shall continue to derive some of our sources and inspiration from that essay.

◌ PART ONE: YOSEF TAKES NO CREDIT

Read – carefully, of course – Chapter 41 verses 25–36, as Yosef discusses Pharaoh's dream in a relatively long speech. Note exactly where the name of God appears! If we were to analyze the structure of Yosef's speech, we would obtain a pyramid-type structure in which God's name is inserted strategically throughout. The underlined verse numbers contain the references to God.

<u>25</u>
26–27
<u>28</u>
29–30–31
<u>32</u>
33–34–35–36

Yosef cites God at the beginning and between each of the parts of his interpretation of Pharaoh's dream. In fact, in v. 32 God is named twice – something not required by Biblical syntax since the subject has not changed in the interim – indicating that Yosef carefully sculpted his reply to Pharaoh

---

[1] Nehama Leibowitz: "How to Read a Chapter of Tanakh." In *Torah Insights* (Jerusalem: 1995), 163–176.

in order to emphasize the central role of God in both the dream and in its interpretation. Pharaoh, in turn, appears to be so impressed with Yosef's deference to God that he refers to it himself not once but twice (vv. 38–39).

As Nehama writes:

> Yosef, at every moment of trial or transition, carries the name of God as a flag, repeatedly emphasizing in an idolatrous world: To Whom does man sin? [Referring to 39:9] Who interprets people's dreams? Who foretells future events? Who declares and does?
>
> He does this without explaining details, just by repeating a word. Pharaoh grasped the point and replied accordingly: "Can such a man be found, a man in whom there is the spirit of God?" (v. 38) And again: "After God has informed you of all this…" (v. 39) (*Torah Insights*, 168).

Lingering momentarily on structures, Nehama calls our attention to the fact that the brothers' first visit to Egypt (42:7 ff.) and their return to their father (42:29 ff.) also follow a detailed, symmetrical structure:

Yosef and his brothers converse	Yaakov and sons converse
Interlude of the three-day imprisonment	Lengthy interlude
They converse again	They converse again

Note: She also notes that "The second visit also has an interesting and deliberate symmetrical structure, though differing from this one." Try to discern the pattern of the brothers' second visit with Yosef (43:15–44:34).

ೞ PART TWO: IT'S ALL A QUESTION OF PERSPECTIVE

Read the first six verses of chapter 42 and note that the Torah refers to Yosef's brothers in four different ways: Yaakov's sons (v. 1); Yosef's brothers (vv. 3, 6); Binyamin's brothers (v. 4); the sons of Israel (v. 5).

Each of these designations signifies a different perspective. Yaakov speaks to "his sons" and sends them on the errand to Egypt. But the moment the word "Egypt" sounds, Scripture prepares us for the reunion by transforming them into "Yosef's brothers." Not sending Binyamin with "his brothers" insinuates the same discrimination that Yaakov earlier practiced with Yosef. Finally, from the perspective of the Egyptians watching them arrive they are "Israelites," a purely ethnic designation.

In a related vein, Rashi notes (42:3):

> Yosef's brothers descended: It doesn't say "Yaakov's sons." This informs us that they experienced remorse over his sale and made up their minds to treat him fraternally and redeem him at whatever price would be demanded.

Note: Additional examples in Bereishit of the use of different designations for the same person or people, reflecting the different perspectives of the participants and/or Scripture, are: 14:12–16, re: Lot, and 21:9–20, re: Yishmael. Examine those verses and see if you can spot, and interpret, the differences.

๕ PART THREE: WHEN "DOWN" ISN'T A DIRECTION, BUT A STATE OF MIND

Nehama, in her essay devoted to Rashi's criteria for citing *midrashim*,[2] remarks:

> Rashi makes sparing use of those *midrashim* that provide metaphorical or figurative explanations to expressions that can be readily understood literally (i.e., according to their *peshat*). Where he does use them, there is generally a linguistic reason (*Torah Insights*, p. 123).

Many *midrashim* interpret the words "ascending" and "descending" in a non-literal sense, indicating spiritual elevation or demotion, or even fluctuating social or economic circumstances. Let us look at several such comments in Rashi and see if we can establish a pattern of usage – as Nehama suggests – the better to understand several appearances of descent in our *sidrah*, which we will cite below.

Let us first compare Rashi on a pair of related verses in Shemot to a pair in Devarim:

1. "Go! Go down!" (*lekh reid*): Descend from your greatness, for I only granted you greatness for their sake (i.e., the people) (Shemot 32:7).

2. "Go, ascend from here" (*leikh 'aleh*): Since the Land of Israel is higher than all other countries it says: "ascend." Alternately, God, in

---

2 See our Preface to Bereishit.

anger, told Moshe: "Go down." Now that He is appeased, He said "Go up" (Shemot 33:1). On the other hand, the next two verses occasion no comment from Rashi, even though they are interpreted by the Midrash.

3. "Ascend *('aleh)* these heights of Avarim": The *Sifrei* comments: "This is an ascent and not a descent" (Devarim 32:49).

4. "Moshe went up *(va-ya'al)*... to Mount Nevo": In the *Sifrei*: "It is an ascent and not a descent" (Devarim 34:1).

Why did Rashi cite the Midrash in the pair of verses in Shemot, but not in the pair from Devarim? The reason, as Nehama indicated, is linguistic. The first verse in Shemot utilizes an "auxiliary" verb: *lekh* (go), which already indicates activity. Since Moshe was atop a mountain, he could only have descended, so adding "down" is either superfluous or metaphorical. Regarding the second verse, the route from Egypt to Israel consists of mostly level country (before any mountains are encountered), so Rashi cites both a *peshat* and a *derash*.

The next set of verses citing ostensible directions is drawn from the *sidrah* we are studying:

1. 42:2, "Go *(redu)* down there"

2. 42:4, "Yosef's brothers went down" *(va-yeredu)*

3. 43:15, "they went down *(va-yeredu)* to Egypt"

4. 43:20, "We indeed came down" *(yarod yaradnu)*

Of these, Rashi comments only on the last, saying, metaphorically: "It is a comedown for us. We who are accustomed to supporting others now need your support." Applying Nehama's criterion of textual justification for the use of a Midrash, Rashi was probably troubled by the repetition of the verb *y-r-d*, which he took as an indication of a state of mind rather than an actual direction.

✍ PART FOUR: INTRODUCING... SUPER-COMMENTARY!

Rashi's commentary on the Torah stimulated almost as much subsequent interest as the Torah itself. Hundreds (literally) of later scholars have sought to explain or elaborate upon his interpretations, probing his motives and cross-examining his proof texts. Their works are known, generically, as "super-commentaries," essentially, commentaries on a commentary. The best known are those composed by Rabbi Eliyahu Mizrahi (Turkey, sixteenth century) and the Maharal of Prague (entitled *Gur Aryeh*, sixteenth century).[3]

Here is what one of them has to contribute to the commentary of Rashi in Part Three.

> **Mizrahi:** Rashi does not base this on the use of the expression "came down" since the Land of Israel is higher than the surrounding countries and whoever enters it goes up, and whoever leaves it goes down [cf. Rashi on 45:9]. Hence, the statement "they went down to Egypt" (43:15) arouses no comment.
>
> What prompted Rashi was the expression "we indeed came down" (43:20), just as the Talmud (*Bava Metzia* 31b) treats other duplications as redundancies... The principle that "the Torah expresses itself in normal human language" is applied only where there is no basis for a homily, but where there is – we apply it.

As we noted at the close of Part Three, the redundancy justified Rashi's use of *derash*.

---

[3] A list of the supercommentaries consulted most frequently by Nehama appears in the essay we cited in the Preface to Bereishit: "Rashi's Criteria for Citing Midrashim."

VA-YIGASH

Life and Death are in the Hands of Language

RESOLVING AMBIGUITIES

&o PREFACE: AMBIGUITY; AGAIN?

In Part One of the *sidrah* of Tol'dot, we discussed the case of ambiguous pronoun reference, illustrating it by means of the two-part commentary of Rashi on the words: *ki tzayid be-fiv.* Yitzhak loved Esav, for the prey was in his [whose?] mouth. There are several ambiguous phrases in the current *sidrah* as well, and we will begin with them.

&o PART ONE: WHO WOULD LIVE, AND (MORE TO THE POINT) WHO WOULD DIE?

Yehudah steps forward to argue Binyamin's case before Yosef. He reminds Yosef that it was his idea to bring Binyamin down to Egypt [now I've gone and done it, too; whose idea was it – Yosef's or Yehudah's?] and that he had cautioned him that Binyamin could not leave Yaakov. Yehudah's exact words are (44:22): "The lad cannot leave his father, for if he were to leave his father – *he* would die."

The obvious question, of course, is: Who would die?

Answer 1: Surely Yaakov, the elderly father. Already bereft of the older son of his favorite wife, he would not recover from the loss of her only surviving child.

Answer 2: Surely Binyamin, the frail and pampered youngest child, whose mother died in childbirth and whose older brother – for all intents and purposes – was also dead.

In the case we cited in Tol'dot, we discovered textual evidence to decide the question of the prey. Is there comparable textual evidence to decide this question?

Answer 1: A subsequent verse (44:3) supports the answer that they feared for Yaakov's life: "When [Yaakov] sees that [Binyamin] is missing, we will be responsible for sending our elderly father to an early grave."

Answer 2: An earlier verse (42:4) supports the answer that it was Binyamin's life for which they were concerned: "Yaakov did not send Binyamin, Yosef's brother, along with his other brothers because he feared that an accident would befall him."

Since we cannot definitively resolve the question through direct Scriptural citation, let us refer it to a panel of experts: the medieval commentators.

Answer 1: Clearly the first interpretation [i.e., Yaakov would die], as Rashbam states [also Bekhor Shor, Shadal, and Ibn Ezra – as cited by Ramban]: "His father would die."

Answer 2: Clearly the second interpretation, as Rashi says [also Targum and Ramban]: "If [Binyamin] left his father we were concerned lest he die *en route,* just as his mother died *en route.*"

Since we cannot resolve the question through recourse to the medieval commentators either, let us refer it to the moderns. [Note that the moderns follow the medievals and utilize the Scriptural support that we have already cited.]

Answer 1: The Jewish Publication Society's Torah Commentary sides with the first interpretation, translating the verse: "The boy cannot leave his father; if he were to leave him, his father would die." In the commentary, Nahum Sarna explains: "Actually, the subject of the Hebrew verb *va-met* is ambiguous. It may be either Benjamin or the father. In light of verse 31, the latter is the more likely."

Answer 2: The ArtScroll Stone Humash clearly supports the second interpretation, commenting: "Jacob reasoned: ... I sent Joseph on a journey and he did not return; the same might happen to Benjamin, for their mother, too, died on the road."

What is the final resolution to be? If there is neither Scriptural evidence, nor medieval commentary, nor modern interpretation adequate to the task of deciding, unambiguously, whose life was in jeopardy, how are we ever to know?

There are actually two answers to this question, too.

Answer 1: We don't have to know. In fact, Talmudic tradition (*Yoma* 52b) acknowledges our inability to resolve every Scriptural ambiguity satisfactorily, relegating such ambiguous verses to a special category called: *she-ein lahem hekhrea'* – unresolved.

Answer 2: If both possibilities have equal textual support, medieval justification, and modern verification, then they are both likely to be right. In answer to the question of whose life was in jeopardy, we would then answer: both Yaakov's and Binyamin's.

Note: Ibn Ezra notes that our verse is not among the five unresolved ambiguities that are listed in *Yoma* 52b. Can this be construed as indicative, let alone conclusive evidence, that it must be resolved?

✸ PART TWO: *'OD AVINU HAY:* REVIVING YAAKOV'S SPIRITS

After their reunion with Yosef, the brothers return to Canaan to prepare their father for the trip to Egypt. They tell him (45:26): "Yosef still lives and he rules over the entire land of Egypt," but "his heart went numb [or: failed] because he did not believe them." In order to convince him, they tell him all the things Yosef told them and they show him the wagons that Yosef sent to transport him. As a result: "Yaakov's spirits were revived" (v. 27).

A close look at these two consecutive verses shows that each one consists of two parts:

> **v. 26:** (a) Yosef still lives, and (b) he rules over the entire land of Egypt;

> **v. 27:** (a) they tell him all the things Yosef told them, and (b) they show him the [royal] wagons that Yosef sent to transport him.

The natural relationship these parts bear to one another is: a:a and b:b. In other words, to convince him that Yosef was still alive the brothers told him what Yosef had said, and to prove that he ruled over Egypt they showed him the wagons. What did Yosef "tell" them that confirmed his identity?

According to Rashbam, he didn't tell them anything as much as give them the opportunity to approach him (45:4) and satisfy themselves, close up (45:14–15), that he was, indeed, their brother (45:12). According to Rashi, who plays on the word *'agalot* (wagons), Yosef gave his brothers a piece of information that only he and Yaakov shared, namely that when they parted 22 years earlier, they had been engaged in a discussion of the laws of the *'eglah 'arufah*.

Note: Why didn't Yaakov's spirits revive immediately upon hearing that Yosef was alive? Why did that await the additional and ostensibly secondary news that he was the ruler of Egypt?

ഔ PART THREE: LIVING AND EATING APART

When Yosef's family is finally reunited with him, he prepares to introduce his father and brothers to Pharaoh. He counsels his brothers: "When Pharaoh summons you and asks you your livelihood, tell him: Your servants have been herdsmen since our youth and in the manner of our ancestors." For what purpose were they to disclose this information? "In order that you shall dwell in the land of Goshen because the Egyptians abhor shepherds" (46:33–34). The Egyptian abhorrence of shepherds, matched by their aversion to eating the flesh of cattle and sheep, was on account of their worship of those animals [see Rashi, here, and Targum on 43:32].

This taboo clarifies an earlier verse in the *sidrah* of Va-Yeshev and raises a challenge to Rashi's commentary thereupon.

After being sold to Potiphar (39:1ff.), Yosef demonstrates his capabilities and quickly rises to the position of overseer in his house. In appraisal of this situation we read (v.6): "[Potiphar] left all that he possessed in Yosef's hands, not concerning himself with anything except the bread which he ate; and Yosef was fair of form and fair to look at." Based on our prior discussion, it appears clear that on account of the taboo we were discussing, Yosef, a Hebrew, was ineligible to oversee the preparation of food for Egyptian consumption. This, in fact, is the interpretation offered here by Ibn Ezra.

Rashi, however, comments: "The bread refers, euphemistically, to [Potiphar's] wife." Why did Rashi abandon the *peshat* in favor of a *derash*? He could have been motivated by the juxtaposition of the bread with a description of Yosef's striking physical appearance. Such a description is certainly more intelligible in relation to Potiphar's wife than it is to his meals.

Note: The matter of Egyptian taboos regarding sheep plays a prominent role in the story of the exodus from Egypt, as we propose to demonstrate in the *sidrah* of Bo'. After the plague of *'arov* (swarms – of either insects or wild beasts), Pharaoh is prepared to allow the Jews to offer the sacrifices they requested, providing that they don't leave Egypt in the process. Moshe rejects the proposition, saying: "It would not be wise to do this, for it is Egypt's abomination which we would slaughter to our God; if we were to slaughter Egypt's abomination before their very eyes – would they not stone us?" (Shemot 8:22).

VA-YEHI

Who Said What to Whom?

ANONYMITY, ELLIPSIS AND REPETITION IN THE BIBLE

❧ PREFACE: DEALING WITH ANONYMITY

In the *sedarim* of previous weeks, we have dealt with the phenomenon of syntactical ambiguity.[1] This week we will continue with syntactically troubling verses, but of a different order. This time, there is not ambiguity regarding the subject – or object – of a verb; there is complete anonymity.

❧ PART ONE: WHO IS DOING ALL THE TELLING?

Read the following verses (48:1–2):

> Afterwards, *he* said to Yosef: Your father is ill. So he took his two sons – Ephraim and Menasheh – with him. *He* said to Yaakov: "Your son, Yosef, has arrived."

The text does not identify either who spoke to Yosef in verse 1, or who spoke to Yaakov in verse 2.

Rashi comments:

> A speaker [anonymously] spoke to him. This is an elliptical verse [*mikra' katzer*].[2] Alternatively: Ephraim customarily kept Yaakov's

---

[1] See, for example, Va-Yigash, Part One.

[2] Ellipsis, sometimes called *derekh ketzarah* (literally: a shortcut), is a form of abbreviation sometimes used in literature. A word, or words, required to make a sentence grammatically or syntactically complete, may be left out providing they are logically obvious and can be supplied by the reader. In Bereishit 41:13, Rashi explains: "This is the way of all elliptical verses: when [it is obvious] who is doing

company to study with him. When Yaakov took ill in the Land of Goshen, Ephraim brought the news to his father in Mitzrayim.

Essentially, Rashi treats both verses the same way – elliptically – as though they said: "[Someone] said to Yosef… and [someone] said to Yaakov." All the "Alternatively" (yesh 'omerim) adds is an Aggadic identification of the "someone."

Similarly, read the following verse (Bemidbar 8:4):

> This is the fashion of the Menorah… according to the appearance that God displayed to Moshe, so did *he* fashion the Menorah.

Since we know that Moshe didn't fashion the Menorah himself, rather he appointed craftsmen to do the actual work (see Shemot 31:1–8, and 37:1–17), to whom is the Torah referring as "he"? Rashi (Bemidbar 8:4) offers two interpretations, just as he does in Bereishit. The first: "Whoever fashioned it," treats the verse as an "ordinary" example of ellipsis. Then, however, Rashi proceeds to cite a Midrash Aggadah [*Tanhuma*] to the effect that "through God, it was fashioned all by itself."

Like most exegetical Aggadot – as opposed to the homiletical variety – this Aggadah has a basis in the straightforward reading of the verse. It presumes that God, who is the subject of the verb "displayed" (her'ah), remains the subject of "fashioned" ('asah), as well. As regards the notion that the Menorah was fashioned "by itself," this, too, is anchored in a verse (Shemot 25:31): "You shall make a Menorah of pure gold; the Menorah shall be made…," using the passive form of the verb tei'aseh (will be fashioned), rather than the same active form [ta'aseh], with which the verse began.

What is the difference between Rashi's treatment of the anonymity in Bereishit and that in Bemidbar?

In Bereishit, as we have just pointed out, his two identifications (someone/Ephraim) are feasible simultaneously. In Bemidbar, however, the two (whoever/God) are mutually exclusive.

[the action] – it remains anonymous." The ambiguity arises when more than one logical possibility exists.

We have treated ellipsis in Va-Yishlah, Part One, and refer to it again (along with metonymy) in Nitzavim, Part Four.

To review and summarize, let us look at an earlier verse in Bereishit in which Rashi "codifies" his treatment of this phenomenon. In 41:13, the chief butler recounts Yosef's dream-interpreting prowess to Pharaoh, saying in conclusion: "It happened just as he interpreted for us; he restored me to my post, and hung him [the baker]." Who did the restoring and hanging? Rashi comments:

> The one capable of restoring, namely Pharaoh who is mentioned above (verse 10: "Pharaoh became enraged..."). This verse is elliptical since it does not note who restored. This is the way of all elliptical verses: when [it is obvious] who is doing [the action] – it remains anonymous.

If Rashi feels that the subject is not obvious, however, as in the case with which we began (since many people could have spoken with Yosef and Yaakov), he might resort to an Aggadic identification.

∞ PART TWO: YAAKOV'S LAST WILL

While our *sidrah* is conventionally called "Yaakov's blessing," it is clear that, quite to the contrary, he does not bless every one of his children. What he has to say to Shimon and Levi, for example, hardly constitutes a blessing (49:5–7):

> Shimon and Levi, the brothers, deal in instruments of violence. Let me not enter into their council, let my reputation not be joined with their assembly; for in their anger they slew a man and by their desire they maimed a bull. Their fierce anger is accursed and so is their intense rage; let them be split up and scattered among Yaakov and Israel.

Yaakov is referring to the incident concerning Dinah (Bereishit 34), in which Shimon and Levi fell upon the men of Shekhem after they had undergone circumcision, and slew them. At the time, Yaakov rebuked them sharply, saying (34:30): "You have sullied my reputation in the eyes of the local inhabitants...."

Here, Yaakov is reiterating that rebuke. The "council" that he condemns is the one that gave the people of Shekhem the insidious advice to undergo the debilitating circumcision, and the "assembly" is the nefarious attack on them that followed.

If the "council" and "assembly" allude to the incident at Shekhem, to the slaying of which "man" and the maiming of what "bull" is Yaakov referring? A glance at Ramban will illustrate the array of the exegetical possibilities.

1. Onkelos interprets *shor* (ox) as though it were vocalized *shur* (a wall). After killing the men of Shekhem, they uprooted its walls.

2. Others say that the ox, the largest domestic animal, represents Hamor and Shekhem, the princes of the land.

3. I [Ramban], however, treat the verse literally: After killing the people, they castrated their cattle.

Why refer to Shimon and Levi, superfluously, as brothers? A *peshat* answer would interpret "brothers" as a code word for concerted action, deriving from the incident at Shekhem for which they were mutually responsible. The Aggadah (*Bereishit Rabbah* 99), however, focuses on the word *ahim*, detecting not only a clear reference to Shekhem (34:25): "Shimon and Levi, Dinah's brothers (*ahei Dinah*), took each man his sword," but also an allusion to the sale of Yosef (37:19): "They said, each man to his brother (*ahiv*), here comes that dreamer...."

In establishing a link between the destruction of Shekhem and the sale of Yosef, this Aggadah leads us to a source that stipulates a direct moral link between the two events. *Seder Eliyahu Rabbah* (chapter 28) states:

> One who can shed the blood of a gentile is capable of shedding Jewish blood, whereas the Torah was given only to sanctify His great name.

✌ PART THREE: REPETITIVE OR SUPPLEMENTARY? A BASIC LOOK AT BIBLICAL POETRY

One of the most recognizable features of Biblical poetry is "synonymous parallelism," the duplication of the first part of a poetic verse in its second part through the use of synonyms. The medieval exegetes disagreed, however, whether the duplicated words are merely repetitious or whether the second part of the verse adds to, or modifies, the first. In this week's *sidrah* we see an example of this disagreement.

The verse reads (49:3): "Reuven, you are my firstborn, my strength and first of my vigor; exceeding in rank (or: loft; *se'et*) and honor (or: force; *'oz*)."

What is the relationship of "rank" to "honor"? Compare the approaches of Rashi and Ibn Ezra.

> **Rashi:** You were entitled to exceed your brothers in the priesthood – [symbolized by] the term "raising the hands" (*nesi'at kapayim*) – and in monarchy, to wit: "He shall give honor (*'oz*) to His king" (1 Shemuel 2:10).

> **Ibn Ezra:** Exceeding in rank: You were entitled to an advantage over all others, to be elevated (*nisa*). Exceeding in honor: The meaning is repetitious (*ha-ta'am kaful*) in the manner of all prophecies.

Rashi views the two parts of the sentence as expressing different, albeit related, propositions, while Ibn Ezra considers them to be virtually identical in meaning. Rashi's position is taken to its logical – if extreme – conclusion by the nineteenth-century exegete, Malbim (Meir Leibush ben Jehiel Michel Weiser, 1809–1879), who wrote in the introduction to his commentary on Isaiah:

> In prophetic discourse, there is no such thing as "repetition of the same idea in different words" [Ibn Ezra's phrase]. No repetitions of speech, no rhetorical repetitions, no two sentences with one meaning, no two comparisons of the same meaning, and not even two words that are repeated.

Let us take Isaiah 1:3 as an illustration:

> An ox knows his purchaser and a donkey his master's trough.

Whereas Ibn Ezra would treat the references to both an ox and a donkey as merely repetitious, Malbim insists that both were mentioned because of certain characteristics that are unique to each one. In fact, he maintains that there are differences between a "purchaser" and "master" as well, and that the two pairs of distinctions – an ox and a purchaser, and a donkey and a master – are intentionally matched![3]

---

[3] The subject of parallelism is given thorough treatment by Prof. James Kugel in his book *The Idea of Biblical Poetry* (Yale University Press: 1981). See 288 ff. for references to Malbim.

Shemot

SHEMOT

Peshat, *Derash* and *Mashma'*

RASHI'S EXEGETICAL TERMINOLOGY

❧ PREFACE: PESHAT IN THE TALMUD

The term *peshat*, in the specific form of *peshuto shel mikra'* (the *peshat* of the verse), appears only three times in the entire Talmud. A brief examination of one such appearance will suffice for our present purpose. The Mishnah (*Shabbat* 63a) stipulates that a man may not carry weapons into the public domain on Shabbat. Rabbi Eliezer disagrees, arguing that weapons are ornamental and may be worn as jewelry. In defense of his argument, he cites the verse: "Hero, gird your sword about your loins; it is your pride and joy" (Tehillim 45:4). This interpretation is challenged by Rav Kahana who states that the verse is universally understood, metaphorically, as a reference to scholars and their words of Torah. He is rebuffed by Mar brei de-Rav Huna, who stipulates: *Ein mikra yotze mi-yedei peshuto*; no verse can be purged of its literal sense.

While *peshat* seems to have meant "literal sense" in the Talmudic period, its usage changed over time. In the preface to Bereishit, we noted the critical works of Sarah Kamin and Benjamin Gelles on Rashi's exegetical terminology; here we shall refine those definitions further.

❧ PART ONE: THE SOURCES

While we have encountered the terms *peshat* and *derash* on several previous occasions, we have not yet examined the significance of the term *mashma'*, which appears prominently in the commentary of Rashi on this week's *sidrah*.

We shall look here at Rashi's commentary on three verses in our *sidrah* and treat them according to Dr. Leibowitz's prescription.[1]

1. 1:12: "As they were oppressing them, so they were increasing and multiplying…"

   Rashi: "As they were oppressing": To the same extent that [the Egyptians] were intent upon oppressing them, so was God intent upon increasing and multiplying them.

   "They were increasing": They increased and multiplied. According to the Midrash: The Holy Spirit spoke [to the Egyptians]: Just so! You said (v. 10): 'Lest they increase,' and I say: So they shall increase.

2. 2:12: "[Moshe] looked here and there, saw there was no one, struck the Egyptian and buried him in the sand."

   Rashi: "He looked about": He saw what he had done to him at home and what he had done to him in the field. According to the *peshat* – it accords with the *mashma'*.

3. 2:14: "Moshe was frightened and said: The affair has become known."

   Rashi: "Moshe was frightened": As its *peshat* [indicates]. According to the Midrash: He worried because he saw wicked informers among the Jews and he thought that perhaps they were not worthy of being redeemed.

   "The affair has become known": As its *mashma'* [indicates]. According to the Midrash: I have come to know that which perplexed me: What crime did the Jews commit that of all the seventy nations they were sentenced to savage servitude? I see now that they deserve it.

In each of these three verses, Rashi offers two interpretations of the same expression. Several questions present themselves.

---

[1] Nehama obtained her Ph.D. from the University of Berlin. Her dissertation concerned a Judeo-German translation of Tehillim and its relationship to Yiddish.

1. Why is the *peshat* interpretation not so labeled in #1 as it is in the two other examples? (Note: In some editions, it does indeed appear.)

2. Why doesn't Rashi suffice with one simple interpretation instead of citing the Midrash each time, as well?

3. What is the difference between *peshat* and *mashma*?

We shall try to answer these questions in the course of examining the three comments.

∞ PART TWO: IN THIS CORNER, THE *PESHAT*...

1. 1:12

This verse is what we might call an equational sentence signifying: "To the same extent that they oppressed them, so did they increase and multiply." However, such a statement cannot be understood as a natural cause and effect and invites an explanation of *deus ex machina,* a divine miracle. This is why Rashi stipulates, "So was God intent upon increasing and multiplying them," emphasizing that He countered the Egyptian intent to limit them by enabling them to increase.

As for his second comment, "[They were increasing] they increased and multiplied," Rashi appears to be responding to a linguistic challenge: Why are all these verbs conjugated in the imperfect tense? Rashi replies, essentially, that they could just as well have been in the perfect; the meaning is the same.

This explanation would also provide Answer 1: Since Rashi is not providing an actual interpretation here, but is only issuing a grammatical clarification, there is clearly no need to label it as *peshat*.

2-3. 2:11–14

Anyone reading these verses understands that when Moshe realized that his killing and burying the Egyptian had become public knowledge, he took fright lest he be arrested, or even executed, by the authorities. In fact, the very next verse reads: "When Pharaoh heard this, he attempted to have Moshe killed." This is what Rashi means by: "Moshe was frightened: as its *peshat* [indicates]," and "The affair has become known: as its *mashma'* [indicates]."

The Midrash, on the other hand, views Moshe and his actions from a completely different perspective and in a different dimension. To see this comprehensively, we must go a few verses back and read them, Midrashically, with Rashi's assistance:

(v. 11) Moshe went out to his brothers to empathize with their tribulations. He spotted an Egyptian taskmaster striking a Hebrew man, the husband of Shlomit bat Divri. The Egyptian, having taken a fancy to her, threw her husband out of his house and came back to have his way with her. When the husband, on his return, realized what had happened, the Egyptian set upon him and beat him all day long.

(v. 12) When Moshe saw what the Egyptian had been doing to the Hebrew both at home [with his wife] and in the field [beating him], and ascertained that none of his descendants would become converts, he slew him....

(v. 13) On the morrow he encountered two Hebrews fighting....

(v. 14) [One of the Hebrews] said: Are you saying I should be killed... [the use of "saying"] indicating that he had slain the Egyptian by reciting the sacred name.

This somewhat long-winded Midrashic recital provides an important perspective on Moshe Rabbeinu. He is not a thoughtless, impulsive killer, as a *peshat* reading alone could imply. He is a man of God who is made privy (by God) to secret contretemps and to future contingencies and who slays evildoers with "the sacred name," i.e., not with brute force but with divine power.

This explanation provides an answer to question 2.

❧ PART THREE: WHAT DISTINGUISHES *PESHAT* FROM *MASHMA*?

We are left with the question: What is the difference between *peshat* and *mashma*? Nehama illustrates the difference by comparing several appearances of the same word, *yad* (hand):

> Literally, a hand is a five-fingered extremity with which one grasps or holds things, gives and takes, writes, etc. However, it has non-literal meanings as well. For example, Eliezer, Avraham's major domo, is said to have departed for Aram "with all the goods of his master in his hand (*be-yado*)" (Bereishit 24:10). It is difficult to

imagine him doing so literally, as much of his master's goods consisted of "sheep, cattle, slaves, and maidservants" (12:16). Therefore, every Hebrew speaker understands that "in his hand," in this instance, means in his possession (compare 31:29). However, when it comes to "[Yaakov] took whatever came into his hand (*be-yado*) as a gift for his brother, Esav" (32:14), Rashi says: "Into his hand, his possession…. According to the Midrash… this refers to precious stones and pearls which people wrap up and carry by hand."

Nehama concludes:

> Here, the *peshat* doesn't follow the literal sense, whereas the Midrash does, since the *peshat* of a verse is its interpretation according to its context and subject, not necessarily according to the literal sense of every one of its words… (*Rashi's Commentary on the Torah*, 469).

In other words, in this verse the *peshat* is non-literal whereas the Midrash is literal! To appreciate Nehama's point, let us reflect on the literal sense of the word *mashma'*. Derived from the verbal root *shin-mem-ayin*, it means "audible," and is used along with *mamash* (tangible), *milluli* (vocable), and *tzurah* (visible), to designate "literal." All four of these words derive from the five senses, implying that *mashma'*, as an exegetical term, signifies that "what you see (hear, taste, or feel) is what you get," rather than an imitation (such as a metaphor).

This explanation provides an answer to question 3.

✍ PART FOUR: TALKING ABOUT HANDS…

Shemot 2:5 describes how Pharaoh's daughter took possession of the box (*teivah*) containing baby Moshe. It says: "She sent forth her *'amah* and she took it." The question is: What was her *'amah*?

Rashi says: "Her maid, but our rabbis treated it homiletically (*darshu*) as an arm." He then proceeds to note, disconcertingly, that "according to Hebrew grammar [were it an arm] the *mem* would have a *daggesh*" [and the *mem* of *'amah* does not].

Our standard question of why Rashi is not satisfied with the *peshat* meaning, "her maid," is surpassed here by an even greater perplexity: Why does he persist in adding the Aggadah ("her arm grew exceedingly long") particularly as he himself notes that it is unacceptable grammatically?

Assuming once again that Rashi utilized the Aggadah primarily when he finds the *peshat* unsatisfactory, it is possible that his problem with the *peshat* of "her maid" lies in the fact that when the princess's maids are introduced at the beginning of the verse, they are called *na'arot*. Rashi may have reasoned: If the princess sent one of her maids after the box, the Torah should have said: "She sent forth her *na'arah*." The use of *'amah*, then, is suspicious and justifies a homily.

Note: Find *teivah* in a concordance. What do you make of the fact that it appears only here and with Noah? See our note to the *sidrah* of Noah at the end of Part One.

VA-'ERA

It's Hard to Say

MOSHE'S SPEECH DIFFICULTY

୫୬ PREFACE: WE'VE BEEN HERE BEFORE

By now, it might appear that most of the time spent by exegetes on their interpretation of Tanakh is concerned with the resolution of syntactical or rhetorical ambiguities. That is correct. It stands to reason that anything that can be understood literally requires no interpretation. In fact, one of the very earliest commentators on the Torah, Sa'adiah Gaon, stipulates in the introduction to his commentary that an exegete should, *a priori*, take everything in the Torah literally and need not comment unless the literal sense contradicts sense perception, reason, another unambiguous verse, or a reliable (i.e., rabbinical) tradition.[1]

We turn, now, to a series of verses which can be seen as ambiguous not on account of deficient syntax, but content. These verses contain references or responses to previous statements, which are not sufficiently clear or unambiguous.

୫୬ PART ONE: GOD'S PROMISE: CAUSE AND EFFECT

In Shemot 6:2–8, we read one of God's inaugural addresses to Moshe. In vv. 2–5, God refers to His appearance to the patriarchs and notes that the oppression suffered by their descendants has prompted Him to recall His covenant. In vv. 6–8, Moshe is instructed to tell the Jews that God will redeem them and bring them to the Promised Land that they will inherit.

---

[1] Moshe Zucker, *Saadya's Commentary on Genesis.* New York: 1982, 191. Also, see our discussion in the *sidrah* of Shemot of "literal" apropos of the term *mashma'*.

Based upon the key word *lakhen* ("therefore"), which appears at the beginning of v. 6, it appears that the relationship between the two halves of the address is causative; whatever is described prior to v. 6 is responsible for what follows it (*post hoc, ergo propter hoc*).

Rashi disagrees, and limits the syntactical and substantive scope of the word *lakhen*, saying: "Therefore: by virtue of that very oath," alluding to an oath that is implied in v. 4 in the reference to the covenant. There is also a relationship – according to Rashi – between the allusion to an oath in v. 4 and the explicit reference to one in v. 8. In fact, Rashi treats the repetitious phrase "I am the Lord" as referring, specifically, to the fulfillment of the oath. Compare his comments on v. 2 and 6:

> **Rashi (v. 2):** *He said to him, I am the Lord:* I am reliable to bestow a reward on those who walk before Me. I sent you only in fulfillment of My word to their early ancestors. This is consistent with phraseology elsewhere, such as: "You have profaned My holy name, I am the Lord" (Va-Yikra 19:12), which signifies the trustworthiness to punish, and "You shall observe My commandments and perform them, I am the Lord" (22:31), which signifies the trustworthiness to reward.
>
> **(v. 6):** *Tell the Israelites, I am the Lord:* Trustworthy [to fulfill] My promise.

Note: See Rashi's commentary on Yehezkel 16:8, in which he cites our verse from Shemot – according to his interpretation – as an illustration of God's trustworthiness in the matter of His promise.

❧ PART TWO: WHEN RASHI RESTRICTS *MIDRASHIM* TO PARTICULAR PASSAGES

On several prior occasions, we have attempted to adumbrate Rashi's position on the use of Aggadah in the resolution of Scriptural difficulties. We have noted that Nehama dedicated an entire essay to this subject from which we now cite again:

Three of his methods in utilizing *midrashim* demonstrate Rashi's viewpoint:

- At times, he notes the existence of certain *midrashim* to a particular verse without actually quoting them. If you carefully examine these *midrashim,* you will understand why he refrained from quoting them, yet could not ignore them to the point of not mentioning them at all.

- He may present a *midrash* that, in its source, deals with several verses in different places in the Torah, and cite it in connection with just one verse or apply it to only some of the verses that it addresses. If you compare all these verses, you see that he could not have applied that *midrash* to any verse other than the one he chose.

- He may transfer a *midrash* from the verse to which it was originally addressed to another verse. If you examine this you will see that from a commentator's viewpoint the *midrash* chosen actually explains only the verse to which Rashi applied it, while the verse on which it originally appears contains no language or subject problem and the *midrash* there really does not shed light on the text as such (*Torah Insights,* 110).

We shall now proceed to illustrate the second of Nehama's three points from within the present *sidrah.*

In Bemidbar 12:13, we read: "Moshe cried out to God, saying: 'Please, God, cure her now!'" Rashi, citing the Sifrei, comments:

Why does Scripture use "saying" (*lemor*)? Moshe said: Let me know whether or not you will cure her. Whereupon God replied: If her father had spat in her face.... Rabbi Elazar ben Azaryah said: Four times Moshe asked [God] to tell him whether he would respond to his requests. The others are:

- (Shemot 6:12) "Moshe spoke before God, saying...." Moshe said: Tell me whether you will redeem them, whereupon God replied (v. 1): "Now you shall see what I will do to Pharaoh."

- (Bemidbar 27:16) "Moshe spoke to God saying, Let God, the master of spirit for all flesh, appoint a leader for the congregation," and God replied (v. 18) "Take for yourself...."

- (Devarim 3:23) "I pleaded with God at that time, saying...." and God replied (v. 26): "Enough!"

Rashi cites Rabbi Elazar's dictum on three of the four verses (the two verses in Bemidbar and the one in Devarim), but not to the fourth (in our *sidrah*)! Since Rashi cites the Midrash only when it fits well into the language of the text [*Aggadah ha-meyashevet divrei mikra*], he could not cite it here because it would require us to reverse the sequence of the verses and regard 6:1 as an answer to 6:12.

∞ PART THREE: HOW "HARD" WAS MOSHE'S SPEECH?

Twice in this week's *sidrah* Moshe refers to himself as *'aral sefatayim* (6:12, 30). A glance at some of the ancient and recent attempts to translate this expression will demonstrate its complexity. Onkelos translates it, figuratively, as "hard of speech," and Yonatan renders it, similarly, as "difficult of speech." The Old Jewish Publication Society translation (OJPS), on the other hand, has, literally, "uncircumcised speech," the New JPS version has "impeded speech," and Aryeh Kaplan, the least literal of all, has "no self-confidence."

Nehama appreciated nuanced translation; indeed, she often commends to us the German translation of Martin Buber and Franz Rosenzweig as singularly sensitive to, and reflective of, the original Hebrew text. A technique she approved of is to ascertain the correspondence between the translators and commentators. For instance, the JPS translation: "impeded speech," appears to correspond to Rashi's interpretation (6:12): *atum* (sealed, closed off). On the analogy of referring to deafness as *"arlah* of the ears" (Yirmiyahu 6:10), incomprehension as *"arlah* of the heart" (op. cit., 9:25), and prohibited fruits as *"arlah* of the tree" (Va-Yikra 19:23), Moshe, here, claims to have *"arlah* of the lips," i.e., he is inarticulate.

Underlying the disagreement over the translation is the question whether this condition was congenital or acquired. "Impeded speech" (NJPS) suggests a congenital defect, "no self-confidence" (Kaplan) is an acquired characteristic, and "uncircumcised lips" (OJPS) leaves it ambiguous. This is congruent with Moshe's previous remarks (4:10): "I am heavy of mouth (*kevad peh*) and heavy of tongue (*kevad lashon*)," which expression is just as ambiguous as "uncircumcised lips." It, too, can refer to either a congenital speech defect or an acquired one. If the former, God would have had to provide him a cure; if the latter – he had to offer reassurance.

In our standard search for textual confirmation of one alternative or the other, we are stymied, since God actually provides both. God's retort: "Who gives man a mouth? Who makes him dumb or deaf, sighted or blind?" (v. 11) implies the correction of a physical impediment, while "I will instruct you what to say" (v. 12) suggests encouragement rather than a cure.

Ibn Ezra, commenting on *kevad peh*, takes the "congenital" approach, saying: "He was born that way, with heavy speech, unable to pronounce labial and liquid consonants [i.e., the letters formed by the lips and the tongue]." A well-known Aggadah, on the other hand, takes the "acquired" approach, suggesting that Moshe was afflicted after placing a hot coal in his mouth. On the other hand, Aryeh Kaplan's translation of "no self-confidence" finds support in Moshe's retort (v. 13): "Make someone else your agent." If neither of God's solutions – separately or together – swayed him, it would appear to favor the interpretation that he lacked self-confidence.

The Midrash *Lekah Tov* combines some of these interpretations:

> Moshe made these remarks three times. One: "I am slow of speech" (4:10); two: "I am a man of impeded speech" (6:12); and three: "I am a man of impeded speech" (6:30). Why so often? In order to transform his speech (*millulo*) into oratory (*tzehut*). He said: Master of the Universe, if I go to Pharaoh with impeded speech, he will say: Was there no better servant to send than you?

> God replied (7:1): "I will place you in the role of a god to Pharaoh." Even though you are a man of impeded speech, you are in the role of god to Pharaoh, for this is the way our God performs miracles: (1) The axe head floats alongside its handle (2 Melakhim 6:6); (2) The bitter water is sweetened by a piece of wood (Shemot 15:25); and (3) During the time of Elisha, brackish water is cured with salt (2 Melakhim 2:21) – all in order to fashion one miracle within another.

BO

The Prerequisite to Ge'ulah

DEALING WITH CONTRADICTIONS

ࣷ PREFACE: CONTRADICTIONS

Anyone who reads Tanakh thoroughly will often encounter a verse that appears to be contradicted or challenged by another verse, sometimes located in another Biblical book. Our Sages referred to these instances as *ketuvim* (verses) *hamakh'hishim* (that contradict) *zeh et zeh* (one another) and advised seeking a third, decisive verse to resolve the contradiction. Their advice is reflected in a statement attributed to R. Avraham ben David (Rabad) of Posquières (thirteenth century):

> We are obliged to study and reconcile any two verses that challenge one another. We may not dismiss one [out of hand], nor may we regard the Torah as being confused.

This week, we shall enumerate some of the kinds of contradictions that verses present to one another, or challenges that they pose to our expectations. The first two examples illustrate discrepancies between what appear to be contradictory sets of instructions. The second set of examples illustrates a contradiction between an instruction and its fulfillment and the third comprises the contradiction between the notice (such as a prophecy) of an impending action or event and the manner in which it actually transpires.

This will be followed by an analysis of the myriad and minute details that governed the original *korban Pesah*.

✂ PART ONE: CONTRADICTORY INSTRUCTIONS

A. Three families of *leviyim*, Gershon, Kehat, and Merari, were selected to perform duties in the *ohel mo'ed* (Bemidbar 4:3). They were entrusted with the responsibility for, serially, taking apart the *mishkan*, packing up its utensils, transporting them, and setting it all up again, as the Jews traveled through the wilderness. Hazal tell us that they were also entrusted with other responsibilities such as musical accompaniment and guard duty.

Seven times the Torah repeats that they serve "from the age of thirty to the age of fifty" (Bemidbar 4:3, 23, 30, 35, 39, 43, 47). However, the Torah also says (8:24–25): "As regards the *leviyim*, from the age of twenty-five and above they shall come to participate in the service of *ohel mo'ed*, and at the age of fifty they shall retire from service." Is the correct minimum age twenty-five or thirty?

B. There is also a discrepancy regarding their habitations. The Torah (Bemidbar 35:1–8, especially v. 7) stipulates that after the conquest they are to receive "forty-eight cities and their environs." With respect to those environs (*migrashim*), however, one verse (3) sets their area as one thousand cubits (*'elef 'ammah*), while the very next verse (4) sets it as two thousand (*'alpayim 'ammah*). What is the actual size?[1]

✂ PART TWO: CONTRADICTIONS BETWEEN INSTRUCTIONS AND THEIR FULFILLMENT

A. In reviewing his forty years' experience with the Israelites, Moshe recollects how he organized their government by appointing captains and officers. He says (Devarim 1:9–15):

> I told you at that time that I could not suffer you alone.... How could I bear the burden of your fractiousness by myself? Nominate wise, understanding, and well-known members of your tribes and I will appoint them to lead you.... I took the captains of your tribes, wise and well-known men, and I made them your leaders: officers of thousands, hundreds, fifties and tens, by tribes.

---

[1] See the *sidrah* of Mas'ei, Part Three.

Whereas Moshe instructed them to nominate people with three qualities (wise, understanding, and reputable), in practice he required only wisdom and reputation. Did he intentionally disregard understanding?

B. When designating Yehoshua as his successor, God instructs Moshe (Bemidbar 27:18): "Take Yehoshua bin Nun... and place your hand upon him." In fulfilling his instructions, however, we read (vv. 22–23) that:

> Moshe did as God instructed him. He took Yehoshua, stood him before Elazar the Kohen and all the people, and placed his hands upon him.

God had instructed him to place one hand upon Yehoshua. Why, then, did Moshe feel it necessary to use both his hands?

C. Another illustration of this point comes from this week's *sidrah*. When Moshe instructs the Israelites on the performance of the *korban Pesah*, he specifies (12:3–5):

> Let each man take one lamb per family and household.... Each person shall eat a quota of the lamb. It shall be an unblemished, one-year-old male lamb, selected from amongst the sheep or goats.

In the review of the laws of Pesah appearing in Devarim, however, we read (16:2): "You shall sacrifice the *Pesah* to the Lord, your God, sheep or cattle."

Was the Pesah sacrifice to be a lamb (or, understood broadly, a sheep or goat), or were cattle permissible?

◈ PART THREE: PROPHETIC NOTICE OF AN EVENT AND HOW IT TRANSPIRES

In the event that God gives an instruction and it is carried out with variation, we assume that the person who was instructed effected the change, and we can dicker over whether the change was necessary, salutary, or prohibited. However, when a prophet transmits a detailed divine warning and the event transpires in a considerably more severe manner than the warning forecast, what sense do we make of it? Did God change His mind (so to speak), or did He intend to mislead the hearers? Such questions have, of course, a decided theological bent to them, which motivates us strongly to seek their resolution.

In Shemot 11:4–8, we read Moshe's forecast to Pharaoh of the catastrophe about to sweep Egypt:

> Moshe said: God has said: At midnight I shall go out in the midst of Egypt. Every firstborn in the land of Egypt shall die... and there shall arise a great cry throughout the land of Egypt.... And all your [Pharaoh's] servants shall descend to me, prostrate themselves before me, and say: "Get out, you and all the people at your feet."

The realization of the forecast, however, states (12:29–30):

> At midnight, God slew all the firstborn of Egypt.... Pharaoh arose at night along with his servants and all of Egypt, and there was a great cry throughout Egypt.... He summoned Moshe and Aharon at night and said: "Get up and get out of the midst of my people, you and the Israelites."

If Pharaoh was destined to beseech Moshe personally to leave Egypt, why did Moshe speak only of his servants coming to implore him? Why did he not deliver the more ominous threat?

✃ PART FOUR: *KORBAN PESAH* – WHY THE MYRIAD AND MINUTE DETAIL?

After the plague of *'arov* (literally: a mixture, it can refer to either a swarm of insects or a horde of wild beasts), Pharaoh offered to allow the Jews to bring sacrifices to God without leaving Egypt. Moshe declined the offer, explaining (8:22):

> It would not be proper because the Egyptians regard our sacrifices to the Lord as abominations. Could we break an Egyptian taboo (*to'avat mitzrayim*) before their very eyes without their stoning us?

We should recall[2] that because the Egyptians held those who ate the flesh of sheep and cattle in the lowest regard. Yosef's brothers were fed separately from the other Egyptians (Bereishit 43:32). Yosef also encouraged his brothers to list their occupations as shepherds in order to keep them

---

[2] See the *sidrah* of Va-Yigash, Part Three.

isolated from the rest of Egypt (46:34). Both of these references feature the word "abomination" (*to'evah*).

We shall now demonstrate, by a series of related questions and answers, that the *korban Pesah* must be understood within this Egyptian cultic context.

Questions:

    A. Why was the fifteenth of Nisan chosen as the date of the sacrifice?

    B. Why was it necessary to select the sacrificial animal four days earlier?

    C. Why was the blood smeared on the doorposts and lintel?

Answers:

    A. The astrological symbol of the month of Nisan is Aries, the ram, and the 15th day is the apex of a lunar month.[3] The ram-god of the Egyptians was to be slaughtered on the evening of the full-moon of its very own month (ostensibly, the height of its powers), and the Egyptians would be powerless to prevent it!

    B. By selecting the sheep or ram four days in advance of the actual sacrifice, the Jews were flaunting their intentions in the faces of their Egyptian neighbors, as though daring them to interfere.

    C. Similarly, the smearing of its blood on the doorposts and lintel was intended to force the Egyptians to suffer the further indignity of seeing the lifeblood of the animal, the essence of many of their pagan rituals, profaned.

Questions:

    A. Why is it forbidden to eat the *korban Pesah* raw (*na*)?

    B. Why may it not be cooked in a pot but only roasted?

    C. Why did it have to be roasted whole – with its head, hind parts, and internal organs, all intact?

Answers:

These details were intended to increase the indignity the Egyptians were meant to suffer and, correspondingly, increase the risk to the Jews participating in the sacrifice.

---

[3] The common astrological signs were known throughout the ancient world. In Egypt, Aries was associated in particular with the god Ammon-Ra.

A and B. Roasting the sheep (or ram), rather than cooking it in a pot or eating it raw, meant that the aroma could not be contained. Even if the Egyptians did not actually see their taboo being slaughtered, they could not avoid the smell.

C. By requiring the principal organs to be kept intact, the identity of the roasting animal could not be disguised or denied.

BESHALLAH

Filling in the "Gaps"

PESHAT, DERASH AND THE MISSING LINKS

❧ PREFACE: WHAT ARE "GAPS" AND HOW ARE THEY FILLED?

Literary texts do not paint a complete picture of the situation they come to describe or provide all the details of events they chronicle. To cite two Israeli scholars who pioneered the literary study of the Bible:

> Anyone who wants to understand a literary work must reply, while he reads, to a series of questions such as: What is the situation being constructed? What is transpiring and why? What is the connection between events occurring now and those that preceded them? What are the intentions of the characters and what are their motivations?[1]

A historical novel, as opposed to a historical chronicle, for instance, moves from one selected episode to another, leaving behind "gaps" for the reader to fill in. Under the best of literary circumstances, the plot will allude to a common characteristic or motive, but often even the allusions are dull or opaque. Some gaps will fill themselves in easily, even automatically, while others will require considerable effort on the part of the reader.

The Tanakh is no different in this respect. Some of its gaps are minor and will not interfere with our comprehension, while others will give us pause to reflect on whether the text can be understood at all without filling them in. Some gaps will be eliminated via *peshat*, while others will resist all but *derash*. We will focus here on several instances and types of gaps in this

---

[1] M. Perry and M. Sternberg, "An Ironic Look at King David." *Hasifrut* 1 (1968–1969): 263.

week's *sidrah* and elsewhere, and reflect on how Rashi, or others, handled them.

❧ PART ONE: FILLING A GAP WITH *PESHAT*

In Bereishit 32:4–6, we read that Yaakov sent messengers to Esav and instructed them on what to say to him. Immediately thereafter (v. 7), we read that the messengers returned and informed him that Esav was on his way to meet him. As we discussed there,[2] the "gap" concerns what happened when the messengers reached Esav and delivered the message. Did they speak to him directly? How did he receive them? Did he question them? Did he reveal his intentions towards Yaakov to them?

Ramban addresses the "gap" as follows:

> It appears to me that Esav did not receive the messengers properly. Perhaps he did not even receive them personally, because if he had, Scripture would have advised us that he asked them, "How are my brother and his family?" "Extend my greetings to him." "Tell him that I am on my way to meet him." And they, in turn, would have reported this to Yaakov. Since Scripture offers no report on the meeting with Esav, [we are left to infer that] he remained angry and was on his way to do him harm. Even the statement, "he comes to meet you" was [only] deduced by the messengers from inquiries they made in Esav's camp.

❧ PART TWO: FILLING A GAP WITH *DERASH*

The Torah describes the circumstances of Moshe's birth and subsequent discovery and adoption by an Egyptian princess in two consecutive verses (Shemot 2:10–11):

> When the child was grown up, [the nurse] brought him to the princess who adopted him and named him Moshe, for she had drawn him out of the water. Once upon a time, when the grown-up Moshe went out to observe his kinsmen's sufferings, he saw an Egyptian beating a Hebrew kinsman.

---

[2] See the *sidrah* of Va-Yishlah, Part One.

In this case, the "gap" consists of what prompted Moshe to sympathize with the Hebrews. Was it a gradual recognition or a sudden realization? Did he struggle with his conflicting identities and loyalties?

Nehama cites three Aggadic explanations that stop part of the gap. The first two are from the Midrash, *Shemot Rabbah* (1:32):

> "To observe their sufferings": What did he see? When he saw their suffering, he cried, saying, I am distressed for you. Would that I could give my life for you, for no labor is more onerous than that of clay. He put his shoulder to it and assisted each and every one of them.
>
> Rabbi Eliezer, son of Rabbi Yossi HaGellili, said: [Moshe] saw a heavy burden [imposed] upon a minor child and a light burden on an adult; a man's burden on a woman and a woman's upon a man; an oldster's upon a youngster and a youngster's upon an oldster. He abandoned his rank of office and relieved their suffering, while pretending to be assisting Pharaoh.

The third comes from a Kurdistani manuscript of the Midrash *Yalkut*:

> To observe their sufferings: What did he see? Rabbi Yehudah says that [the Egyptians] were burdening children like adults and adults like children, the young like the old and the old like the young. Moshe came before Pharaoh and said to him, "I see that your project is doomed to fail." He replied, "Why so?" He said, "Your workers are going to die because they are all being burdened alike, young and old. Give me permission to assign each one according to his ability." He replied, "Do it; the permission is granted." Immediately he ordered them treated according to their abilities.[3]

In her typical fashion, Nehama then contrasts the three sources and characterizes them:

> The first describes Moshe having compassion on his brethren and aiding them. The second describes his reaction in the guise of a state official who pretends to be fulfilling a civic responsibility. The third exercises the imagination with considerable liberty, delineating how Moshe manipulated Pharaoh into improving their working

---

[3] Menahem Kasher, *Torah Sheleimah* 9/89, note.

conditions by professing concern about the project (*Rashi's Commentary on the Torah*, 358).

Note: The related question of how much time elapsed between Moshe's birth until he took the initiative to protect his brethren is dealt with in other Aggadic sources. One speculates that he was twenty years old when this incident occurred, while another suggests that he was forty. The latter opinion reflects the rabbinic notion of the symmetry of history, positing – by implication – that Moshe's life is divisible into three forty-year periods. In the first, he grows up in the palace; in the second, he establishes himself in Midian; and in the third, he leads the Jews from slavery to freedom.

✍ Part Three: "Intentional" Gaps

One of the gaps in the text filled by Aggadah is the absence of explicit intent or purpose. One of the means utilized by the Aggadah to supply these intentions is the *mashal*, the parable. These parables are generally drawn from daily life and circumstances: from agriculture, family, or even the royal court, and their purpose is to provide a descriptive answer to a conceptual problem in a manner that most people will readily understand and assimilate. Sometimes, the Aggadah will provide its own explanation of the parable [*nimshal*]; sometimes, the commentator will provide a missing explanation by citing the Aggadah; sometimes, only the parable itself is cited and we can be left wondering about its full meaning and import.

In his commentary to this week's *sidrah* (Shemot 17:8), Rashi attempts to explain the connection between the episode of Amalek and that of *masah u-merivah* which precedes it:

> [The Torah] linked the following episode to the previous verse (17:7; "… they tested God saying, 'Is God in our midst or not?'"), to say, I [i.e., God] am always in your midst and prepared to meet all your needs, and you dare ask, "Is God in our midst or not?" I swear that a dog will come and bite you, you will cry out to me, and then you will know where I am.

> This resembles (*mashal*) a man who placed his child upon his shoulders and went on the road. Whenever the child saw something he wanted, he would say, Father, give that to me, and he would give it to him. This happened twice, and three times. Then

they met another traveler and the child asked him, Have you seen my father? His father replied: You don't know where I am? He threw him down and a dog came and bit him.

The intent [*nimshal*] of the parable is that God is the father, the Jews are the child, the objects the child desires are the water, the manna and the quail, and the dog is Amalek. Its moral is that if you cannot recognize the presence of God after several demonstrations of His proximity and responsiveness, then the only way you may come to appreciate Him is when you cry to Him for help when you are endangered.

Compare this relatively straightforward *mashal* to the one Rashi utilizes earlier in the *sidrah* (Shemot 14:20):

> "[The pillar of cloud] came between the Egyptian and Israelite camps; there were cloud and darkness and it illumined the night": This resembles a man walking with his son going before him. When robbers approached, he placed his son behind him; when a wolf stalked him from behind, he placed the boy before him; and when robbers came from the front and wolves from the rear, he took the boy on his shoulders and fought them.

The intent [*nimshal*] of this parable is that the father is the pillar of cloud that represents God, and the child is Israel. The robbers are the sea, the wolves are the Egyptians, and placing the child on the father's shoulders represents the crossing of the sea. However, the details of the *mashal* and the *nimshal* do not correspond exactly. In the parable, the father starts off in the rear, whereas in the Torah the cloud starts off in front.

Rashi continues:

> "Illumined the night": the pillar of fire [lit] the night for Israel and preceded them, as usual, [to enable them] to go by day and night. The darkness of the cloud was [cast] towards the Egyptians.

By importing the pillar of fire from 13:21, Rashi is trying to alleviate a difficulty in the verse.

The second half of the verse implies that the cloud and darkness "illumined the night." This presents two difficulties. One, clearly, is that clouds and darkness are not a source of illumination. Secondly, how does God help the Israelites by shedding light on the Egyptians? Therefore, Rashi explains that the cloud and darkness were behind the Jews in order to obscure the way for the Egyptians, while the pillar of fire continued to go before them to light their way.

&o PART FOUR: YOU HAVE TO GET UP VERY EARLY IN THE MORNING....

Another question about Rashi's methodology in his use of *midrashim* is: If a Midrash appears in the context of several verses, why does Rashi often cite it only to one of those verses and not to the others? An example occurs in conjunction with this week's *sidrah*.

The theme of "Love/hatred corrupts habit" (*ahavah/sin'ah mekalkelet et ha-shurah*) is cited in conjunction with the following two matched pairs of verses:

A. **Bereishit 46:29:** Yosef hitched up his chariot and rode to greet his father.

B. **Bereishit 22:3:** Avraham arose early in the morning and saddled his donkey.

A¹ **Shemot 14:6:** Pharaoh hitched up his chariot and assembled his forces.

B¹ **Bemidbar 22:21:** Bil'am arose in the morning and saddled his donkey.

Avraham and Yosef illustrate the principle that "Love corrupts habit," as they personally undertake a task that would ordinarily be left to their servants. Pharaoh and Bil'am, on the other hand, illustrate "Hate corrupts habit" as, overcome by their hatred for the Jewish people, they personally perform tasks otherwise left to servants.

The Midrash goes further yet. It describes the earliest of each pair as "anticipating" the latter. Pharaoh's attempt to get credit, as it were, for hitching his own chariot, was offset by the earlier example of Yosef, and Bil'am's attempt to earn credit for saddling his own donkey was neutralized by the earlier instance of Avraham. In the language of the Midrash, God addresses the evildoers, saying: *Rasha', kevar kedamkha* – Wicked one, you have been anticipated!

While the Midrash cites this phrase to each of the two pairs, Rashi cites it only apropos of Avraham and Bil'am. Bearing in mind our habitual caveat –

101

that Rashi uses Aggadah to resolve textual difficulties – if we look very closely at the wording of these verses, we ought to be able to see what motivated him to cite the "anticipation" only there and not apropos of Pharaoh and Yosef. While the language concerning Yosef and Pharaoh is identical, there is a subtle yet significant difference between the verb describing Avraham's action (*va-yashkem*; he rose early) and that which describes Bil'am (*va-yakam*, he rose).

Rashi understands that *kevar kedamkha* cannot simply mean that Avraham and Yosef preceded Pharaoh and Bil'am chronologically, because that, per se, would not provide them with any advantage. He implies, then, that Avraham preceded Bil'am in time of day as well. Bil'am, inspired by his hatred, merely arose in the morning, while Avraham, on account of his love, got up *early* in the morning. That is his merit and that is why it overcame the animosity of Bil'am.

YITRO

When Two Are One

RASHI'S PROFICIENCY IN HEBREW GRAMMAR

✆ PREFACE

A frequently overlooked feature of Rashi's commentary is his proficiency in Hebrew grammar. While modern philologists (and many medieval ones, too!) are often critical of his assumptions (such as the notion that Hebrew verbs are generally bi-literal; i.e., of two-letter roots, rather than three), he was so intimately familiar with the entire corpus of biblical and rabbinic literature that he was often able to arrive at incisive conclusions through his powers of deduction.

✆ PART ONE: ADVICE OR INSTRUCTIONS?

Our *sidrah* begins (18:17–26) with Yitro advising Moshe on restructuring the Israelite judiciary system by recommending divisions of responsibilities by tens, fifties, hundreds and thousands.

These verses can be divided, literarily, into two parts: the advice (17–23) and the implementation (24–26). One phrase, however, is repeated in both parts: "They shall judge (*ve-shaf'tu*) the people at all times" (22, 26). Given the ever-present stipulation that the Torah does not engage in unnecessary duplication or redundancy, we should note that the word *ve-shaf'tu* is ambivalent (having two meanings) and can serve for both the advice and its implementation.

This dual usage is reflected in Rashi. In v. 22, he cites the Aramaic *ve-ydunun*, calling it "a form of instruction (*leshon tzivuy*)," while in v. 26, again citing the Aramaic Targum, he translates it as *ve-dayenin*, adding that "the earlier verse is a form of instruction, while [the latter] is implementation ('asiyah)."

When Rashi speaks of *leshon tzivuy*, he does not mean what modern grammarians call the "imperative." He wants to emphasize that the intended actions are unfulfilled – what we call the "future" and what grammarians, more precisely, call the "imperfect." In other words, when spoken by Yitro they constitute advice; the second time around, however, they indicate a standard practice that Moshe introduced, which is why they were translated [into Aramaic] in the active participial form.

In essence, the first time the phrase should be translated: "They shall judge" [and the *vav* is "conversive" (*ha-hippukh*)], and the second time: "they judged" [and the *vav* is "conjunctive" (*ha-hibbur*)].

◎ PART TWO: HOW MANY OF THEM WERE THERE?

Along with examples of Rashi's grammatical and syntactical virtuosity, we have also come to appreciate that he rarely describes the difficulty he treats. He generally jumps right into the resolution of an aberration or ambiguity and leaves us to deduce the problem from its answer. Here is such an instance from our *sidrah* (19:2): "They traveled from Refidim, they came to the wilderness of Sinai, and Israel [he] camped opposite the mountain."

There is an obvious discrepancy between the two plural verbal forms at the start of the verse and the singular one at its conclusion. Capitalizing on this incongruity, Rashi comments:

> "Israel – he camped there": As one person, with one heart; the remainder of their encampments, however, were marked by turmoil and disunity.

A comparable difficulty exists in Shemot 14:9–10. Whereas in v. 9 the Egyptians are described in the plural: "They pursued... they caught up...," in v. 10 the Egyptians are singular: "They beheld Egypt – he was following them." Here, Rashi offers two solutions. The first, like the example in this week's *sidrah*, states: "As one person, with one heart." The second states: "They saw the [angelic] minister of the Egyptians coming from heaven to their assistance."

Whereas we might incline to identify both explanations as *derash*, we can actually make a case for the first explanation as *peshat*: 14:9 provides an actual report of the Egyptians' activities; therefore it – properly – refers to them in the plural. Verse 10, however, reflects the Israelites' perception of the Egyptians' activities. From their intimidated perspective, we can well imagine that the Egyptian "host" gave the appearance of a single, consolidated mass.

❧ PART THREE: IS THAT REALLY "ENOUGH"?

When God first appeared to Moshe at the burning bush and instructed him to secure the release of the Jews from Egypt, He said: "This is your sign that I dispatched you; when you take the people out of Egypt you will worship God on this mountain" (3:12). Since the avowed – and oft-repeated – purpose of the exodus was to receive the Torah at Sinai, how can we sing at every Seder: "If He had brought us near Mount Sinai and not given us the Torah – it would have been sufficient (*dayyeinu*)"?

Rashi's Midrashic observation on the singularity of Israel's stance opposite Mount Sinai contains the potential answer to this question. Since the stance before Sinai entailed a form of Jewish unity that was unparalleled subsequently (and remains so elusive particularly in our own troubled times!), had we been able to freeze that moment and preserve it forever – "it would have been sufficient."

❧ PART FOUR: IT'S THE "THOUGHT" THAT COUNTS

Rashi – contrary, perhaps, to the impression we may have inadvertently created in these weekly lessons – does not only deal with problems of literary contradictions and ambiguity. He is deeply immersed in the beliefs and opinions of the Torah and deals with them substantively as well. Here is an example from this week's *sidrah* of the consideration Rashi gives to a series of contradictions with considerable philosophical and halakhic consequences.

> **Rashi (20:8):** "Remember" (*zakhor*) and "Practice" (*shamor*) were recited simultaneously. So were: "Her transgressors will surely die" (Shemot 31:14) and: "On the Sabbath day, two sheep" (Bemidbar 28:9); "Do not wear *sha'atnez*" (a mixture of wool and flax; Devarim 22:11), and "Make yourself fringes" (ibid., v. 12); "Do not expose your sister-in-law's nakedness" (Va-Yikra 18:16), and: "Her brother-in-law is to come to her" (Devarim 25:5). This is what is

meant by the verse: "God speaks [but] once, [yet] we hear twice" (Tehillim 62:12).

This principle, which we might label "simultaneity," accomplishes an exegetical purpose in each case:

- "Remember" is accomplished mentally (or verbally), while "Practice" presumes overt physical activity. The effect of Rashi's Midrashic observation is to blend together, in Shabbat, both of these aspects: the sanctification in word and thought [*kiddush*, *havdalah*, *tefillah*] together with the physical aspect of the abstinence from work.

- Were it not for the "blending" of these two verses, they would create a dilemma: How can I fulfill the commandment of sacrifice on Shabbat if it constitutes a forbidden activity for which the punishment is death? The answer is that sacrifice, per se, remains prohibited, save for communal offerings for which specific license was given.

- Ordinary garments in the Biblical period were made of flax, while the "sky-blue thread" required in *tzitzit* was, necessarily, made of wool. How can I fulfill the mitzvah of *tzitzit* if it is prohibited to mix flax and wool in the same garment? Ordinary mixing, as in weaving, is forbidden, but an exception was made for the tying of *tzitzit*.

- A brother's wife is one of the forbidden incestuous or adulterous relationships ['*arayot*]. On the other hand, the Torah specifically prescribes the union of a widow with her late husband's brother [*yibbum*]. The assumption of "simultaneity" is that ordinary sexual relations between in-laws are forbidden, but the "levirate" marriage arranged after the death of the husband permits the relations between his brother and his widow.

We would do well to note, however, that the first of these four pairs of verses differs from the others in that the first pair offers a contrast only, while the remaining three pairs actually contradict each other.

❧ PART FIVE: IBN EZRA ON FORM VS. CONTENT

In a very lengthy commentary on this week's *sidrah*, Ibn Ezra takes issue with the assumption underlying Rashi's interpretation, namely that the two formulations of the Shabbat laws in the two "versions" of the Ten Commandments are mutually exclusive. He proposes, instead, to resolve this case by formulating a principle of his own: *ha-'ivri shomer ha-te'amim ve-lo ha-millot*; i.e., Biblical literary style is concerned with meaning more than with phraseology. In other words, as long as there is no overt contradiction between *shamor* and *zakhor*, they can be dealt with linguistically or literarily rather than philosophically or theologically.

Ibn Ezra rejects the dictum of "simultaneity" because it is unscientific. Utilizing principles established by Greek science, he explains that even if it were possible – for argument's sake – for God to *say* two different things at exactly the same time, it would require a suspension of the laws of nature for people to *hear* them simultaneously, and the Torah gives no such indication.

Note: Compare Ibn Ezra's phraseology here to that of Radak, which we cited in the note to the *sidrah* of Hayyei Sarah. Bear in mind that Ibn Ezra (Spain, twelfth century) preceded Radak (Provence, thirteenth century) by a century.

MISHPATIM

Rashbam – More Than Meets the Eye

RASHI VS. RASHBAM: PLUMBING THE DEPTHS OF *PESHAT*

✌ PREFACE: ALL IN THE FAMILY – GETTING REACQUAINTED

In the *sidrah* of Va-Yetze', we made the exegetical acquaintance of Rashi's grandson, Rashbam, and compared their respective interpretations of Yaakov's journey and dream. In this *sidrah*, we will compare their interpretations of several items of halakhic importance.

✌ PART ONE: HOW LONG IS FOREVER?

In Shemot 21:5–6, the Torah states that an indentured Hebrew servant who refuses his freedom at the end of six years of service shall have his ear pierced and serve his master *le-olam*. Our inclination, of course, would be to take the word *le-olam* literally, and to consign the servant to an eternity (or, at least, a lifetime) of servitude. Rashi, however, notes that the stipulation in Va-Yikra 25:10 that every servant goes free in the Jubilee (*yovel*) year, contradicts the literal sense of our verse.

Rashi resolves the contradiction by asserting that the fifty-year period of a *yovel* constitutes "forever" (*le'olam*). Indeed, Rashi – in line with the Midrash (Mekhilta) and Gemara (Kiddushin) – stipulates that the balance of any *yovel* cycle comprises "forever" and that servants go free at the *yovel* year even if fewer than six years are actually served.

Rashbam, however, offers a very different interpretation. He takes *le'olam* literally, saying: "According to the *peshat* – all the days of his life, as it says of Shemuel: 'and he will remain there forever' (*'ad 'olam*)" (1 Shemuel 1:22).

We shall attempt to explain how Rashbam can blithely ignore the Midrash and Gemara, let alone disregard the verse in Va-Yikra.

🔊 PART TWO: A LOOK AT THE RECORD

Before we answer this specific question, let us look at several other places where the commentary of Rashbam appears to contradict the halakhic norm.

1. Shemot 13:9: "It shall be like a sign for you on your arm, and like a souvenir for you between your eyes…" Rashi understands the verse as designating the mitzvah of *teflillin* and comments: "Write these portions [of the Torah] and tie them to your head and arm." Rashbam, however, comments as follows:

   According to the depths of the *peshat*, it shall be like a perpetual souvenir for you as though it were inscribed on your arm, as in the verse: "Place me as a signet upon your heart" (Shir ha-Shirim 8:6)… like jewelry, such as a gold chain, placed upon the forehead for ornamentation.

   Here, Rashbam seems to blithely ignore the halakhic consequences of his metaphorical interpretation. Did he not wear *tefillin*?

2. Bereishit 1:5: "God called the light day, and He called the darkness night; it was nightfall and it was daybreak: one day." Hazal adduce this verse as proof that a halakhic day commences with nightfall; Rashbam, however, says:

   Daylight always precedes darkness. The verse does not say "It was nighttime and it was daytime," rather it says, "It was nightfall and it was daybreak." Namely: the first day ended with the setting of its sun and then the night broke with the rising of the dawn. This completed one day of the six days of which God spoke in the Ten Commandments and [thereafter] the second day began and God said "Let there be a firmament…."

   The verse does not intend to stipulate that a setting [sun] and a rising [sun] constitute a day because our only need, here, is to describe how there were six days wherein the breaking dawn ended the nighttime, marking the passage between one day and the next.

Once again, Rashbam seems to ignore rabbinic interpretation and produces an interpretation at great odds with received tradition.

◌ PART THREE: *DEREKH ERETZ* PRECEDES TORAH

Before we account for Rashbam's ostensible iconoclasm, let us take a look at an introductory note that Rashbam prefaces to this *sidrah*:

> Rationalists will understand that I have not come here to interpret the *halakhot* even though they are paramount – as I indicated in Bereishit [37:2] – because they are derived from extraneous words... and can be found in the commentary of my maternal grandfather, Rashi.
>
> I have come to interpret the text straightforwardly [*peshat*] and will interpret [even] laws and *halakhot* according to prevalent norms [*derekh eretz*].

Rashbam is interpreting the *sidrah* of Mishpatim [and, by extension, other halakhic portions of the Torah – such as those cited above] in a dimension that is not necessarily halakhic, and by means of a method of inquiry called *peshat*, which is supported by a contingency called *derekh eretz*.

In Va-Yetze, we translated *derekh eretz* – as it affects narrative – as "common usage;" we shall now offer a refinement of that understanding as it applies to Halakhah.

In his commentary on Va-Yikra 13:2, "Should a man develop a swelling, rash, or discoloration on the skin of his body," Rashbam notes:

> In all of the chapters of afflictions to humans, animals, or buildings; their appearances, the calculation of their quarantines and the matter of white, black, or yellow hairs; we have no recourse to the literal sense of Scripture (*peshuto shel mikra'*) at all, nor to human expertise (*beki'ut... shel benei 'adam*) based upon prevailing norms (*derekh eretz*).

In other words, whenever the definitive halakhic position or decision rests on the appreciation of a true-to-life reality that can no longer be empirically observed, Rashbam – without denying the normative force of Halakhah! – rests his interpretation of the Halakhah entirely upon the visible, textual evidence. The result may appear to contradict the Halakhah – as in the three cases we cited – but actually serves as its underlying explanation.

✦ PART FOUR: THE ANSWERS, PLEASE

Answer #1:

In the case of Bereishit 1:5, we cannot argue with Rashbam's *peshat* of the verse. He correctly notes the difference between the terms for day (*yom*) and daylight (*'or*), nighttime (*laylah*) and darkness (*hoshekh*), and correctly observes that the verse states that "a day" followed *boker*, which is to say that it began after the break of dawn – and not, as the halakhah would have it, after dusk. He hastens to point out, however, that this pertains only to the six days of Creation (i.e., the days about which God spoke in the Ten Commandments), which is to say, the only six days for which there is no recovering their true-to-life reality since they were not [yet] under human observation.

Reconstructing the entire verse under Rashbam's exegetical guidance, we obtain the following understanding: After creating light, God separated the newly created light from darkness. Which darkness? Not the primordial darkness (mentioned in v. 2), but that which followed the setting of the first day's light. God then proceeded to name the period of light (*'or*) – day (*yom*), and the subsequent period of darkness (*hoshekh*) – night (*laylah*). With the breaking of a new dawn (*boker*), one full day had been completed.

Answer #2:

When Rashbam, in Shemot 13:9, offers an entirely metaphorical explanation of *'ot* and *totafot*, he is, similarly, trying to reconstruct the rationale supporting the mitzvah of *tefillin* from the textual evidence alone.

By citing the examples of the signet and the gold chain, he is attempting to establish a true-to-life reality that would account for the choice of the specific locations of the arm and forehead: they are the places on which people customarily displayed jewelry and other items of value. By citing the clearly metaphorical verse in Shir ha-Shirim ("place me as a signet upon your heart"), he signals his appreciation that it is not the signet, per se, which is of value, but what it represents – the affection of the lover.

Similarly, it is not the box-like *tefillin* that is of value, but what is represented by the *parashiyot* it houses: that is to say, the miracle of the exodus. The reason we place *tefillin* upon our hearts and foreheads is to proudly display the textual recognition of our gratitude to God for redeeming us from bondage.

ೂ PART FIVE: IF IT TAKES FOREVER...

Answer #3:

Finally, we return to the verse with which we began. It should be clear by now that if Rashbam had been approached by a master and his indentured Jewish servant and asked to rule on the length of his extended servitude, Rashbam would undoubtedly have followed Talmudic precedent and committed him to serve only until the Jubilee year – just as there is no doubt that Rashbam wore *tefillin* (although I could not tell you whether he wore those of Rashi or his brother, Rabbeinu Tam), and observed Shabbat and festivals beginning with sundown.

The exegetical question he is addressing here is rhetorical: If the Torah intended him to serve only until the *yovel*, why not just say so? The verse could easily have said: "He shall serve him until *yovel*." Why complicate matters unnecessarily by using the word *le'olam*? His answer is that the Torah thinks he should really serve out the rest of his natural life; it is just too compassionate to oblige him to do so. Therefore, in a subsequent clarification of the laws of servitude (i.e., Va-Yikra) it makes the limited term of service explicit.

Is this explanation credible? Surely. After all, Rashi himself, in his commentary on the previous verse – explaining why the servant's ear is to be pierced – cites the Talmudic explanation that voluntary servitude is a violation of the spirit – if not the letter – of the first of the Ten Commandments, which acknowledges God primarily in His role of the liberator from slavery. Someone who goes and "acquires his own master" is denying the mastery of God and ought to forfeit his personal freedom forever.

ೂ PART SIX: HOW DOES THIS AFFECT EYES AND TEETH?

A comparable explanation recommends itself for the resolution of another longstanding question: If one who blinds another only has to pay compensation, why does the Torah appear to suggest that he is, himself, to be blinded (*'ayin tahat 'ayin*; Shemot 21:24)?

Using Rashbam's rhetorical analysis, we offer the following interpretation: The Torah regards the resort to violence as completely unacceptable. The image of two Jews locked in struggle with one another conjures up that of the two Hebrew slaves whose struggle precipitated Moshe's flight from Egypt. Free men must learn to solve their differences peacefully. To motivate the peaceful resolution of conflict, the Torah stipulates the penalty that the attacker deserves: exactly what he meted out to his fellow. Out of preference for a non-violent solution, however, it allowed the retributive punishment to be mitigated, in practice, to the payment of compensation.

TERUMAH

It's Ibn Ezra's Turn

IBN EZRA'S EXEGETICAL PROGRAM: *KABBALAH* VS. *SEVARAH*

❧ PREFACE: WHERE *DERASH* MEETS ITS MATCH

As Nehama observed on innumerable occasions, the way one resolves textual difficulties depends upon one's exegetical orientation, and Rashi and Ibn Ezra indeed give very different responses to Scriptural challenges. We shall now examine their respective responses to the challenge of *'atzei shittim* (25:2) and relate them to the basic exegetical propositions that underlie their respective commentaries.

❧ PART ONE: WHERE DID IT ALL COME FROM?

At the start of this week's *sidrah*, God instructs Moshe on the solicitation and collection of the "free-will offerings" (*Terumah*) that were to provide the material for the construction of the Mishkan and its furnishings. The items on God's "wish list," as it were, include: "Gold, silver, bronze; blue-violet, royal purple, scarlet [yarn], byssus and goats' hair; rams' skins dyed red, tanned leather skins, acacia wood...." (25:3–5).

Where did the Israelites obtain these exotic materials in the wilderness? Several of these items are mentioned earlier (Shemot 12:35 mentions objects of silver, gold, and clothing), so the assumption is that these materials were part of the "spoils of Egypt." After serving so many years of slavery, the Jews were entitled to compensation and items of gold, silver, bronze, etc., have intrinsic worth. Why, however, would anyone want to complicate their rapid departure from a "house of bondage" by transporting acacia wood? What value could it have had?

> **Rashi:** Where did they get [trees] in the desert? Rabbi Tanhuma explained: Our patriarch, Yaakov, foresaw prophetically that the Israelites would build a tabernacle in the wilderness, so he brought cedar trees to Egypt and planted them, and commanded his sons to take them along when they left Egypt.

> **Ibn Ezra:** Some of our predecessors said that Yaakov planted them and the Israelites removed them under Moshe's orders, as [a later] verse says: "Whoever had acacia tress with him donated them" (35:24).

That later verse seemingly supports the "predecessors'" point by stipulating that there were people who already had acacia trees with them, and there is no logical explanation for that other than they took them out of Egypt.

If you are asking yourself: "But that only begs the question: Why would they have taken trees along with them at the time of the exodus?", then you are still keeping pace with Ibn Ezra, who goes on to ask:

> Even if we were to stipulate this, the question would remain: Why would they take out acacia trees? What purpose could they serve?

In considering Ibn Ezra's question, we might assume, like Rabbi Tanhuma, that there was a purpose to carrying out trees and that even if the people themselves could not articulate it, Moshe could, having been so informed by God, or recalling the instructions of an ancestor.

❧ PART TWO: THE TREES AND THE EXODUS

If you are saying to yourself: The logistics of the exodus militate against the trees being carried out during the exodus, Ibn Ezra is proud of you. He continues in that very vein:

> Moreover, the Egyptians thought they were only going [for three days] to offer sacrifices and that they would subsequently return, which is why they agreed to lend them [the silver, gold, and clothing we mentioned above]. That being the case, how could they have carried out numerous wooden planks – each one at least ten cubits in length, not to mention the crossbars [which had to be even longer]?

Note: Ibn Ezra's reasoning would also exclude the possibility that the trees were for the sacrificial fire, since ten-cubit lengths of wood (15–20 feet) are hardly useful for kindling.

Why not assume that, in order to avoid just such a problem, they detoured around the population centers on their way out of Egypt so as not to arouse their suspicions? Anticipating this, Ibn Ezra adds:

> They passed the royal palace of Egypt on their way out! What explanation could they have given for carrying acacia trees if they were only on their way to celebrate a three-day festival?

Indeed, Shemot 12:31 supports Ibn Ezra's contention that the actual exodus took them past the royal palace, citing Pharaoh as summoning Moshe and Aharon – presumably to his palace – and imploring them, and all the Israelites, to "arise and go out from the midst of my people."

◈ PART THREE: RELATING THE COMMENT TO THE METHODOLOGY

Back in the beginning,[1] we cited Rashi's remarks in his commentary to Bereishit 3:8 regarding the use of Aggadah. He said:

> There are numerous Aggadic *midrashim*... but I have come only to [establish] the *peshat* of Scripture and those *aggadot* which settle the language of Scripture, as "a word fitly spoken."

The difficulty in our *sidrah* is the one we cited at the outset: where did they get trees in the wilderness, and the resolution – to Rashi's way of thinking – is the one suggested by Rabbi Tanhuma: There was a method to the Israelite madness in removing them from Egypt; the trees were "destined" for the *mishkan*.

On the other hand, Ibn Ezra takes a considerably dimmer view of the historicity or facticity of Aggadah. In the Preface to his commentary on *Eikhah,* he compares *aggadot* to garments and Scriptural verses to bodies, saying: "Some [i.e., garments=*aggadot*] are like fine silk while others are coarse as burlap." Given this indisposition, it stands to reason that Ibn Ezra would reject an Aggadah with whose basic historical premises he finds such fatal flaws as those he finds here.

---

[1] In the *sidrah* of Bereishit, to be exact.

✌ PART FOUR: WHAT, THEN, IS THE ALTERNATIVE?

If the acacia trees were not taken out of Egypt, where did the Israelites get them to donate to the *mishkan*? In setting up his reply to this question, Ibn Ezra passes some of the most critical, but eminently reasonable judgment ever leveled against an Aggadah:

> Indeed, we are in a quandary. If our ancestors had an historical tradition (*kabbalah*) that the trees were removed from Egypt, we, too, shall take them at their word. If it is only speculation (*sevarah*), however, we are entitled to seek an alternative approach, and to say that adjacent to Mt. Sinai there was a forest of acacia trees.

In other words, in the absence of objective confirmation of its historicity, and in consideration of the several challenges to its accuracy, Aggadah remains in the realm of speculation and, as such, is optional. It is not mandatory, as it would be if it had independent verification.

A final question, though, remains: If, as Ibn Ezra claims, the trees were not taken from Egypt but were cut down in the wilderness, how are we to understand the verse, which he cited himself, "Whoever had acacia trees with him donated them" (35:24)?

Ibn Ezra explains:

> Upon their arrival there they were informed that they would tarry there a while – without cloud cover, as I have already explained (in 15:22) – so each one made himself a booth (*sukkah*) while the princes made courtyards (*hatzerot*), each according to his rank. This depleted the forest completely, since they were so numerous and made so many booths.

> Moshe, however, did not address them on the subject of the Tabernacle until after Yom ha-Kippurim; this explains "whoever had acacia trees with him" (i.e., left over from the construction of the booths).

TETZAVEH

Rashi Was French, After All

LEXICOGRAPHY AND FRENCH "GLOSSES" (*LE'AZIM*)

℘ PREFACE

The smallest linguistic unit of Tanakh is the individual word, and one of Rashi's greatest contributions to our understanding of Tanakh is providing definitions for difficult words. In this week's *sidrah,* there appear numerous unusual words, which refer to parts of the Mishkan, its furnishings, and the uniforms worn by the *kohanim.* This lesson will serve as an opportunity to examine how Rashi obtains his information about the meanings of difficult words, and how he conveys that information to us.

℘ PART ONE: *LE'AZIM*: RASHI'S USE OF THE VERNACULAR

Interspersed throughout Rashi's commentaries to the Tanakh (and to the Talmud as well) are numerous translations of individual words into Old French. These "glosses" – which comprise one of the major sources for the history and development of the French language in the Middle Ages – were used by Rashi and other Northern French exegetes when they had no other or better way to explain or describe something to their French-speaking Jewish audience. Some even went so far as to provide Old French translations, called *pitronim*, of all difficult words in the Bible.[1]

---

[1] Later copyists and printers often replaced these French words with glosses in their own languages, most often Judeo-German, which created the mistaken impression that Rashi knew Yiddish. Other *le'azim*, which derived from Slavic languages, were designated *leshon kena'an* (literally: Canaanite) on account of the curse of abject slavery that Noah placed on his grandson Canaan (*'eved 'avadim*; Bereishit 9:25).

We shall take the opportunity this week to examine his use of glosses in his identification of items in the *mishkan* or amongst the priestly vestments.

(1) Let us start with the word "vestments." In commenting on 28:41, *u-mileita et yadam,* Rashi comments:

> Every instance of "filling the hands" signifies instruction. Whenever someone enters [a situation] in order to become entrenched in it, from that day onwards he is "filled." In *la'az,* whenever someone receives an appointment, the sovereign places a leather glove – called a *gant* – in his hand, by means of which he certifies him. This giving over (of the glove) is called *revetir,* and it means filling the hands.

Both of the French glosses that Rashi employs here have English equivalents. The first, *gant,* is cognate with the English "gauntlet," which also means a glove, and the kindred expressions "to throw down/take up the gauntlet," which mean to issue and accept a challenge, not unlike the bestowal and acceptance of authority.

The second gloss, *revetir,* is more significant in our context since it is cognate with the English "invest."[2] For this same semantic reason, we referred (in the Preface) to the *bigdei kehunah* as "vestments," meaning, literally, to clothe, and, figuratively, to endow. Consistent with Rashi's interpretation, then, we should translate *miluy yadayim* as "investiture."

(2) The Ephod

Rashi begins his interpretation of this word with a most remarkable statement:

> I have not heard (*lo shama'ti*), neither have I found (*lo matza'ti*) in the *baraita* a description of its configuration. My heart tells me, however (*ve-libi omer li*)…

Lacking either an oral or written tradition of the interpretation of *ephod,* Rashi relied upon his intuition and produced the following:

> [The *ephod*] is belted about him at his back, its width the width of man's back, in the fashion of an apron called *pourceint,* which the noblewomen wear when they go horseback riding.…

---

[2] Webster's also lists: "revest: to clothe again."

In other words, an *ephod*, according to Rashi, is a riding habit. Capitalizing on the fact that the word habit, which designates feminine riding apparel, shares an etymology with the word habit that designates a characteristic or usual behavior, we can end this part of the lesson by posing the age-old question: Does the man make the clothes or do the clothes make the man?

❧ PART TWO: ASSOCIATION

Sometimes, Rashi associates a difficult word with a similar word from the same *shoresh*, or verbal root (called a cognate), with a clearer connotation elsewhere in Tanakh. In Bereishit 24:63, for example, Yitzhak is described as going out to the field *lasuah* as Avraham's major domo was returning with Rivkah. Rashi explains *lasuah* on the basis of the appearance of a cognate word in Tehillim 102:1 ("he poured out his *siah*") as: "an expression of prayer." In other words, the unambiguous use of the word in Tehillim (its poetic parallel in the first half of the verse is *tefillah*) enables Rashi to determine its meaning in Bereishit. [Ibn Ezra and other medieval exegetes often refer to a "cognate" word as "a brother" (*ah*) or "a friend" (*rea'*).]

In Bemidbar 11:31, to cite another example, "The divine wind blew quail in from the sea, *va-yittosh* upon the camp." Ordinarily, the root *n-t-sh* means "to forget, to abandon" (see Bereishit 31:28, 1 Shemuel 12:22), but it cannot retain that meaning here. Rashi recognizes the root as a homonym and cites its appearance in 1 Shemuel 30:16 to determine that it has the additional meaning of "to spread out."

In general, if the meaning of a word is reasonably well-known, Rashi forgoes its definition. If the meaning, however, is either esoteric or, as in this case, homonymous, he provides its interpretation.

❧ PART THREE: RELIANCE UPON PREDECESSORS

At other times, Rashi relies upon the interpretations of Hazal or his medieval predecessors. As Lot invites the two "men" home (Bereishit 19:2),[3] he instructs them: "*Suru na* to the house of your servant." What exactly does he expect from them? Rashi says: "Take a roundabout [literally: crooked] path

---

[3] See our elucidation in Va-Yera'.

to my house so people will not notice you entering. That is why he used the word *suru*." Rashi recognizes that the verb *lasur* means to turn away, and uses the Midrash *Bereishit Rabbah* here to lend Lot's instructions the conspiratorial nuance that the context requires. Without assuming the precautions implied by *suru*, we would question Lot's sanity in so publicly flouting the municipal code of Sedom.

Shemot 19:13 prohibits the people from ascending Mount Sinai until "the draw of the *yovel*." What kind of a sign was that? Rashi cites the Talmud (*Rosh ha-Shanah* 26a) to the effect that "In Arabia, a ram is called a *yuvla*," and the "draw" of the *yovel* is the blowing of a ram's horn.

Coming now to our own *sidrah*, what are *kela'im* (27:9), and what are *hashukim* (10)? Here, Rashi relies on the Aramaic translation [Targum] of Onkelos, and renders the former as nets ("holed like a sieve"), and the latter as belts or buckles.

On occasion, however, Rashi will cite an interpretation of Hazal only to reject it in favor of his own, or that of a medieval predecessor. For instance, Bemidbar 11:8 describes the taste of the manna as resembling *leshad ha-shemen*. Rashi cites the interpretation of the Sifrei, which derives *leshad* from the word *shadayim* (breast) and *shemen* from *shamen* (fat; i.e., treating it as an adjective rather than a noun). He then proceeds to reject that interpretation on three separate grounds:

1. there is no relevance of breast to oil;

2. if the root of *shemen* were the same as *shamen*, the *mem* would require the vowel *tzeireh* (which he calls *kametz katan*) and would be accented on its final syllable (*milera'*);

3. the *kametz* of the *shin* – as opposed to the *patah* we would expect – is on account of the pausal form at the end of a sentence.

Instead, Rashi prefers the interpretation of Dunash Ibn Labrat, a tenth-century Spanish grammarian and lexicographer: "The moisture (or freshness – *lahluhit*) of oil."

৯০ PART FOUR: PASSING OVER

In Shemot 12:13, God advises the Israelites that when He sees the blood on the doorposts, He will not allow the pestilence to enter their homes. The verb that describes God's action is *pasahti*, the same root (*p-s-h*) from which the name of the holiday *Pesah* is derived.

Rashi first cites his own opinion: "I shall pity you," as in "to pity and to rescue" (Yeshayahu 31:5). He then appears to directly contradict himself, adding: "But I say that every instance of *p-s-h* signifies skipping and jumping over... as in 'How long will you skip (*poshim*) over the sides of the threshold?'" (1 Melakhim 18:21).

Why contradict himself? If he thought better of his initial explanation, why not just delete it? In reality, the phrase "But I say..." is part of the Midrashic text (*Mekhilta*) that serves as Rashi's inspiration, and that attributes these two opinions to R. Yonatan and R. Yoshiya. Rashi himself appears to favor the latter interpretation (skipping), since God did not "pity" the Israelite houses in Egypt, but He did skip (or pass) over them.

Ki Tissa'

The Sin of the Golden Calf – A Biblical Whodunit?

THE MAJOR EXEGETES ON AHARON'S COMPLICITY

✍ PREFACE

Fewer than forty days after hearing the voice of God at Sinai, fewer than eighty days after seeing the sea split and swallow the Egyptians, fewer than ninety days after the firstborn of Egypt perished in a plague, the Israelites constructed and proceeded to worship a golden calf. How could they have been so ungrateful? How could they have been so stupid?

✍ PART ONE: GOES TO MOTIVE, YOUR HONOR

The first questions investigators ask after a crime has been committed concern motive and opportunity. Let us, too, begin by asking who stood to profit from the golden calf in order to determine who bore responsibility for its construction.

The Torah assigns initial responsibility for proposing the calf to "the people" (ha'am; 32:1), although a careful reading of the verse shows that they requested an *elohim*, ostensibly a generic form for a deity and not a specific one.[1] The first appearance of the calf is later, in verse 4.

If the people sought a deity, why did Aharon specifically construct a calf?

Answer 1: It was somehow implicit in their request. Perhaps the phrase: "who took us out of Egypt" triggered the association with the calf – one of the principal gods of Egypt.

Answer 2: It was not fashioned by design.

---

[1] See our discussion of the homonymous form *elohim* in Va-Yishlah, Part Three.

How can we countenance the (outlandish) assertion that the calf was unintentional when v. 4 explicitly states: "He [Aharon] took [the gold] from them… and made it into a molten calf"? The answer comes from the transcript of his subsequent interrogation by his brother Moshe (v. 24):

"They gave me [the gold]; I cast it into the flames and out came this calf," to which Rashi comments: "I had no idea that a calf would emerge, and yet it did."

To reconcile these two verses and assign blame properly for the incident, the most straightforward approach would be to presume that if Aharon had truly been guilty of deliberately fashioning a calf, he could not have hidden his culpability from Moshe. Therefore, he spoke the truth when he said that he had no idea that a calf would emerge, in which case v. 4 is not stating, categorically, that Aharon fashioned the calf, only that he was instrumental in its coming into existence.

❧ PART TWO: AHARON'S ALIBI

If Aharon did not plan on fashioning a calf, what was he planning to do with all the gold he had collected? What did he expect to emerge from the flames? Aharon's plan, according to Rashi (v. 2), was to stage a delaying action, so to speak, pending Moshe's imminent return: "Aharon thought: Women and children are possessive of their jewelry. Hopefully, they will dally and Moshe will arrive in the interim."

Continuing Rashi's defense of Aharon, we can assume that after the people fooled him and quickly turned in all their jewelry, he tossed it – as a lump – into the fire assuming, again, that Moshe would return before he had to go any further.

Once more, if Aharon was not responsible for the calf, where did it come from? According to Rashi (v. 4), the transformation of the gold into a molten calf was accomplished by sorcerers of the 'eirev rav, the mixed multitude that accompanied the Israelites from Egypt at the time of the exodus (12:38). Later on, in verse 7, Rashi notes the unusual reference to the Israelites as "Your [Moshe's] people," rather than "the people," and remarks: "These were the mixed multitude which Moshe converted on his own recognizance without consulting God."

An alternative explanation that Rashi provides (v. 4) is that the calf received its shape from an icon that Moshe had used to retrieve the coffin of Yosef from its burial place in the Nile[2] and that was cast into the lot of jewelry unbeknownst to Aharon.

The golden calf episode – like many others – is reiterated in Sefer Devarim. If we examine Devarim 9:20, what would our verdict be regarding Aharon's guilt or innocence? It says: "God was enraged with Aharon, too, to the point of his destruction." This would seem to place a burden of guilt squarely on his shoulders. Can we continue Rashi's spirited defense of Aharon in spite of this verse? Yes, because if he had been guilty as charged, how could Moshe's prayers (v. 11ff.) ever have earned him a reprieve?

‮ﻼ‬ PART THREE: WHAT DID THE PEOPLE EXPECT?

If the people did not specifically request a calf, what did they think they were going to get when they requested an *elohim*? Since they raised no objection to Aharon's collection of their golden jewelry, one would have to assume that he was fulfilling their expectations, implying that they expected him to make something out of gold. This, perhaps, is the key to understanding Rashi's comment on v. 1: "That shall go (*yelekhu*) before us: They desired for themselves many deities." Ordinarily, the use of a plural verb or adjective with the collective noun *elohim* is unremarkable (as in the ubiquitous *elohim aherim*); here, as Rashi maintains, the context mitigates in favor of the desire to produce a number of molten images.

Were they really so foolish as to regard molten images as "the deities that took them out of Egypt?" Here we turn to the commentary of Rashbam (v. 4), who asks, rhetorically: "Were they fools imagining that the calf, which had just been fashioned, had actually taken them out of Egypt?" In his response, he provides a valuable insight into the primitive, pagan mind:

> All idolaters know that our God in heaven created the world; their error lies in thinking that statues possessed an impure spirit just as the prophets possessed a holy spirit. They believed that the calf, which was really motivated by the impure spirit, was animated by the holy spirit, which is why they referred to it as the deity who had taken them from Egypt.

---

[2] According to Devarim 33:17, the symbol of Yosef was an ox (*shor*).

Was the calf really animated? Did it actually speak? Does Rashbam, then, believe in sorcery? He continues:

> The spirit of impurity is used to test Israel. All forms of sorcery, including *'ov* and *yid'oni*, have the capacity to challenge heaven by telling the future, thereby testing the people's loyalty to God.

Rashbam says, in essence, that the power that appears to give animation to works of idolatry is the power of God, Himself, which He utilizes, periodically, to test mankind.

Indeed, Ramban (v. 1) infers from the fact that they referred to it as "the god who liberated us from Egypt" – rather than "the God who created heaven and earth" or "the God who gives life on Earth" – that they did not actually regard the calf as a god, per se, but only as a representation of a deity.

This explanation is somewhat reminiscent of Rambam's (Maimonides') account of the origins of idolatry in the beginning of *Hilkhot 'Akum* in the Mishneh Torah. There he explains that Adam certainly recognized the exclusive existence of God, as did his earliest descendants. At some later point, however, mankind erred by imagining that just as a mortal king demands obedience to his servants, so God demands the recognition of, and obedience to, His servants – namely, the heavenly bodies. From the recognition of the sun, moon and stars as God's servants, however, evolved their erroneous designation as deities within themselves.

∞ PART FOUR: IBN EZRA: THE DEFENSE SUMS UP

Ibn Ezra (31:18) combines several of the elements we have already discussed:

> God forbid that Aharon made an idol, neither did the Israelites request an idol. They thought that Moshe had died.... He had been away for forty days and people cannot last that long without food.... The word *elohim* refers to a physical representation of [divine] glory....[3] Since this was a reverential request, Aharon complied by building an altar and announcing that on the morrow they would offer sacrifices... and only a minority [the three thousand who were slain?] thought it was an actual deity.

---

[3] Similar to the pillars of smoke and fire which led them out of Egypt?

VA-YAK'HEIL

Who Turned Off the Lights?

INTRODUCING THE KARAITES

℘ PREAFACE

In two separate portions of the Torah, the laws of Shabbat intrude upon the enterprise of the *mishkan*, first, in Ki Tissa' (31:12–17) and, second, here (35:2–3).

In this lesson, we shall try to establish a very specific relationship between Shabbat and the Mishkan. We shall also be making the acquaintance of the Karaites, who tended to a more stringent interpretation of some of the laws of Shabbat, and the manner in which Ibn Ezra, in his commentary to our *sidrah*, deals with their interpretation of the prohibition against kindling fire on Shabbat.

℘ PART ONE: MEET THE KARAITES (*KARA'IM*)

In the middle of the seventh century, the Persian Empire, with its large Babylonian Jewish community, was conquered by the Muslims. For reasons both theological and practical, the Muslims allowed the Jews to maintain their two principal self-governmental institutions, the Gaonate and the Exilarchate.[1] The *Ga'on,* or *Rosh Yeshivah* (of Sura or Pumbedita), was the

---

[1] Under Islamic law, Jews were entitled to the special status of tolerance (*dhimma*) that Islam awarded to "the people of the Book," the adherents of three Scriptural-based religions: Judaism, Christianity and Zoroastrianism. The practical reasons relate to the difficulties which the Muslim conquerors originally faced as a religious and ethnic minority amongst the vastly more numerous Zoroastrian Persians. Their predicament led them to deal more leniently with the population of Persia. The Jews were mollified by the recognition of their communal authorities, while the

spiritual head of Islamic Jewry, while the *Reish Galuta* (also: *Rosh ha-Golah*, i.e., exilarch), was its temporal head. In approximately 750 CE, the incumbent exilarch died, leaving two sons. On account of an unspecified character flaw, the elder son, Anan, was passed over in favor of his younger brother Hananiah, in spite of the former's acknowledged superiority in Talmudic learning. Hananiah's appointment was made by the Ge'onim – as tradition required – and confirmed by the Muslim Caliph.

Anan's revenge on the rabbinic establishment that had spurned him is the origin of Karaism. According to a rabbinic historical narrative,[2] Anan protested his brother's appointment and was consequently arrested by the Muslim authorities on the charge of treason. In jail, awaiting execution, he was approached by a Muslim sectarian leader[3] who advised him to circumvent the verdict by acknowledging his brother as exilarch of the "Talmudic" Jews, while claiming for himself the exilarchate of the "Scriptural" Jews.

Anan made the claim, the Caliph bought it, and the rest is history. The "Talmudic" Jews came to be known as "Rabbinites," while the "Scriptural" Jews eventually came to be known as the "Karaites."[4] In the ninth century, Anan's challenge to rabbinic authority was renewed by a Persian Jew, Binyamin al-Nahwendi. By the tenth century, Karaism, with its center in Jerusalem,[5] had taken firm root throughout the Jewish world.

✍ PART TWO: SOME EXAMPLES OF KARAITE HALAKHAH

Anan composed a *Sefer ha-Mitzvot*, a compendium of laws, which illustrates his approach to the interpretation of the Torah. While certainly

---

Zoroastrians were coddled by the extension of the privileges of *dhimma* to them despite the essential dualistic nature of their religion.

[2] The text, attributed to Sa'adiah Gaon (but without any conclusive evidence of his authorship), appears in a twelfth-century book by a Karaite named Elijah ben Abraham. Selections in English translationcan be found in Leon Nemoy, *Karaite Anthology,* New Haven: 1952, 4–5.

[3] Identified as Abu Hanifah, founder of the Hanafi school of Muslim jurisprudence, who is said to have died in prison c. 767.

[4] Until late in the ninth century they were known, simply, as Ananites.

[5] This emphasizes Karaism's association with the Scriptures, as opposed to Rabbinite Jewry, whose focus on the Talmud made it "Babylo-centric."

fundamentalist, he was *not* a strict literalist. Indeed, some of his interpretations are examples of sophisticated exegesis. Here are two examples of Shabbat laws:

> (a) [Anan the Prince] permitted light objects to be transported on Shabbat, saying, transport occurs only when borne upon the shoulder, to wit, "they shall bear them upon their shoulders" (Bemidbar 7:9).[6]

Upon reflection, this law, in spite of its antinomian conclusion, is modeled upon the rabbinical exegesis that was Anan's forte – recalling that even his rabbinical adversaries acknowledged his mastery of Talmudic learning. The verse cited by Anan relates to the Levitical clan of Kehat. When the princes of Israel donated wagons for the work of the *mishkan*, Moshe gave none to Kehat because "in order to perform the holy work they bore [the utensils of the *mishkan*] upon their shoulders" (Bemidbar 7:9). According to the Talmud, the prohibited labors on Shabbat derive from the principal labors of the *mishkan*. If the labor of transport, as it pertained to the *mishkan*, meant carrying on the shoulders, then surely the labor of transport to be prohibited on Shabbat must be the same.

> (b) [Anan] said: One might perhaps say that it is only the kindling of fire on the Sabbath which is forbidden, and that if the fire had been kindled on the preceding weekday it is to be considered lawful to let it remain over the Sabbath? Now the Merciful One has written here, "Ye shall not kindle fire," and elsewhere, "Thou shalt not perform any work" (Exodus 20:10), and both prohibitions begin with the letter *taw*.[7] In the case of labor, of which it is written, "Thou shalt not perform any work," it is evident that even if the work was begun on a weekday, before the arrival of the Sabbath, it is necessary to desist from it with the arrival of the Sabbath. The same rule must therefore apply also to the kindling of fire, of which it is written, "Ye shall not kindle," meaning that even if the fire has been kindled on a weekday, prior to the arrival of the Sabbath, it must be extinguished.[8]

---

[6] *Liqqutei Kadmoniyot*, edited by S. Pinsker. Vienna: 1860, 69.

[7] *lo-teva'aru; lo-ta'aseh.*

[8] The translation is from *Karaite Anthology op. cit.,* 17–18.

Upon examination, this, too, is considerably more sophisticated than the term "literal" implies. Like the Talmud, Anan uses inferential logic in order to compare a specific type of forbidden labor (i.e., kindling) with the general prohibition against laboring on the Sabbath. Even the specific hermeneutic device he employs is Talmudic in origin, although he uses it in a distinctly antinomian fashion. I refer to the principle called *gezeirah shavah*, a particular type of inference which draws upon the similar phrasing of disparate verses. Whereas the Talmud strictly limits its use to entire words, Anan seeks to utilize it in regard to but a single letter. Whereas the Talmud restricts its use to examples which have been in continuous traditional use, Anan is clearly giving it an unprecedented usage.

Pointedly, whenever Ibn Ezra cites an opinion of Anan ben David, he adds a pejorative epithet, *yimmaheh shemo ke'anan* (may his name evaporate like a cloud), which puns on the literal meaning of the name.[9]

✇ PART THREE: WHEN DOES THE "DAY" BEGIN?

In his commentary on our verse, Ibn Ezra commends his illustrious predecessor, Sa'adiah Gaon, for his refutation of Anan's interpretation of the prohibition against kindling fire on Shabbat. He then proceeds to record a disputation he personally held with a Karaite on the related question of when that prohibition begins. Ibn Ezra offers to debate the Karaite without resort to tradition, and the following exchange (which we have abbreviated) ensues:

> I asked him as follows: What is the source of the prohibition against kindling a fire on the eves of Shabbat after sunset? He replied: The verse, "You shall kindle no fire." I responded: But that verse only mentions [Shabbat] which, like "circumcise his foreskin on the eighth day" (Va-Yikra 12:3), is exclusive of the night. He responded [with the verse], "It was evening, it was morning, one day" (Bereishit. 1:5), [signifying that] they are, together, called "a day," with the evening preceding the morning....

---

[9] See his Introduction to his commentary on the Torah, part IV. The Karaites are referred to there (and elsewhere in medieval Hebrew literature) as *Tzedokim*, which should be understood as descriptive of their antinomian tendencies and not taken as an indication that they were actually descended from the Second Temple sectarians known as "Sadducees."

He [also] responded with, "Keep your Shabbat from one evening to the next" (Va-Yikra 23:32), but I replied that this verse deals exclusively with the Day of Atonement, to wit the verse says "your Shabbat," in the singular, rather than "your Shabbatot" – as it actually says [elsewhere], "Observe My Sabbaths" (Va-Yikra 19:30). Furthermore, Shabbat is not called "your" Shabbat but "God's" Shabbat, as in "Observe My Shabbatot" (Shemot 31:13), whereas the Day of Atonement is referred to as, "It shall be your Sabbath of Sabbaths" (Va-Yikra 23:32)....

He left in anger and returned a month later,[10] pleased with himself for having found the verse: "This day is a day of annunciation" (2 Melakhim 7:9), of which it is said, "We shall wait until the light of day" [implying that even the night before was called "day"]. I replied: Is that the only such "day" you could find? What about, "the day on which I smote all firstborn" (Bemidbar 3:13), since the plague of the firstborn occurred at midnight! Rather, the word *yom* can be interpreted in two ways. One refers to day [as opposed to] night, while the other means a period of time, as in, "It shall be on that day" (Yesha'ayahu 17:4)....

I have mentioned all these things because an astute person can interpret Scripture variously, so we require Tradition, Custom and the Oral Law for all matters of mitzvot, as I have explained at the outset of this work.

Ibn Ezra, like Sa'adiah before him, learned a lesson about polemics that appears to be lost on many contemporary defenders of the faith. Rather than take refuge in a tradition that is obviously not respected by the other party to the dispute ("I'm right because the *Shulḥan Arukh* says so!"), they sought to meet the Karaites on the mutually acknowledged grounds of philosophy and philology, and to demonstrate that Karaite arguments were unsupportable even by the standards to which they themselves subscribed.

---

[10] One cannot help but wonder how the Karaite would have fared if he had a concordance. We might as well wonder how Ibn Ezra – or Rashi or any other exegete – fared without what we regard as the single most irreplaceable tool of Biblical scholarship. We can only assume that they had committed the text of the entire Tanakh to memory in such a way (with mnemonic devices?) that they could locate not only whole words, but even such philological fragments as kindred roots and conjugations.

ഇ PART FOUR: THE MISHKAN, SHABBAT, AND THE GOLDEN CALF

We return, now, to the anomaly we posed in our Prologue: Why do Shabbat laws intrude upon the enterprise of the *mishkan*? The Sages and exegetes, attuned to all the nuances of the text and the context,[11] recognized the significance of the two interpolations, saying, in the first case, do not take license to defer Shabbat on account of the labors of the *mishkan*, and, in the second case, to instruct us that the labors of the *mishkan* do not supersede Shabbat.[12]

The laws of Shabbat (31:12–17) are contiguous to the *mishkan* on the one side (25:1–31:11) and to the episode of the golden calf (32:1ff.) on the other. In light of the sensitivity to context that we have just admired, we must presume the relevance of Shabbat to the golden calf no less than to the *mishkan*, but just what is that relevance?

The interposition of the episode of the golden calf between the instructions concerning the construction of the *mishkan* and their actual implementation indicates that we are dealing with the use and abuse of symbols. The calf demonstrated that the people – with the illustrious exception of the *leviyim* – had confused the symbol with what was being symbolized. That, I believe, is why Moshe inverted the sequence of his instructions when it came to their implementation. He therefore fashioned the *aron ha-kodesh* (the first to be described) last, doing so in the privacy of the inner sanctum (which was the last to be described and the first to be built), lest the sight of the *keruvim* cause the same consternation as the golden calf. It also explains why Aharon and the *leviyim* were the only Israelites who regularly glimpsed the Ark and *keruvim*, since they, alone, were unaffected by them.[13]

Shabbat, too, is a symbol, yet of another kind altogether. Even before the revelation at Sinai, Shabbat had been introduced to the Jewish people (at Marah) as the day on which they would not find manna in the field (Shemot 16:25). The Jews ought, then, to have been able to make their own *a fortiori* deduction that if Shabbat deferred even the life-sustaining labor of collecting

---

[11] For the significance of "nuances," particularly for the rabbinic exposition of the Law, see our lesson on the *sidrah* of Yitro.

[12] So Rashi on Shemot 31:13 and 35:2.

[13] Recall that Aharon, after fashioning the calf, could yet declare: *mi la-shem eilay.*

food, it surely ought to defer the labors of the *mishkan*. After they fell prey to the golden calf, however, God reminded them of the Shabbat, emphasizing its value as "an eternal sign between Me and the children of Israel" (31:17). The Jews were now to have a *mishkan*, a controlled symbolic environment, but not at the expense of the original, authentic "sign," the Shabbat.

PEKUDEI

The Enterprise of the Mishkan and the Labor of Cosmic Creation

MELAKHAH VS. *AVODAH*; MAN AS CREATOR

ഔ PREFACE

Nehama marshals seven literary parallels between God's creation of the universe and the Israelites' construction of the *mishkan*, concluding:

> God created heaven and earth and all therein to be the abode of mankind. He created them in six days, resting on the seventh. Moshe, similarly, was summoned [by God] into the cloud in order to view the structure of the *mishkan* he was to erect to be the abode of God upon earth. Man is called upon to emulate his Creator in actions and attributes, and is required to be His partner in primordial creation (*Iyyunim be-Sefer Shemot*, 352).

ഔ PART ONE: *MELAKHAH* VS. *AVODAH:* AGENCY VS. SUBSERVIENCE

The noun *melakhah* is used in the creation story (thrice in Bereishit 2:2–3 alone) and also appears about a dozen additional times in reference to the labors prohibited on Shabbat and *yamim tovim*, including the two "intrusions" into the enterprise of the *mishkan* about which we spoke in the *sidrah* of Va-Yak'heil. The *mishkan* narrative, however, while using *melakhah* predominantly (twenty-five times, mostly in Shemot 35–36), also uses forms of the noun *avodah* (five times), although almost always as part of the combined form: *melekhet avodah*.

While both these synonyms designate work, they derive from two distinctively different verbal roots, which set them apart from one another in spite of all their semantic similarities. The noun *melakhah* derives from the verbal root *l-'-k*, to send or minister (although it never actually appears in Tanakh as a verb), which also produces the noun *mal'akh*, a messenger, agent, or "angel" (which is actually Greek for a messenger or agent, often leading to its confusion with a winged and haloed creature of the same name).[1] The noun *avodah*, on the other hand, derives from the root *'-v-d*, to work or serve, which also produces the noun *eved*, a slave.

The difference between these words is nuanced: *melakhah* appears to be work that is done by an independent agent while *avodah* is (the same) work done by a servant. The former implies a measure of equality between the principal and his agent, while the latter just as clearly implies the subordination of the laborer to a master. In addition, the former signifies that the laborer contracts to complete a job, guided and informed by his own experience and expertise, as opposed to the latter where the laborer contracts to complete a job according to the instructions and specifications of the principal.

This distinction enables us to derive a "moral" regarding the *mishkan*. By designating man's labor in the construction of the *mishkan* as "agency," and "informed" agency at that (*melekhet mahshevet*), God is calling upon man, to use Nehama's expression, "to emulate his Creator in actions... [and] to be His partner in primordial creation."

℘ PART TWO: MAN AS CREATOR

There are only three contexts in the Torah in which verbal root *r-k-'* is utilized: in the Creation story (Bereishit 1:6ff.), here, in the fashioning of the *ephod* (39:3), and in the episode of Korah (Bemidbar 17:3–4). Given our ongoing comparison between Creation and the *mishkan*, we may conclude from this correspondence that the *mishkan* was a virtual "micro-cosmos," a universe in miniature, whose construction intentionally parallels the creation of the world. The flattening of gold threads to be woven into the sky-blue fabric of the *ephod* deliberately emulates God's interposition of the flattened-out firmament to separate the sky-blue waters.

---

[1] The question of whether divine agents are heavenly or mortal beings is debated by Rambam and Ramban, *inter alia*, with regard to Avraham's visitors and Yaakov's antagonist. We refer to this dispute in our lesson on the *sidrah* of Va-Yishlah. Also, see Va-Yeshev, Part Three: B.

We may account, in a similar fashion, for the appearance of *r-k-'* in the Korah episode, where the copper fire pans of Korah's followers were flattened into plating for the altar. Its avowed purpose, "that no outsider... should presume to offer incense" (v. 5), captures the symbolism of the primordial *rakia'* as an instrument of separation of jurisdictions.

The *ephod*, of all the priestly vestments, is the only item whose actual construction – and not just material composition – is cited in detail. Ramban speculates that this indicates a creative innovation on the part of the artisans, namely: "the first time gold was ever hammered flat and transformed into threads as malleable as wool or flax."

❧ PART THREE: SYMMETRY AND AESTHETICS

Having established the patent symmetry of Creation and the *mishkan*, we may pose a final question: Why does the construction of the *mishkan* not conclude with an explicit aesthetic judgment comparable to *tov me'od* (Bereishit 1:31)? The answer is that while *tov me'od* climaxes Creation, it does not conclude it. The conclusion of Creation comes only with Shabbat, which God greets by blessing and "ordaining" it (Bereishit 2:3). [Our choice of "ordain," rather than "sanctify," derives from the appreciation that the essence of holiness is to be set apart for a specific function.]

Harold Fisch, Professor of English and Comparative Literature at Bar Ilan University, makes the following observation in an essay entitled, "What Is Beautiful?"

> And yet there is surely something wrong with a scheme that makes the "very good" [*tob me'od*] of Gen. 1:31 the moment of supreme aesthetic gratification that comes when a work of art has been completed.... The moment "when the artist steps back a little and surveys his handiwork with delight" would more fittingly correspond with the contemplative posture of the day of rest, when indeed there is a completion... the "goodness" of the six days carries us to the supreme moment of completion of the seventh day. But when we get to that moment, we find not a moony space of aesthetic delight, not the category of *tob* at all, but rather that of holiness (2:3). For God declares the seventh day not *yafeh* or *tob*,

but *qadosh*. For six days the work had been beautiful; to the seventh day, when it arrives, he awards the title of holy.[2]

Professor Fisch also adduces the commentary of Ramban to the effect that, "Creation carried with it the notion that the world would go on being made throughout the 6,000 years of its existence," and alludes to a portion of the daily liturgy that praises God for the daily renewal of "an open-ended act of creation" [*ha-mehaddesh be-tuvo be-khol yom tamid ma'aseh bereishit*].

A comparison between Bereishit 2:3 and Shemot 39:43 and 40:9 offers a final correspondence in this regard. Moshe, too, greets the conclusion of the construction with a blessing and, rather than pronouncing aesthetic judgment over it, he too "ordains" it.

Following Professor Fisch's lead, we may now pass our own judgment on the Torah's aesthetics, concluding that ultimate beauty resides in function more than in form. The earth was indeed beautiful, but the climax of its creation was the purpose for which it was "ordained," namely, an environment for man's cultivation of a Torah-specific culture and civilization. The *mishkan*, too, was a genuine work of art, but its ordained purpose, the service of God, overshadows even its many aesthetic accomplishments.

❧ PART FOUR: SHABBAT AND *MISHKAN* – COMPLETING THE HERMENEUTIC CIRCLE

We now have the opportunity to bring to full circle the discussion we began in the *sidrah* of Va-Yak'heil regarding the relationship between the *mishkan* and its creative endeavors, and Shabbat and its prohibited labors. The *mishkan* was to be God's abode on earth; since it behooved Him that its construction meet the highest aesthetic standards, He endowed its principal architect with the keenest possible sense of aesthetic values. That endowment made Bezalel "His partner in primordial creation" in the fullest sense of the word, as it simultaneously made the enterprise of the *mishkan* the epitome of creativity.

When the Sages came to delineate the specific nature of forbidden Shabbat labor, they were struck by the identity of the linguistic form *melakhah*, which is the hallmark of both Shabbat and the *mishkan*, as well as

---

[2] *Poetry with a Purpose*. Indiana: 1988, 21.

by the implied identity of the primordial Creator with His partner, the artisan. Ergo, they inferred that the very labors that preceded the benediction and ordainment of the "micro-cosmos" of the *mishkan* should be forbidden on the day that marks the conclusion of the "macro-cosmos" of the universe.

&o EPILOGUE: MAN AS *"ELOHIM"*

In a previous lesson, we touched, briefly, upon the multiple significances of the word *elohim*.[3] We noted, *inter alia*, that as a noun it signifies divinity or authority (particularly judicial authority), but that it also functions as an adjective signifying majesty or grandeur. The combination of *ru'ah elohim* has evoked various translations according to its several appearances in *Tanakh*, betraying a fundamental uncertainty on the part of the translators concerning its precise meaning.

In its *locus classicus* of Bereishit 1:2, it is best known in the King James translation as "the spirit of God," while the New JPS prefers "a wind from God" (which, I assume, it thought more appropriate for the context of "sweeping [KJ: hovering] over the water"). When Pharaoh uses it to describe Yosef (Bereishit. 41:37), NJPS reverts to "the spirit of God" (i.e., still a noun), yet when describing the attributes with which God endowed Bezalel (Shemot 31:3), even NJPS uses the adjectival form, "divine spirit" (comprising yet another striking linguistic link between creation and the *mishkan*!).

Rambam, in the *Guide for the Perplexed* (1:2), analyzes the phrase *yod'ei tov va-ra'* (Bereishit. 3:5), distinguishing between the objective categories of true/false and the subjective categories of good/bad. The former are called "necessary truths" (Hebrew: *muskalot*, because they derive from the immutable properties of the intellect) and these were already possessed by Adam and Eve. The Tree of Knowledge – so the serpent promised – was supposed to provide them with the knowledge of "apparent truths" (Hebrew: *mefursamot*, so-called because they are only a matter of general agreement).

We submit, then, that if an *elohim*, by Torah definition, is one who can make the subjective value judgment of good/bad, then *ruah elohim* (viewed

---

[3] Va-Yishlah, Part Three.

adjectivally, while recognizing that it might often be nominal, as in the case of Yosef or Sha'ul) means a divinely endowed aesthetic sense.

To press the point a bit further, if *tov/ra'* constitute aesthetic judgments, then the recurring phrase, *ki tov*, with which God punctuates Creation, and the *tov me'od* with which it climaxes, are paradigmatic expressions of aesthetic satisfaction. This observation, if correct, allows for a new answer to the question: Why is Creation associated specifically with the divine name *e-lohim* rather than *ha-shem*? We would venture to say that the former (signifying the attribute of justice) implies the particular faculty of discrimination, which is an aesthetic function. It requires an *elohim* to judge whether something is good or bad.

Va-Yikra

VA-YIKRA

Saying You're Sorry

SEFER HA-HINUKH: ACTIONS AND INTENT

℘ PREFACE: BY DEFINITION

Nehama frequently quoted, with obvious approval, the postulate of the *Sefer ha-Hinukh*: *aharei ha-pe'ulot nimshakhim ha-levavot* – feelings are prompted by actions. In this week's *sidrah*, we shall see this manifested in the matter of *korbanot*.[1]

The Hebrew word *het'* is usually translated into English as "sin." That, as we shall now demonstrate, is a "sin" in itself. Whereas "sin" (from the Anglo-Saxon) denotes evil or wickedness, the Hebrew verb *h-t-'* means to miss the mark (see Shoftim 20:16). This significant difference manifests itself in the complementary term *teshuvah*, as well. Whereas the Hebrew verb *sh-u-v* means to return, or repeat, the English word "penitence" (or: repentance) shares an etymology with "penalty." The distinction is clear: for committing an evil or wicked deed, one must pay a penalty; if one misses the mark, however, the remedy is to try again.

Note: For purposes of comprehension, however, we shall continue to use the colloquial terms: "sin" and "repentance."

---

[1] Usually translated as "sacrifices" (from the Latin: to make sacred), there is a lot to be said for Everett Fox's preference for "near-offerings" in his translation of the Torah: *The Five Books of Moses* (NY: Schocken, 1995), *passim*.

❧ PART ONE: THE INFLUENCE OF ACTIONS UPON THOUGHTS

The laws of the sin offering, which begin with Va-Yikra 4:2, make it clear that it is brought only for a sin committed through error (*shogeg*). The author of the *Sefer ha-Hinukh* (thirteenth-century Spain) explains:

> Have I not emphasized time and again that the inclinations of the heart depend upon actions? Therefore, when a man sins, he cannot cleanse his heart merely by uttering between himself and the wall, "I have sinned and will never repeat it." Only by doing an overt act to atone for his sin, by taking rams from his enclosures and troubling himself to bring them to the Temple, give them to the priest, and perform the entire rite as prescribed for sin-offerings – only then will he impress upon his soul the extent of the evil of his sin and will take measures to avoid it in the future.... And the Torah has promised that when the sinner has done this great action and has fully repented, the sin committed through error will be forgiven. In [the case of] sin committed intentionally and presumptuously, however, this symbolic action is inadequate because he who sins intentionally will not be moved by symbols (Mitzvah #95).

While this gives an insight into the nature and symbolic significance of the sin offering, it leaves a fundamental question unanswered: What is the "sin" of someone who acts in error? Why should anyone be held accountable for forgetfulness or ignorance? Rabbi Samson Raphael Hirsch (1808–1888) provides the following answer:

> The sinner through error is he who sins from carelessness. In other words, at the moment of omission he did not take full care with his whole heart and soul that his act should be in keeping with the Torah and commandments.... The lack of anxiety and the lackadaisical unconcern for his way of life – these are the elements of commission in the sin of omission. This is the transgression (*pesha'*) that resides in the sin (*het'*), as it is stated: "And because of their transgressions [within] all their sins" (Va-Yikra 16:16).

In Talmudic parlance, such a sinner by error is called *shogeg karov le-meizid*.

❧ PART TWO: *HET'* VERSUS *PESHA'*: DOES INTENT MATTER?

Does intention (*kavvanah*) determine whether an action was deliberate or not? Rabbi David Tzvi Hoffman (1843–1921), like Hirsch, a German Orthodox rabbi, provides the clarification in his commentary to our *sidrah*:

> Even a sin committed through error is a sin. In this respect, the term *het'* (omission) differs from other terms that denote sin – such as *pesha'* (transgression) – in that the latter denotes only intentional sins, whereas the former refers also to unintentional sins. According to rabbinical tradition, there are two kinds of sin through error: (1) Error with respect to the law; that is, he was ignorant of the fact that the act was prohibited; (2) Error with respect to the act; that is, although he knew that the act was prohibited by law, he did not realize – through negligence – that he was performing the prohibited act. The sinner through error needs atonement because he did not take proper care and precaution.... Not so he who sins unwillingly, from compulsion. He need bring no offering because "the All-Merciful absolves him who acted under duress" (*'ones, rahmana patreih*).

❧ PART THREE: THE BIGGER THEY ARE....

Although forgetfulness would appear to be a universal constant, all negligent sinners do not bring the same offering. Since the absence of the intention to sin does not absolve the sinner from his responsibility, the greater the sinner's status – the greater his burden of responsibility and, hence, the greater his need for atonement. Indeed, our *sidrah* lists a variety of "sinners through error," stipulating a different atonement for each.

The sequence in which sinners through error are listed is: (a) the anointed priest; (b) the whole congregation; (c) the prince (*nasi'*); (d) one of the common people. Since it is inconceivable that "the whole congregation of Israel" should err – all at once! – over the same matter, Hazal refer this phrase, euphemistically, to the Sanhedrin.

A close reading of the relevant verses, however, reveals an anomaly. While items a-b-d are introduced by the Hebrew particle *'im* (if), making them conditional, item c (the *nasi'*) is introduced by *'asher* (that), implying that it is unconditional. Since "no righteous man on earth will do only good and never err" (Kohelet 7:20), it is perhaps inevitable that even a prince among men will sin. Compare this passage from the Talmud Yerushalmi (*Horayot* 3:2):

> Rabbi Yohanan ben Zakkai said: Fortunate is the generation (*'ashrei ha-dor*) whose ruler brings a sin offering for his sin of omission. If the ruler brings an offering, need we speak about the common man? And if for his sin through error he brings an offering, need we speak of his willful transgression?

The word "fortunate" (*'ashrei*) is a play on the word *'asher* that appears in our text. While it is not "fortunate" that a prince sins, it is fortunate, according to Rabbi Yohanan, that if he acknowledges even an inadvertent mistake, he can rectify it.

✍ PART FOUR: SOME OTHER OPINIONS

In explaining why the Torah uses the word *nefesh* (soul)[2] to designate a man here, rather than the word *'adam*, Ramban says (1:2):

> The reason why it is necessary for sacrifices to be brought for an inadvertent offense is because every sin causes a spiritual blemish to the soul.... For this reason, the soul of the inadvertent offender is required to offer a sacrifice conferring upon it the opportunity to draw nearer to God.

Note: How is this interpretation of the sin offering different from those of Hirsch and Hoffman cited above?

Abrabanel notes:

> When the prophets extolled Jewish sacrifices, they referred to the burnt offerings (*'olah*)[3] as in: 'Then You will delight in the sacrifices of righteousness, in burnt offerings and whole offerings' (Tehillim 51:21). Yesha'yahu utters a similar sentiment regarding sacrifices in the future: 'their burnt offerings and sacrifices shall be acceptable

---

[2] While on the subject of etymologies (see previous note), we should note that all three Hebrew synonyms for the English word "soul" — *neshamah* and *ruah*, along with *nefesh* — derive from breathing, suggesting that the capacity for autonomous respiration is the sine qua non of living.

[3] Curiously, an early English translation of *'olah* was "holocaust," from the Greek for "burnt whole."

on My altar, for My house will be called a house of prayer for all nations' (56:7).

Note: Why are sin offerings not mentioned in either verse?

TZAV

It's *Deja Vu* All Over Again!

COMPARING THE *KORBANOT*

ဆာ PREFACE

Having noted on several occasions Nehama's concern over ostensible repetitions and duplications in the Torah, we are obliged to address the question of why many of the laws of sacrifices that appeared in last week's *sidrah* reappear in this week's as well. A close reading will, again, reveal comparison and contrast.

ဆာ PART ONE: WATCH WHOM YOU'RE TALKING TO

The first observation we may offer on the comparison is that the form of address used in 1:2 differs from that which is used in 6:2. The former instructs Moshe to "speak to the Israelites," whereas 6:2 instructs him to "command Aharon and his sons." The sequence of sacrifices in Tzav also differs from that of Va-Yikra.

Va-Yikra:		Tzav:	
'olah (burnt offering)	Ch. 1	*'olah*	6:1–6
minhah (meal offering)	Ch. 2	*minhah*	6:7–11
shelamim (peace offering)	Ch. 3	*hatat*	6:17–23
hatat (sin offering)	Ch. 4, 5:1–3	*'asham*	7:1–10
'asham (guilt offering)	Ch. 5:14–26	*shelamim*	7:11–21

Indeed, the contrast we noted between the respective forms of address can explain the differences in the sequence. When the Torah is speaking to the Israelites, in general, it says: "If a man should bring a sacrifice," therefore, it gives precedence to the voluntary sacrifices such as *'olah, minhah,* and *shelamim*, and only afterwards does it refer to the obligatory offerings such as *hatat* and *'asham*. On the other hand, when the Torah addresses the *kohanim*, the sequence it chooses is that of holiness, beginning with *'olah*, *minhah*, *hatat* and *'asham*, which are called *kodshei kodashim* (sublime sanctity), and then moves on to *shelamim*, whose status is that of *kodashim kalim* (subordinate sanctity).

❧ PART TWO: A MISSING LINK

There is even a link between the last item of Va-Yikra (*'asham*) and the first item of Tzav (*'olah*). According to the Midrash (Tanhuma):

> "Command Aharon... This is the law of the burnt offering...." (6:2). Said the Holy One, Blessed be He: Observe that which is written in the passage immediately preceding, and after that: "This is the law of the burnt offering." Why [does one follow the other]? "For I, the Lord, love judgment, I hate robbery for burnt offering [*be-olah*]" (Yesha'yahu 61:8), even in a burnt offering. What is written in the preceding passage? "Then it shall be because he has sinned and is guilty, that he shall restore that which he took violently away" (5:23), and afterwards: "This is the law of the burnt offering." If you wish to offer a sacrifice, do not take it from someone else violently.... And when will I accept your burnt offering? When you wash your hands of robbery. As David said: "Who shall ascend the Mount of the Lord and stand in His holy place? One who has clean hands and a pure heart" (Tehillim 24:3–4).

Why do we need a Midrash to tell us that we may not bring a stolen animal as a sacrifice when, in addition to being contrary to ordinary Torah law, it is an explicit verse in Malakhi (2:16): "And you bring that which has been stolen?" By utilizing the verse in Tehillim, the Midrash indicates that it is not talking about the actual use of a stolen animal for a sacrifice, but the bringing of a sacrifice by someone who is unfit – as though by a conviction for robbery.

As Nehama writes:

> Thus one of the central concepts of the prophetic messages of Yesha'yahu, Hoshea, Amos and Yirmiyahu that sacrifices

unaccompanied by good deeds and pure intentions are worthless, underlies the connection between the two *sidrot* – Va-Yikra and Tzav – which contain the principal sacrificial laws (*Iyyunim hadashim be-sefer Va-Yikra'*, 60).

Note: Regarding the *Midrash Tanhuma* cited above, is "burnt offering" the correct translation of the word *be-olah* in Yesha'yahu? It is a proper translation, but not the only one. Our translation follows the commentaries of Rashi, Ibn Ezra, and Radak, whereas Targum Yonatan [along with the JPS translation] treats it as a form of the word *'avlah*, meaning iniquity.

✄ PART THREE: ASHES, ASHES...

The first specific responsibility assigned to the *kohanim* in this week's *sidrah* is *terumat ha-deshen*, lifting the ashes of the sacrifices off the altar. The *Sefer ha-Hinukh* explains its purpose as follows:

> The purpose of the mitzvah is to enhance the sanctuary and beautify it to the utmost of our ability.... Beauty is added to the altar by cleaning out the ashes from where the fire has to be kindled, and moreover, the flame burns well when there are no ashes beneath (Mitzvah #131).

If removing the ashes serves a purely technical function – cleaning the altar and keeping the flame burning clearly – would the Torah have devoted a special instruction to it? If the only purpose of cleaning the altar was utilitarian, would the Torah have to require the *kohen* to change out of his vestments to do it?

Some commentators presume that the reasons for these activities were symbolic. Rabbi Bahya ibn Pakudah, for instance, remarks:

> [A man] should belittle his own accomplishments and criticize himself for his inadequacy in spiritual matters before both God and man, seeking help and courage from Him...and forsaking greatness and honor whenever he acts for God – in private or public – as it is written with regard to Aharon concerning the loftiness of his station: "And he shall remove his linen garments and put on other garments and lift out the ashes," in order to humble and remove the haughtiness from his heart. A similar humbling is implied in the description of David in 2 Shemuel 6, as seen through the eyes of

[his wife] Mikhal: "And she saw King David leaping and dancing before the Lord" (*Hovot ha-Levavot*, Chapter 6).

Rabbi Samson Raphael Hirsch, however, has a slightly different take on these instructions. In his commentary (*ad loc.*), he writes:

> "And he shall lift out the ashes": The relics of the previous day's work need clearing away before the new day's work can be begun, in a clean and renovated place. This explains the importance of the instruction to perform the removal of the ashes – a symbol for the occupation with the previous day's work – in worn-out and old clothes. One must not don the smartest clothes in honor of something performed in the past.

Rabbi Hirsch is suggesting that it is our daily duty to bring a fresh zeal to our observance of mitzvot.

Shemini

You Are What You Eat: A Look at Kashrut

YITZHAK ARAMA AND DAVID TZVI HOFFMAN

ഇ PREFACE

Nehama, ever the conscientious pedagogue, highly approved of incorporating and highlighting *ta'amei ha-mitzvot,* rationales for mitzvot, in explaining the Torah. In this week's *sidrah,* we shall explore some of the rationales that have been provided for kashrut.

ഇ PART ONE: FOR WHAT PURPOSE?

The dietary restrictions reported in this week's *sidrah* were not the first to be recorded; Adam was already instructed concerning permissible and prohibited fruits. According to the Midrash *Tadshe* (Bereishit 2:16–17), the purpose behind that restriction was:

> In order that his gaze should be continually directed towards [the prohibited tree] and thereby call to mind his Creator and be conscious of the yoke his Maker placed upon him, lest he be overwhelmed by his passions.

This logic resembles that which is offered for the prohibition against slaughtering a heifer and its calf on the same day: It is educative; i.e., its reason is not intrinsic to the prohibited act, but serves to train or educate the performer.[1]

There are, of course, other explanations for the laws of kashrut such as the one offered by Maimonides, who argues that they possess an inherent advantage, namely the prevention of illness and other detrimental physical

---

[1] We treat this subject at length in our study of the *sidrah* of Emor.

effects (Guide 3:48). Yitzhak Arama (fifteenth-century Spain, author of *Akeidat Yitzhak*), on the other hand, disagrees sharply:

> God forbid that we should imagine that the prohibition of foods is dependent on hygienic considerations. If that were the case, the Torah, far from being the work of the living God, would be no better than any medical treatise. Furthermore, the so-called harmful effects of such foods could always be counteracted by various drugs. Antidotes could always be discovered rendering the prohibition null and void and the words of our Torah of no lasting value....

The real reason is quite different. The dietary prohibitions are motivated by spiritual considerations, to keep the soul healthy and pure and preserve it from being defiled and tainted by unclean and abominable passions, thoughts and ideas.

As Nehama elaborates:

> Arama offers a further variation on the motive for the prohibition of certain foods. It was not that their consumption was detrimental to the soul of man, but rather abstention from them was conducive to self-control and discipline in life. Self-control, he states, is the distinctive feature marking man as superior to animal. By not being allowed to eat just anything that comes to his mouth or that he fancies, he will be disciplined, from his childhood, to exercise the same self-control that he is called on to display in the dietary field in other fields, in accordance with the thought expressed at the end of the daily *Shema'*, in the paragraph concerning the wearing of *tzitzit*: "Do not go astray after your own heart and after your own eyes" (Bemidbar 15:39) (*Studies in the Weekly Sidra*, first series, 5715 #25).

ಏ PART TWO: *BEIN YISRAEL LA-AMIM*: KASHRUT AS A HEDGE AGAINST ASSIMILATION

Yet another explanation of kashrut was advanced by Shmuel David Luzzatto (Shadal; Italy, 1800–1865):

> Every Jew must be set apart from the nations in laws and ways of life and not imitate their deeds, always cleaving to the God of his

forefathers: "Sanctify yourselves and be holy, for I am holy" (Va-Yikra 6:44).

His explanation prompts the following question: If all the gentiles started keeping kosher, would the laws of kashrut then lose their validity? Logically, the answer is: Yes, they would. For this very reason, perhaps, Rabbi David Tzvi Hoffman, in his commentary, said:

> Some tend to regard these laws as designed to make a fundamental cleavage between the Jewish people and the other nations. A special diet was imposed on the Jewish people, to make them feel separate or specially singled out as a holy nation, as the people of the Lord....
>
> In actual fact, the verses quoted make no mention of the idea that certain foods were prohibited to Israel in order to separate them from the nations. On the contrary, it is stated that since God has [already] separated the Jewish people from other peoples, Israel is obliged to observe the divine precepts that teach us to make a difference between clean and unclean beasts, just the same as Israel is obliged to keep other mitzvot.

Out of apparently the same consideration, Shadal added:

> But besides this reason – which varies with time and place (for instance, if all the world were to worship the true God and keep just laws, this separation would not be necessary) – the multiplicity of mitzvot and statutes is of benefit at all times and places in improving our moral behavior on two counts:
>
> 1. The mitzvot we observe remind us of God who commanded them... and act as a restraint on our passions... that we should not sin;
>
> 2. The only method by which man can overcome his passions and rule over himself lies in habituating himself to forgoing material enjoyments and the endurance of pain and difficult circumstances....

The numerous mitzvot and statutes of our Torah accustom man to exercise self-control, to endure and abstain.

❧ PART THREE: PURITY AND DANGER[2]

Another approach to the laws of kashrut – early in the modern period – argued that they were borrowed from the non-Jewish environment. One such theory found their source in the dualistic Zoroastrian religion of Persia, which made a sharp distinction between forces of good and light (represented by the god Ahura Mazda) and those of darkness and evil (represented by Ahriman). The distinction between "clean" and "unclean" animals, it was argued, followed from this dualism.

In response to this argument, Rabbi Hoffman wrote:

> This theory is untenable, since the precepts of purity and holiness in the Zoroastrian scriptures and Judaism are not identical.... For instance, all the beasts without cloven hooves, such as the horse and the donkey, the dog and the fox, are, according to Zoroaster, clean animals, whereas according to the Torah, they are unclean.... According to the Torah, defilement is a subjective term, which only exists in relation to man.... There is no point of contact between Zoroaster and the Mosaic Law beyond the fact that both list categories of clean and unclean animals, and this is a feature common to all ancient peoples. Indeed, the Torah, no doubt, takes for granted the existence of a tradition common to all the peoples.

In support of Rabbi Hoffman's position, we may point to other Torah laws that do not distinguish between clean and unclean animals, such as:

- not hitching an ox and a donkey to the same plow;

- helping adjust the load on a donkey;

- returning [all] stray animals to their owners.

In addition, Noah, who represents mankind in the pre-Sinaitic era, is instructed to bring the animals into the ark according to their division into clean (seven of each) and unclean (two of each). This, too, would seem to imply that the distinction between clean and unclean animals is (in Hoffman's words): "a feature common to all ancient peoples."

---

[2] *Purity and Danger* is actually the title of a book by anthropologist Mary Douglas that includes a chapter on the laws of kashrut.

Note: If clean and unclean animals are essentially alike, and a pair is sufficient to ensure the survival of a species, why was Noah commanded to bring seven of the clean species? Was the intention to propagate more of the "kosher" species that the non-kosher ones?

Right after the flood, Noah expressed his gratitude to God for his rescue by offering Him sacrifices. Since sacrifices could only be offered from "clean" animals, there had to be more than a pair for those species to propagate.

TAZRIA'

Purity and Impurity, *Niddah* and "Catharsis"

NEHAMA AND YESHAYAHU LEIBOWITZ AND JOSEPH B. SOLOVEITCHIK

❧ PREFACE

As in the previous *sidrah*, we shall again explore the subject of *ta'amei ha-mitzvot*: providing rationales for the commandments. We will begin with a general look at the concepts of *tum'ah* and *taharah* (impurity and purity) and then narrow our focus to the laws of *niddah* (menstruation) that are stipulated in this week's *sidrah*. Along the way, we will compare Nehama's views with those of her brother, Yesha'ayahu, which we will also compare with a selection from the writings of Rabbi Yosef Dov ha-Levi Soloveitchik.

Note: It is a coincidence worth noting that Yesha'ayahu and Nehama Leibowitz, along with Rabbi Soloveitchik, were students in the University of Berlin at the same time.

❧ PART ONE: PURITY AND IMPURITY: FOR WHAT PURPOSE?

Nehama wrote:

> The laws of impurity and purity elude us. We neither know their reasons nor are we able to investigate them. Even the very concepts of impurity and purity have us groping blindly (*Iyyunim hadashim be-sefer Va-Yikra*, 145).

Nehama's observation is in line with Rashbam's comment on this week's *sidrah* (13:2):[1]

---

[1] Which we have cited previously, cf. Mishpatim, Part Three.

In all of the chapters of afflictions to humans, animals, or buildings; their appearances, the calculation of their quarantines and the matter of white, black, or yellow hairs; we have no recourse at all to the literal sense of Scripture (*peshuto shel miqra'*), nor to human expertise (*beqi'ut... shel benei 'adam*) based upon prevailing norms (*derekh 'eretz*).

On the other hand, however, it contrasts sharply with what her brother Yesha'ayahu Leibowitz wrote:

The major part of this *sidrah* deals with the blood of childbirth and that of menstruation, and of ritual impurity and purity – of the biological foulness of human existence. The mitzvot related to this comprise the worship of God, because the worship of God was imposed on man in that he is human. It was not imposed on man in that he is a spiritual being, but in that he is a physical creature, who must worship God not only with his soul but also with his body – because the body and the soul together constitute the man (*Accepting the Yoke of Heaven*. Jerusalem: Urim, 2002, 110).

Professor Leibowitz compares the laws of impurity-purity of this week's *sidrah* to those of kashrut in last week's *sidrah*, noting that:

[Man] does not just eat; he eats in accordance with the mitzvot of God. The same is true with marital relations, this possibly being the most profound of all areas in man's existence in that he is a living creature.... Both man and woman must maintain a specific discipline in their sexual lives, and as this is a discipline that man accepts upon himself only for the reason that he is observing a mitzvah which has no other reason – not a social reason, not a hygienic reason, not a moral reason – it is the supreme expression of the worship of God (*op. cit.,* 111).

✥ PART TWO: LEIBOWITZ AND SOLOVEITCHIK ON *NIDDAH*

While acknowledging that the laws of ritual purity and impurity lapsed two thousand years ago, Professor Leibowitz notes that one such law remains "on the books," so to speak, and that is the law of *niddah* (menstruation) and *tevilah* (immersion), which he categorizes not so much as a matter of ritual purity as a religious prohibition that is imposed on both men and women. In arguing that the observance of these laws for their own sake comprises "the supreme expression of the worship of God" (*ibid.*), Leibowitz cites a Midrash on Shir ha-Shirim, whose overt description of the relations between a lover and her beloved is understood, traditionally, to symbolize the relationship between Israel and God. The Midrash states:

> A man longs to see himself under the bridal canopy, because there is no day that is dearer to a man than that, where he will rejoice with his wife. He comes to be with her, and she says to him: "I saw something like a rose" [i.e., I saw a drop of menstrual blood]. He separates himself from her and she separates herself from him. The one turns his face to this side and the other turns her face to the other side. Who separated them? What snake bit them? What scorpion harmed them? What fence is there between them? But these are the words of the Torah, as it states: "You will not approach a woman in her menstrual impurity to have intercourse with her" (Va-Yikra 18:19) (*Shir ha-Shirim Rabbah,* 7:2–3).[2]

Interestingly, Rabbi Yosef Dov ha-Levi Soloveitchik (the Rav) cites the identical Midrash while making a similar point about the laws of *niddah.* He writes:

> Bride and bridegroom are young, physically strong and passionately in love with each other. Both have patiently waited for this rendezvous to take place. Just one more step and their love would have been fulfilled, a vision realized. Suddenly the bride and groom make a movement of recoil. He gallantly, like a chivalrous knight, exhibits paradoxical heroism. He takes his own defeat.
>
> There is no glamor attached to his withdrawal. The latter is not a spectacular gesture, since there are no witnesses to admire and to laud him. The heroic act did not take place in the presence of jubilating crowds; no bards will sing of these two modest, humble young people. It happened in the sheltered privacy of their home, in the stillness of the night. The young man, like Jacob of old,

---

[2] The Midrash addresses the verse: "Your belly is like a heap of wheat, set about [alt: fenced off] with roses."

makes an about-face; he retreats at the moment when fulfillment seems assured ("Catharsis," *Tradition* 17:2 [Spring 1978]: 45).[3]

❧ PART THREE: THE FOCUS ON WOMAN: THE '*EZER KE-NEGDO*

The relationship between men and women that is governed, partially, by the laws of *niddah*, is discussed by Nehama, who devoted one of her earlier *gilyonot* to the subject of the creation of woman.[4] She begins the discussion with a citation from *Akeidat Yitzhak*, the Torah commentary of R. Yitzhak Arama:

> God's wisdom saw fit that the union of man and woman should not be based exclusively on sexual relations, like all other animals. Rather, they should have a special personal relationship that will strengthen their love and companionship and allow them to assist one another mutually in all matters as befits them. This way all males and females should not be, individually, like other animals that can graze alongside one another without requiring one another's company. Rather [humans] are capable of creating a proper mutual society as need be. For this purpose, woman serves man as the worthy and proper assistant to whom he is equal (Bereishit 5713 [1952]).

The word in the verse (i.e., Bereishit 2:18) from which Arama derives the identification of woman as man's assistant is, clearly, '*ezer*, while the word that seems to support his stipulation that man and woman are equal is *kenegdo*. Two things that are juxtaposed one with the other (which is quite the literal meaning of *neged*)[5] are, ostensibly, equal. Indeed, this interpretation is consistent with the well-known Midrash (*Bereishit Rabbah* 17:2): "If he is

---

[3] See my presentation of this essay in *A Study and Program Guide to the Teachings of Rabbi Joseph B. Soloveitchik* (Brookline: The Rabbi Joseph B. Soloveitchik Institute, 2003), 42–47.

[4] The weekly *parashah* sheets (*gilyonot*) began to be circulated in 5702 (1941) and continued for thirty years until 5742 (1971). Nehama was awarded the prestigious Israel Prize for this enterprise.

[5] Nehama cites the commentary of S.D. Luzzato who compares the word to its rabbininc usage [e.g., *keneged arba'ah banim dibberah torah*], meaning in relation to. The verse, then, designates woman as one who relates to man and to his needs.

worthy, she assists him; if he is unworthy, she opposes him," because her opposition would hardly be consequential if she were not his equal.

Rashi's citation of this Midrash, however, comprises a striking instance of the freedom he often takes with his sources. To the text of the Midrash as we have cited it, Rashi adds, at the very end, the word: *le-hillahem*, to combat. In explanation of the argumentative, often combative nature of marital relationships, Nehama offers the insight of the Gur Aryeh, the super-commentary on Rashi of the Maharal of Prague (sixteenth century):

> Rashi should be understood as follows: I shall make for man an assistant [i.e., woman] who can assist through opposition, because this assistant is unlike the assistance of a father to a child or vice versa, for they will never oppose one another. This assistant, however, will be an "assistant in opposition" because woman is equal to man in importance and she assists him. Alternatively, man brings something and woman perfects it. This is called *'ezer ke-negdo.* Similarly, if man is unworthy, she will oppose him completely, whereas a father will never oppose his child. This must be regarded as the *peshat* of the verse; otherwise Rashi would not have cited it.
>
> There is also an esoteric side to this (*davar ne'elam*). Male and female are opposites.... If they are worthy, they combine into one complete force just as all opposites unite into one force. If they are worthy, God reconciles the opposing forces and unifies them. When they are unworthy, however, the fact that they are two opposites prompts her to oppose him.

METZORA'

"Beware of the Affliction"

MIDRASH VS. MAIMONIDES; *TZARA'AT* AS METAPHOR

ဆ PREFACE

Nehama writes:

> *Tzara'at* is not an illness that comes upon a person. According to most commentators, it is supernatural; it afflicts a person through divine providence as a sign and indication that he has erred, and as a summons to him to repent (*Iyyunim hadashim be-sefer Va-Yikra*, 157).

Accurately, the Torah term *tzara'at* is not leprosy. Leprosy is a contagious skin disease which is spread pathologically, by bacteria. *Tzara'at*, while designated an affliction (*nega'*), is neither a disease nor contagious. First of all, there is no indication in the Torah or elsewhere (such as in the story of the *metzora'im* which comprises the *haftarah*), that a *metzora'* suffers a serious health problem. Secondly, if *tzara'at* were contagious, we would be required to quarantine every suspected *metzora'* immediately. According to the protocols prescribed by the Torah, however, we delay isolation pending a formal declaration by the *kohen*.[1]

For the sake of convenience, however, we will continue to use the word "leprosy" throughout this essay as though it were identical with *metzora'*.

---

[1] In a similar vein, the Mishnah (*Nega'im* 3:2) instructs us that a bridegroom is not inspected during the week of his wedding and that no inspections were conducted at all during the *shalosh regalim*. If *tzara'at* were a contagion, it would be unthinkable to suspend the inspection process under any circumstances.

✌ PART ONE: ABRABANEL

In the *sidrah* of Shemini, we reported on several points of view concerning the laws of kashrut. Some saw them – from a hygienic point of view – as dietary laws, while others found in them symbolic significance. The same holds true for the laws of *tzara'at*.

Don Yitzhak Abrabanel (1437–1508) belongs to the first group. He suggests that the laws of *tzara'at* help us deal with something that (outwardly) resembles the contagion of leprosy. The isolation of the *metzora'* is intended to prevent the affliction from spreading, and the Torah further advises him not to use contaminated garments or utensils after his recuperation. The challenge to his position, though, is the question: Of all the diseases from which mankind has suffered (and continues to be afflicted), why did the Torah pick just this one to treat?

Alternatively, there are interpretations of *tzara'at* that view it symbolically.

✌ PART TWO: MIDRASH *RUTH RABBAH*

The Midrash draws our attention to one particular aspect of the laws of *tzara'at* – the gradual progression that characterizes the onset of these afflictions. In every case, a waiting period of seven days is prescribed from the onset of the first symptoms to see how matters develop:

> The All-Merciful does not mete out punishment immediately upon people themselves, as we learn from *Iyyov* (Job)[2] ...So it is with the afflictions (*nega'im*): First they descend upon one's house. If he repents – well and good; if not, the stones have to be removed. If he repents – well and good; if not, they have to be burnt. After that, the afflictions beset his body. If he repents – well and good; if not, the *kohen* comes and goes. If he repents – well and good; if not, "he shall dwell alone, making his residence outside the camp" (*Ruth Rabbah* 2:10).

While *tzara'at* clearly existed during Biblical times (see, again, the *haftarah*), it seems to have disappeared by the time of the Talmud. As the

---

[2] First his oxen were captured, then his servants slain, then his house collapsed on his children, and finally, he was afflicted with boils.

Talmud (*Sanhedrin* 71b) says: "An afflicted house never existed." What prompted the change between the two eras? Sforno offers the following explanation for the difference:

> When the generations no longer rose to the moral heights warranting this divine compassion, no sign of such afflictions visiting the house was ever again evident.

๛ PART THREE: MAIMONIDES

As we have noted previously, whenever the question of *ta'amei ha-mitzvot* (rationales for commandments) arises, Rambam will surely have something to say.[3] In his *Mishneh Torah,* he writes:

> *Tzara'at* is a homonymous term denoting dissimilar subjects... The change in the color of garments and houses – termed *tzara'at* by the Torah – is not a natural phenomenon, but constituted a sign and wonder for Israel to warn against evil talk.... As the Torah warns us (Devarim 24:8): "Beware of the affliction of *tzara'at*, remember what the Lord your God did to Miriam on the way."
>
> This refers to the words she spoke against her brother Moshe.... Indeed, she had not even spoken ill of him but had only erred in equating him with other prophets. [Furthermore,] Moshe himself had taken no umbrage.... In spite of this, she was immediately punished with *tzara'at*. How much more so [deserving of punishment, are] wicked and foolish people who indulge in idle and boastful talk.... But the worthy of Israel indulge only in words of Torah and wisdom. Therefore, the Holy One, Blessed be He, helps them and credits them for it (*Tum'at Tzara'at* 16:10).

๛ PART FOUR: *TZARA'AT* AS A METAPHOR: THE BIGGER THEY ARE...

Why would *tzara'at* be a punishment for "evil speech" [*leshon hara*]?[4] The Talmud denies a share in the world to come to anyone who "blanches

---

[3] See our discussions of rationales for mitzvot in the sections on Shemini and Emor.
[4] A linguistic word about *leshon hara'* is in order. Since (a) the noun for speech in Hebrew is *lashon*, and (b) it is feminine in gender, "evil speech" (i.e., a noun and adjective) should be translated as: *lashon ra'ah*. The combination of *leshon* and *ha-ra'* can only be explained as a construct of two nouns (i.e., a possessive relationship, Hebrew: *semikhut*), signifying "the speech of the evil [one]." That is to say, the way

[*malbin*] someone else's face in public." Causing someone's face to turn white is, arguably, *shefikhut damim*, spilling blood (*Baba Metzia* 58b); i.e., equivalent to murder. Reciprocal retribution (*middah ke-neged middah*) would call for the spilling of his blood in turn. Since it is only metaphorical murder, the whitening of his appearance through the affliction of *tzara'at* is tantamount to his execution. Indeed, this explains why the Talmud regards someone afflicted with *tzara'at* as though he were dead (*hashuv ke-met*; *Nedarim* 64b).

The ritual purification of the *metzora'*, which uses "a piece of cedar wood, a crimson thread, and a clump of grass" (Va-Yikra 14:4), is also fraught with symbolism.

Cedar trees are the natural symbols of great stature, while a clump of grass is the quintessence of lowliness. Their combination in the ritual purification of the *metzora'* emphasizes his need to learn humility. The crimson thread leads us back to the point we made just above about the equivalence between slander and spilling blood.

Indeed, these items are reminiscent of two other rituals prescribed by the Torah: The sprinkling of the ashes of the *parah adumah* (red heifer; Bemidbar 19:6), and the original *korban Pesah* (Shemot 12:22). This is hardly a coincidence. All three rituals have a common denominator that can account for the similarities between them: they all provide purification from death or its metaphorical equivalent.

While the cases of a *tame' met* and the *metzora'* (as per our discussion above) fit this description, how does it suit the *korban Pesah*? The *korban Pesah* marked the rejection of idolatry,[5] and the essence of Egyptian idolatry was the worship of and obsession with death. (Just think of the pyramids and the vast and magnificent burial chambers of the Pharaohs.)

Note: There appears to be another distinction borne by the *korban Pesah*: Its ritual involved only the clump of grass, without either cedars or crimson threads. The ram's blood, however, substituted for the crimson thread as the symbolic equivalent of lifeblood, and the notion of stature is adumbrated by

---

in which the evil one, i.e., Satan, speaks – as opposed to the manner of speech of the Holy One, which is designated *leshon ha-Kodesh*. [In the linguistic tradition of many of the *eidot ha-mizrah* (Oriental Jewish communities, such as Yemenites), God is regularly referred to as *ha-Kodesh, barukh hu* (rather than *ha-Kadosh*).]

[5] See our study of the original *korban Pesah* in the unit on Bo.

the application of the blood to the lintel (the top of the door), since there were not likely to be cedar trees in Egypt in any event![6]

---

[6] See our discussion in Terumah regarding the *shittim* trees from which the *mishkan* was constructed, and which are identified in the Aggadah with cedars.

AHAREI MOT

Straying from the *Peshat*

RASHI'S USE OF *AL TIKREI, GEMATRIA* AND *NOTARIKON*

∾ PREFACE

Of the numerous homiletic interpretations that fall short and wide of *peshuto shel mikra*, Nehama wrote:

> With respect to Biblical exegesis, it was not the intention [of the Sages] in any which way to suggest that the meaning of the verse was other than its text implied, rather that even the supplementary significance – such as that obtained by alternative readings – is somehow contained within the implication of the text (*Rashi's Commentary on the Torah*, 339).

Until now, we have consistently attempted to reconcile Rashi's use of Aggadah with his pronounced tendency towards *peshat*. In this week's *sidrah*, however, we choose to highlight some of the instances in which it is patent that Rashi's interpretations stray considerably not only from the *peshat*, but from the Masoretic text itself. Such deviations include homiletic readings (i.e., *al-tikrei*) and the use of either acrostics (*notarikon*) or alpha-numerics (*gematria*).

To "redeem" Rashi, however, we will conclude with an instance in this week's *sidrah* in which he emphasizes the complementary nature of Halakhic Midrash and *peshuto shel mikra* – just as Nehama indicated.

❧ PART ONE: *GEMATRIA*: HOW MUCH IS THAT WORD'S WORTH?

Rashi makes spare use of *gematria* – barely a dozen times in his commentary on the entire Tanakh.[1] One of those uses is Bereishit 14:14, which describes how Avraham drafted his 318 household retainers to rescue his nephew Lot. On their number, Rashi comments: "Our rabbis said that it was Eliezer alone, the numerical value of [whose name] is 318."

Keeping with our tendency to justify Rashi's every recourse to Aggadah as an attempt to resolve a textual difficulty or anomaly, we surmise that Rashi found the Torah's furnishing a specific number problematic. Since we do not know how many soldiers there were in the Mesopotamian raiding party that captured Lot, why should we be impressed with the number of men in Avraham's posse? When Moshe instructed Yehoshua to "select some men" and counter the Amalekite attack (Shemot 17), the Torah gives no indication of their number; why do so here? And if the point is to magnify the miraculous nature of the victory over a considerably larger force, Gideon, we recall, was also able to rout an entire Midianite army with only three hundred warriors (Shoftim 7).

In Bereishit 32:5, Rashi resorts, again, to *gematria* in his interpretation of Yaakov's message to Esav informing him that he had spent this considerable time "abiding with Lavan" (*im lavan garti*), noting:

> *Garti* has the value of 613, as though to say: I abided with the wicked Lavan while observing all 613 commandments and not coming under his pernicious influence.

In keeping with that same tendency, we suggest that Rashi was influenced here by the Aggadic view of Lavan as a prime nemesis of the Jewish people. As the *Pesah* Haggadah observes: "Pharaoh only declared [war] on the males, while Lavan sought to uproot everything." In this light, Yaakov's ability to abide in Lavan's company must be viewed not only as a hallmark of physical endurance, but of spiritual survival as well.

By way of contrast, Rashi's reluctance to cite other Aggadic *gematriot* indicates that he did not find their Torah phraseology problematic. For instance, he declines to note the well-known *gematria* on Bereishit 42:2: "Yaakov said to his sons: Go descend [to Egypt] and acquire some grain for

---

[1] Nine times in the Torah, once in Yirmiyahu and once in Iyyov.

us," in which the numerical value of the Hebrew word *redu* (descend) is taken as a sign of the 210 years they were destined to spend in slavery in Egypt. Since all references in the Torah to travel to and from Israel and Egypt are phrased in terms of "descent" (cf. 12:10, *va-yered* and 13:1, *va-ya'al*), there is no need here to remove it from its *peshat*.

✌ PART TWO: *NOTARIKON*; INITIALIZING TORAH

Rashi is even more sparing in his use of *notarikon*, by which the initial letters of words (usually consecutive) are assumed to spell out Midrashic messages, employing it only eight times altogether.[2]

Bemidbar 11:8 describes among the properties of the manna: "Its taste was that of the *leshad* of oil." Rashi notes:

> *Leshad* is a *notarikon*, standing for *layish shemen devash*; dough kneaded with oil and smoothed with honey.

In this case, it appears that Rashi's recourse to "initialization" was prompted by the fact that the word *leshad* is, otherwise, a veritable *hapax legomenon*; a word found uniquely here (and, possibly, in Tehillim 32:4), with no other clue to its meaning.[3]

In Bemidbar 22:32, the "angel" who sought to frustrate Bil'am's venture remarks that but for the donkey, "the path turned contrary (*yarat*) to me." Rashi, unable again to precisely define the unique word, comments:

> The Sages of the Mishnah interpreted it homiletically (*darshu*) as the initials of "it feared (*yar'ah*), saw (*ra'atah*) and turned aside (*natetah*)."

On the other hand, the Torah reports (Bereishit 41:42) that Pharaoh had Yosef driven about in the chariot of the viceroy, while "they called before him *abrekh*." The Midrash (*Sifrei* Devarim 1) considers this a *notarikon* representing "venerable [*ab*] in wisdom yet tender [*rakh*] in years." Rashi, however, declines this comment, indicating that he saw no difficulty here. Indeed, it is likely that he recognized *abrekh* as a form of the verb *b-r-kh*, which he correctly defined (in Bereishit 24:11) as: "to cause [animals] to kneel."

---

[2] Seven in the Torah and once in Tehillim.

[3] We discussed *leshad ha-shamen* in Tetzaveh, Part Three.

❧ PART THREE: *AL TIKREI*: "A VERY BEAUTIFUL POETIC FIGURE OF SPEECH"

Rashi's use of homiletical readings is equally sparse, limited to just a half-dozen instances in the Torah.

Upon recapitulating the deaths of Nadav and Avihu, Moshe tells Aharon that God had previously warned of just such an incident: "This is what God said: I shall be glorified by My sacred ones" (Va-Yikra 10:3). Where, exactly, did God issue this admonition? Citing an *al-tikrei* in the Midrash, Rashi replies: "'I shall keep appointments there [i.e., in the Mishkan], and it shall be sanctified by My glory' (Shemot 29:43); do not read My glory (*kevodi*), but My sacred ones (*mekhuvadai*)."

The specific nature of such homiletical readings of Scripture is best illustrated by the following example. In Devarim 23:10–15, the Torah stipulates some military ordinances, such as the requirement that soldiers' gear include a trenching tool [*ve-yated tiheyeh lekha al azeinekha*] with which they can maintain field hygiene. In the Talmud, however, Bar Kappara interprets this phrase homiletically [*darash*] in a manner totally unsuited to the context:

> Do not read the word as *azeinekha* [gear] but as *aznekha* [ears]. If one overhears something improper, let him stick his fingers in his ears (*Ketubbot* 5a).

Notably, the relationship between the *peshat* and *derash* of this verse is addressed by Rambam himself in the *Guide for the Perplexed* (3:43) as follows:

> I do not think that an educated, rational person will believe [that Bar Kappara thought this to be the literal meaning of the verse]. Rather, this is a very beautiful poetic figure of speech that inspires a lofty principle. Namely, just as it is prohibited to say something improper, so it is prohibited to listen to it. [Bar Kappara] attached this [principle] to this verse in the manner of [coining] proverbs or poems. Indeed, everything in the category of *al tikrei* should be understood in this fashion.

To which, Nehama adds:

> It would be wrong to say that there is no connection between [the *peshat*] of our verse and Bar Kappara's ethical principle. Covering

physical pollution is a requirement understood by every civilized person; but covering verbal pollution, i.e., refraining from listening to improprieties, is a comparable obligation that every civilized person should undertake (*op. cit.,* 340).

🔊 Part Four: Effecting a Reconciliation

As promised in the Preface, we shall conclude this unit with a citation from Rashi's commentary relating to this week's *sidrah* in which he effects a fundamental reconciliation between *peshat* and Halakhic *derash*. The occasion is Va-Yikra 18:16, which prohibits sexual relations between a man and his sister-in-law. The problem Rashi perceives here is the seeming contradiction between this prohibition and the fact that in the case of the brother's death without having fathered children, marriage with that same sister-in-law becomes mandatory (*yibbum*). He relates to this ostensible contradiction, along with several similar instances, in Shemot 20:8:

> "Remember" and "Observe" were both pronounced in one utterance. "Transgressors will be put to death" and "On the Sabbath [sacrifice] two lambs" were both pronounced in one utterance. Similarly, "Do not wear *sha'atnez*" and "Make yourself fringes [i.e., *tzitzit*]." Similarly, "Do not uncover the nakedness of your brother's wife," and "Her brother-in-law shall unite with her." This is the meaning of the verse: "God speaks but once [yet] we hear twice,"[4] and: "Is not My word like a fire? says the Lord."

In other words, Rashi emphasizes that what may superficially appear to be contradictory turns out, upon rabbinic examination, to be complementary. Such is the power of Midrashic reconciliation.

---

[4] Paraphrasing Tehillim 62:12, which states: "I hear twice." Gerald Blidstein explains that the author of the Midrash switched the Biblical 'I' with 'we' for the sake of the homily, since it is speaking about the Jewish people, in general (*De'ot* 44 [1975]: 272).

KEDOSHIM

The "Body" of Torah

GUFEI TORAH AND NEKAMAH, MALBIM AND KANT

✍ PREFACE

Nehama writes:

> The complete fulfillment of the Torah depends upon its acceptance
> at all levels and social strata of the nation.... No individual, even
> the most righteous, can accomplish it all individually. That is why
> this portion was recited in full assembly because only "the entire
> congregation of Israel" is capable of its fulfillment (*Iyyunim hadashim
> be-sefer Va-Yikra*, 210).

✍ PART ONE: ONE AT A TIME OR ALL AT ONCE?

The opening words of Kedoshim (19:1–2) differ from those of other *sedarim*
(if you prefer: *sidrot*) in Va-Yikra. Whereas the "standard" opening is: "Speak
to the Children of Israel, saying...," our *sidrah* begins: "Speak to the entire
congregation of Israel."

Of what significance is this deviation? According to Rashi (ad loc.):
"This instructs us that this parashah was recited in full assembly (*hakhel*),"
i.e., at a specific time when the entire congregation of Israel was actually
assembled. What necessitated this variation from standard procedure?
"Because most of the fundamental rules of the Torah (*rov gufei torah*) are
derived from it."

This raises a simple logistical question: If the people were not always
gathered together in one place and at one time, how did they learn whatever
Torah laws they needed? The answer, says Rashi, is through an educational
process, which he describes (Shemot 34:32) as follows:

> How was the Torah expounded? Moshe would learn from the Almighty Himself. Aharon entered, and Moshe taught him his portion. Aharon retired, and sat on Moshe's left. His sons entered, and Moshe taught them their portion. They retired, Elazar sitting on Moshe's right and Ittamar on Aharon's left. The elders entered, and Moshe taught them their portion. They withdrew, and seated themselves at the side. All the people entered, and Moshe taught them their portion.

> Thus, the people received it once, the elders twice, Aharon's sons three times, and Aharon four times.

Of course, an alternative argument can also be made: If ordinary rules and regulations had to be taught individually and repetitively, how much more so the laws that constitute *rov gufei torah*! Should they not have been taught to every section of the population, each according to its capacity and intelligence, rather than to the entire congregation at once? R. Moshe Alshekh (Italy and Tzefat, 1521–1593) states that the underlying idea behind this assembly was to emphasize that even the highest and most noble principles of the Jewish faith can be attained by any Jew, provided he makes the effort.

R. Eliyahu Mizrahi (Constantinople, 1450–1526), however, has a different explanation for the requirement of the entire congregation:

> They all had to be together so that if doubts arose over a ruling the others would be able to correct them. If they had received these laws in separate groups, however, the members of one group would not be able to correct the members of another group since the latter could claim that they had never heard Moshe say such a thing.

The Korban Aharon (Aharon ben Avraham ibn Hayyim; Morocco, 1545–1632) cites the explanation that Rashi brought, and then adds yet a third interpretation:

> In other words, he taught each one in accordance with his capacity, so that the people received the essentials of the Law that are conveyed by its plain meaning – [i.e.] the body, while the elders received the soul of the Law and its spiritual implications.

Since most of the rulings in this chapter must be grasped and fulfilled in accordance with their literal "bodily" meaning, all the people were equal in respect of them. Accordingly, Moshe assembled them all together.

Note: Both Rashi and the Korban Aharon are indulging in a play on words. Rashi called the laws of this *sidrah*: *gufei torah*; *guf*, literally, means "body."

❧ PART TWO: VENGEANCE IS... WHOSE?

One of the specific "fundamental rules of the Torah" contained in this *sidrah* is: "You shall not avenge (*tikkom*) or bear any grudge (*tittor*) against the members of your people" (19:18).

[Without looking inside: Do you remember the continuation of this verse? If you don't – you may look now.]

What is the difference between *nekamah* – retaliation or revenge, and *netirah* – bearing a grudge? Rashi explains the difference by means of a concrete illustration. We paraphrase:

A asks to borrow something from B, who refuses. On the morrow, B asks to borrow from A. If A refuses to lend to B, citing B's prior refusal to lend to him, that is vengeance. If A consents to lend to B, but states that this is in spite of his prior refusal, "this is termed 'bearing a grudge' since he bears a grudge in his heart but does not actually take vengeance."

If one is not supposed to make reference to a prior injury or insult, does that mean one is not entitled to legal redress? Doesn't that allow the wicked party to "get away with it?" Not so. The Torah specifically states (Va-Yikra 24:19): "As he did, so shall be done to him."

Ramban explains the distinction:

> Where monetary liability or damage is involved, one is not required to forgo one's just claim, but it should be claimed in court... and the one who inflicted the damage is obliged to make good.

As Nehama writes:

> The prohibition against vengeance does not imply any foregoing of just claims or due process of law, neither in respect of money matters nor human life. It does not imply a demand to love the

wicked and the one who perverts justice, a course of action which can only strengthen the forces of evil in the world (*op. cit.,* 294).

✍ PART THREE: SELF-CONTROL

One is expected to achieve self-control – restraining and controlling feelings of animosity – in order to refrain not only from vengeance but even from bearing a grudge. Rambam writes:

> Revenge is a grave failing… since for the discerning, everything is vanity and trivial and not worth avenging…. A man should rather erase the matter from his heart and not [even] bear a grudge since as long as he bears a grudge… he will come to commit vengeance.
>
> For this reason the Torah cautioned us not to bear a grudge… and this is the right manner of conduct by which civilization and human relations can be maintained (*Hilkhot De'ot* 7:7–8).

Sefer ha-Hinukh, however, states:

> We should bear in mind that anything that happens to man, whether good or bad, comes from God. Whatever man suffers at the hands of his fellow must be ultimately traced to Divine Providence. Man should adopt the attitude that his own sins are to blame for any hurt he suffers and not think of taking vengeance. King David reacted in this way in the case of Shim'i ben Gera who cursed him. Rather than take vengeance, he stated: "Leave him alone and let him curse, for the Lord has bidden him" (2 Shemuel 16:11) (Mitzvah #247).

The difference between these two opinions concerns the reasons for the prohibition and the explanation of the evils of vengeance. According to Rambam, the provocation is real; it is just not worth risking vengeance over it. According to *Sefer ha-Hinukh,* however, the provocation is, essentially, self-inflicted; a man should not blame anything but his own inadequacies.

✍ PART FOUR: A GLIMPSE AT THE CONTINUATION

Earlier, we alluded to the continuation of the verse that prohibits vengeance and bearing a grudge. It is: *ve'ahavta le-re'akha kamokha.* Ordinarily, this is translated as: "Love your neighbor/friend/fellow as yourself." Is it really possible for someone to feel as much love towards another as for oneself?

What, for example, of the law that says: "If your life and the life of another are at risk – save yourself first" (*hayyekha kodmim*); doesn't this contradict the principle of loving another as oneself?

As Malbim notes in his commentary:

> Exegetes have already pointed out that it is impossible for one to love another as he loves himself since this is not within the capacity of the soul.

Malbim explains that the verse is misinterpreted. It is also mistranslated in the standard English versions. If the intent of the Torah had been to require one to love another – to whatever degree or extent – it would have had to place the particle '*et* between the verb and its direct object (i.e., *ve'ahavta et re'akha*), as it actually does in the case of the love of God (Devarim 6:5; *ve'ahavta et hashem*). The function of the prepositional *lamed* (*le-re'akha*) is to separate a verb from its indirect object. The correct translation of the verse should be: "Love for (or: on behalf of) another as you would for yourself," and its converse would be the statement of Hillel (*Shabbat* 31a): "Do not do to another that which you despise."

Note: It is noteworthy that in explaining *ve'ahavta le-re'akha kamokha* according to his grammatical insight, Malbim refers to something he calls *hok kollel*, which invokes man to regard his fellow as an end rather than a means and consider whether he would want to be treated by all men the way he would treat this particular fellow. This is actually the categorical imperative of Immanuel Kant, with whose philosophy Malbim was acquainted and to which he makes additional references in his commentaries.

EMOR

Of Cows and Calves

MIDRASH, MAIMONIDES, *SEFER HA-HINUKH* AND SHADAL

✍ PREFACE

On the verse: "Do not slaughter a cow or ewe together with its young on the same day" (Va-Yikra 22:28), Nehama notes:

> In order to underline the eternity of this Divine attribute of "compassion on all His works," this verse is placed in the mouth of the patriarch Jacob, even before the giving of the Torah, before Moses had actually recorded it from Sinai. The concept underlying the verse was timeless and was contained in the "Torah" that Midrashic homily regards as having been in existence prior to the creation of the world [1] (*Studies in the Weekly Sidra*, first series, 5715, #28).

Throughout Sefer Va-Yikra, we have taken note of differences of opinions amongst the classical and medieval commentators regarding the purposes that are served by some of the Torah's more opaque legislation. From "dietary laws" (if that is what kashrut really is) to "leprosy" (if that is what *tzara'at* is), we have seen the opinions range from the hygienic to the mystical. This week we look at one of the classic locations of this debate.

✍ PART ONE: THE HUMANISTIC INTERPRETATION

The Torah prescribes (22:27–28):

---

[1] The allusion is to the Midrash *Bereishit Rabbah* (32:9), which imputes this verse to Yaakov as an expression of his anxiety over his impending reunion with Esav. See, further, in Part Three.

When a bullock, sheep, or goat is born, it shall remain with its mother for seven days; from the eighth day on it becomes acceptable as a sacrifice to God. Do not slaughter a cow or ewe together with its young on the same day.

Rambam:

It is also prohibited to kill an animal with its young on the same day, in order that people should be restrained and prevented from killing the two together in such a manner that the young is slain in the sight of the mother; for the pain of the animals under such circumstances is very great. There is no difference in this case between the pain of man and the pain of other living beings, since the love and tenderness of the mother for her young ones is not produced by reasoning, but by imagination, and this faculty exists not only in man but in most living beings. This law applies only to ox and lamb, because of the domestic animals used as food these alone are permitted to us, and in these cases the mother recognizes her young (*The Guide for the Perplexed,* 3:48).[2]

Sefer ha-Hinukh:

The plain reason for this mitzvah lies in the psychological influence of a deed performed in a wholly perfect manner. The sacrifice cannot be considered perfect until eight days old, since prior to that it is not fit for anything, and no one will desire it to partake of it, or to do business with it, or even to give it as a gift (Mitzvah #313).

Va-Yikra Rabbah (27:11):

Rabbi Berekhiah ben Levi said: It is written (Mishlei 12:10), "The righteous man knows the soul of his beast, but the tender mercies of the wicked are cruel." The [first half] refers to the Holy One, blessed be He, who wrote in His Torah, "When a bullock, sheep, or goat is born, it shall remain with its mother for seven days...." The [second half] refers to Haman, the wicked one, who sought "to utterly destroy, to slay, and to cause to perish."

---

[2] According to Rambam, the same rationale applies to the sending away of the mother bird (Devarim 22:6–7) prior to taking her chicks.

There is a basis in the text of the *sidrah* for the association of the eight-day provision with the perfection of sacrifice, being that the *sidrah* earlier spoke of the blemishes which disqualify animals for sacrifices. According to this approach, there is also a connection between this prohibition and that of the following verse: slaughtering mother and offspring together. It is a paradigm of insensitivity, just as Haman – cited in the Midrash – is a paradigm of cruelty.

ஸ PART TWO: THE LOYAL OPPOSITION

Neither Ramban nor Shadal, who shares his view, is opposed to the humane consideration of animal life. They are, however, opposed to that interpretation of this Torah legislation.

Ramban (Devarim 22:6–7):

> The reason for the prohibition of slaying the mother and young on one day, as well as the ordinance of sending away the mother bird, is to eradicate cruelty and unkindness from man's heart... not that God had pity on the mother bird or the mother and young.
>
> Were that the case, God would have entirely forbidden *shehitah*! But the real reason is to cultivate in us the quality of mercy.... Since cruelty is contagious, as is well known from the example of animal killers by occupation, who often become inured to human suffering....
>
> These precepts regarding bird and beast are not motivated by pity on them but are decrees of the Almighty to cultivate good moral qualities in man.

Note: (1) Does the Torah only prohibit the slaughter of the young before its mother's eyes or is the slaughter of the mother before its young also prohibited? How would the disagreement between Rambam and Ramban be affected by the answer to this question?

(2) The Mishnah (*Megillah* 25a) states: "[A *shali'ah tzibbur*] who says: May your mercies reach the bird's nest... should be silenced." The Gemara stipulates the reason: "Because he makes God's attribute one of mercy and in reality it is a decree." Whose opinion does the Gemara seem to support: Ramban or Ramban? How do you think the Gemara is interpreted by whoever it doesn't seem to support?

ஐ PART THREE: "HIS MERCIES COVER ALL HIS CREATURES."

Two *midrashim* place nearly identical words about compassion and cruelty in the mouths of two different Biblical characters: Yaakov (see our Preface) and Moshe.

> **Bereishit Rabbah (73:13):** "Yaakov said: If Esav shall come and destroy one camp... and slay mothers and children" (32:9). In that hour Yaakov said: Master of the Universe! You wrote in the Torah, "Do not slaughter a cow or ewe together with its young on the same day." Should this wicked one come and destroy my children and their mothers, the Sefer Torah that You are destined to give on Mount Sinai – who will read it?

> **Eikha Rabbati (Petihta):** Moshe spoke up and said: Master of the Universe! You wrote in the Torah: "Do not slaughter a cow or ewe together with its young on the same day." But behold, they have slain children and their mothers in countless numbers while You remain silent.

Note: Which slayers of mothers and children did Moshe witness?

From the context (*Midrash Eikhah*), it would appear to be the Babylonians slaying the defenders of Jerusalem. According to this Midrash, Moshe was given the ability to see far into the Jewish future.

BEHAR

Finding Freedom in Servitude

NEHAMA ON THE SEARCH FOR TRUTH

❧ PREFACE: THE WORD THAT LEADS

One of the features of Biblical literature that Nehama used to great advantage is the *leitwort* (leading word), a word (better: a verbal root) that appears a disproportionate number of times in a relatively concise text, giving the impression that its function is to lead us to a particular conclusion or observation. Nehama was indebted to Martin Buber for the identification and designation of this literary feature, and she openly acknowledged that indebtedness even though it opened her to the criticism of being "soft" on non-traditional sources.[1]

❧ PART ONE: SLAVE OR SERVANT?

In Va-Yikra 25:25–47, the word *ahikha* (your brother) appears often enough to give the appearance of a *leitwort*. Indeed, in every case in which the Torah refers to the impoverishment of another Jew, it designates him "your brother" as it delineates our responsibilities towards his financial and social rehabilitation.

Based on the accepted notion that "leading words" are of considerable significance, the conclusion at which we can arrive regarding the Torah's use of *ahikha* in this context is that it is forbidden to view an indentured Hebrew servant as chattel. At all times and in all circumstances, you should remember that he is, above all, your brother.

---

[1] See our Epilogue, here.

In treating the subject of slavery in Tanakh, Nehama calls our attention to the German Jewish philosopher, Hermann Cohen,[2] who observed that the Torah has no special term for servant and master; rather, everyone who labors is called an *'eved*, servant. One who has sold himself is an *'eved* and one who has been sold (ostensibly against his will) is an *'eved*, but the God-fearing man is also an *'eved* and even the Messiah is called the *'eved* of the Lord.

In her words:

> The whole institution of servitude in the Torah is in complete harmony with the altruism of the monotheistic faith. The servant can never become merely chattel, but always remains an individual, a human being (*Studies in the Weekly Sidra*, first series, 5715, #29).

This is reflected in the limitations that halakhah imposes on a "master" with regard to the employment of his "servant." Rambam lists the restrictions (which, out of the interests of space, we shall paraphrase):

> He may not put him to such menial tasks as carrying his belongings to the bath house or untying his shoes, nor can he be made a public bath attendant or barber, nor may he force him to learn and apply a new trade. Why? Because he has already been humiliated by being sold and this would add insult to his injury (Hilkhot Avadim 1:7).

We might wonder, however, if it is embarrassing to be a bath attendant or barber, why is it permissible for a Jew to serve in those professions at any time? We must differentiate, as Rambam himself does, between a freeman who undertakes these professions of his own volition and the servant who does so only at his master's behest.

❧ PART TWO: "ONE WHO BUYS A SERVANT HAS ACQUIRED HIMSELF A MASTER" (KIDDUSHIN 20A)

In 25:42–43, God prohibits the imposition by Jews of slavish treatment (*avodat eved*) or rigorous labor (*perekh*) upon one another on the grounds that "they are My slaves/servants whom I took out of Egypt."

---

[2] *Die Religion der Vernunft aus den Quellen des Judentums* (Religion of Reason out of the Sources of Judaism), 179. Later in the same study, Nehama cites Salo Baron: *Social and Cultural History of the Jews* (vol. I, 267) in reference to Hebrew slavery.

Rambam defines *perekh* labor as "busy work"; i.e., work that serves no purpose other than to keep the worker occupied and thereby constantly aware of his subservience to his master.

Speaking of leading words, we ought to recognize the word *perekh* from another, related context. It appears in the first chapter of Shemot (1:13, 14) as a description of the manner in which the Egyptians subjugated the Hebrews. This correspondence led Nehama to remark:

> Neither the idea of human equality nor even the idea of human freedom underlies this motivation, but rather the subservience of every human being to his Maker who, alone, is Master of all. "For they are My servants" and not servants of servants, commented our Sages.

And she concludes with a citation from a poem by Yehudah ha-Levi:

> The temporal servant (or: the servants of time) are servants of servants; the servant of the Lord is the only one who is truly free (*Iyyunim hadashim be-sefer Va-Yikra*, 439).

Note: Connect Nehama's thought with the Mishnah (*Avot* 6:2):

> "The tablets were divine handiwork and the script was also divine, engraved (*harut*) upon the tablets" (Shemot 32:16). Do not read *harut* (engraved) but *herut* (liberty), for the only free man is the one who is occupied with Torah study.

ɞ EPILOGUE: "ACCEPT THE TRUTH FROM WHOEVER UTTERS IT"

Nehama's attribution of the importance of the *leitwort* to Martin Buber (see Preface) was expensive; it cost her dearly in the effort she was forced to exert in defense of the proposition that one could properly utilize tools of Biblical research and insights into Tanakh without thereby granting legitimacy to those who had developed them.

In her correspondence with Rabbi Yehudah Ansbacher, a Tel Aviv rabbi, on this very subject, Nehama also defended her numerous citations from Benno Jacob, a German Reform rabbi, noting that while Jacob had composed a superlative critique of the Documentary Hypothesis, Moshe David Cassuto, a strictly Orthodox Jew, had written things about the authorship of the Torah that she found problematic from an Orthodox perspective.

In conclusion, she wrote: "I do not take the [identities of the] authors into consideration; only what they wrote."[3]

---

[3] *Pirkei Nehama,* 658.

BEHUKOTAY

Tokhehah; Constructive Criticism

SEFER HA-HINUKH AND *KELI YAKAR* ON REBUKE

❧ PREFACE

Nehama Leibowitz was a genuine *ohevet yisrael.* Yet although her love for the Jewish people was universal and unconditional, it was not indiscriminate. Nehama did not devalue the coin of her love by dispensing it without qualification; if she thought you were wrong, she would say so.

The concluding portion of the Book of Va-Yikra is known, traditionally, as the *tokhehah.* We shall capitalize upon that title to examine several aspects of the mitzvah of *tokhehah.*

The noun *tokhehah* derives from the root *y-k-h,* to decide or prove, and means to correct or rebuke. According to Va-Yikra 19:17: "Do not hate your brother in your heart; offer rebuke to your fellow, and do not bear him a sin." Two other verses in Tanakh offer complementary perspectives. In Mishlei 3:12 we read: "God rebukes whomever He loves," and in Devarim 8:5: "God chastises you as a parent chastises a child."

❧ PART ONE: WHAT PURPOSE DOES *TOKHEHAH* SERVE?

According to the Biblical sources, *tokhehah* is a gesture of love. Just as rebuke demonstrates a parent's love for a child, it indicates the love of whoever offers it to whoever receives it. There is, of course, an underlying assumption that the objective of the *tokhehah* is the improvement of the one who receives it and that anyone would be grateful for such advice.

As the Talmud states (*Tamid* 28a):

Rabbi [Yehudah] said: Which is the straight path which a person should choose? To accept rebuke; for as long as rebuke is offered, the world is pleasant, filled with goodness and blessing, and emptied of evil.

Similarly, in *Bereishit Rabbah* (54:3):

"Avraham rebuked Avimelekh" (Bereishit 21:24). R. Yossi ben Haninah said: Rebuke leads to love, as it is written (Mishlei 9:8): "Rebuke a wise person and he will love you." This is the opinion of R. Yossi ben Haninah who used to say: "Love without rebuke is not really love." Reish Lakish said: "Rebuke leads to peace."

Sefer ha-Hinukh, in accounting for the rationale of the mitzvah, states:

The grounds for this mitzvah are that it establishes harmony and peace among people. Whenever a person is wronged by another, if he rebukes him – privately – he will apologize, his apology will be accepted, and they will reconcile. If he does not rebuke him, however, he will bear him a grudge and will cause him harm, either immediately or subsequently.[1] So it is written about a wrongdoer: "Avshalom did not speak with Amnon about matters good or evil" (2 Shemuel 13:22). All the ways of the Torah, however, should be pleasant and all its pathways peaceful (Mitzvah #218).

According to these rabbinic sources, the principal purpose of *tokhehah* is to demonstrate our love for one another, even for someone who has wronged us, and to attempt to repair the damage to our personal relations. Here the underlying assumption is that *tokhehah* consists not merely of word of encouragement and improvement but also of rebuke for injury or insult.

To summarize, then, the concluding portion of Sefer Va-Yikra is known as the *tokhehah* because it consists of advice that God has given us – out of His great love for us – by means of which we may prosper by knowing what to do to please Him and from what to refrain lest we anger Him.

✂ PART TWO: OTHER GROUNDS FOR *TOKHEHAH*

Other sources, however, posit different objectives for *tokhehah*. According to the Talmud (*Shavuot* 39a):

---

[1] See our explication of "holding a grudge" in the *sidrah* of Kedoshim.

What is the meaning of the verse: "They shall stumble over one another" (Va-Yikra 26:37)? They shall stumble over one another's sins. This teaches us that all Jews are responsible for one another.

And (*Shabbat* 54b):

Anyone who can protest against [the wrongdoing of] his family and does not protest will be caught in their [wrongdoing]. Against [the wrongdoing] of his city – will be caught in their [wrongdoing]. Against the entire world – will be caught in their [wrongdoing].

According to the Talmudic sources, the purpose of rebuke is the satisfaction of a mutual, legal obligation to prevent one another from doing wrong. Yet, these last cited sources are not quite identical. According to the Talmud in *Shavu'ot*, Jews would appear to be responsible only for the wrongdoing of other Jews, on account of their legal responsibility towards one another [*arevut*]. According to *Shabbat*, however, Jews are required to protest even against the whole world, implying Jews and gentiles alike.

The *Keli Yakar* (Ephraim of Lunschitz; Poland, 1559–1619), whose Torah homilies often serve as a super-commentary on Rashi,[2] describes this mutual obligation by way of an example:

This can be compared to the case of a man who was drilling a hole in the bottom of a boat. All the passengers shouted at him: What do you think you're doing? He replied: I am drilling only under my own seat! They retorted: Even if the water enters only under your seat, the entire boat will sink in any case.

According to this alternative rationale, the *tokhehah* which God offers us illustrates the verse in Yesha'ayahu (63:9): "In all their adversity, He is distressed." Although God's existence is wholly independent of our own, were we to "drill beneath our own seats," His universe would still suffer in consequence. Since He committed Himself to its continued existence by creating us, He rebukes us and challenges us to improve.

---

[2] See more about him in our Preface to Ha'azinu.

Bemidbar

BEMIDBAR

It's the Order that "Counts"

RASHI VS. RASHBAM: CHARTING THE ORDER OF MARCH

҂ PREFACE

As a seasoned pedagogue, Nehama had a repertoire of didactic strategies (she called them, in Hebrew slang, *trick-im*) that she used to great advantage. In an examination of this week's *sidrah*,[1] she incorporates a chart to facilitate our understanding of the census that was conducted at the outset of the Israelites' journey across the wilderness. We shall duplicate that chart here and attempt to further our understanding of the *sidrah* through its analysis.

҂ PART ONE: WHY ANOTHER CENSUS?

According to Rashi, God's love for the Israelites makes itself manifest in the frequent conduct of a census.[2] They were counted at the exodus, again after the sin of the golden calf and, presently, after the erection of the *mishkan*, as God came to rest His presence upon them. Rashbam, on the other hand,

---

[1] The reference is to *Studies in the Weekly Sidra:* first series (5715 [1954–1955]), translated and adapted from the Hebrew by Aryeh Newman and published by the Department for Torah Education and Culture in the Diaspora of the World Zionist Organization. According to the publisher's introductory note: "The author's aim is, as she herself has written, to enable the student to appreciate the inspired qualities of every letter of the Torah, and this includes both the written and oral law, rabbinic comment and exegesis, endearing both Holy Writ and its Revealer to its devotees."

[2] A comparison of Rashi's comments to the initial verse of Shemot reveals that the relationship he posits here between counting and love is a recurring theme in his commentary. Moreover, his comments to the initial verses of every book of the Humash reflect, to one extent or another, the theme of *ahavat yisrael* that appears to have characterized Rashi himself.

says that the present census was in preparation for the actual advance into the Land of Canaan.

Using Nehama's technique (another "*trick*") of concise characterization, the difference between their interpretations is that Rashi sees the census as a *means* (of displaying God's love), while Rashbam views it as an *end* within itself.

In such a case of exegetical disagreement, Nehama taught us to seek other textual support for one interpretation or the other. Following her prescription, we note that the date on which this census was instituted, according to Bemidbar 1:1, was the first day of the second month (*Iyyar*) of the year following the exodus. We also note that, according to Bemidbar 10:11–12: "On the twentieth day of the second month, the cloud was lifted from upon the *mishkan*... and the Israelites commenced their journey through the wilderness of Sinai."

Arguably, this juxtaposition supports Rashbam's position. The proximity of the conduct of the census on the first of *Iyyar* to the "lifting" of the cloud of God's Glory (*anan ha-kavod*) on the twentieth of *Iyyar* suggests the connection between the two events that Rashbam assumes. Rashbam's interpretation also receives support from the exclusion of the *leviyim* from the census. If census is a sign of love, why not count the *leviyim*? If it is for military preparedness, however, the *leviyim*, who were exempt from military service, are understandably excluded.

As Shadal (Shmuel David Luzzatto; Italy, 1800–1865) comments:

> After the *mishkan* had been erected and they were proceeding towards the promised land to conquer it under divine leadership, it was desirable for them to be divided in accordance with their standards and groupings so that everyone would know his place and the camp would be properly ordered so that they would not appear as runaway slaves but constitute a people ready for battle. They were therefore counted as a part of the policy of instituting order. In this connection, our Sages rightly made the point that, "when He came to rest His divine presence amongst them, He counted them."

Note: An argument could be made that Shadal is hedging his interpretation. His emphasis on military preparedness follows Rashbam, but the reference to the statement of the Sages comes directly from Rashi.

ಱ PART TWO: FROM CENSUS TO A "TABLE OF ORGANIZATION"

The principal question that engages Nehama about this census is what rhyme or reason lies behind the distribution of the encampment and the order of march of the tribes.

According to Ramban (in his Preface to Bemidbar), this arrangement mirrors the organization of the people as they stood at Sinai and awaited the revelation of the Law: "He set bounds around the *mishkan* in the wilderness just the same as He set bounds about Mount Sinai when His Glory rested there." S.R. Hirsch comments, similarly (Shemot 40:23):

> Just as it is recorded regarding Mount Sinai (Shemot 24:16) that "the Glory of the Lord rested above/upon Mount Sinai," so it was now that the Torah had found its earthly resting place in the *mishkan*, in the place set aside for the revelation of God's Glory below.... Just as it reported about Mount Sinai that "the cloud covered it six days and on the seventh day He called unto Moshe out of the midst of the cloud" (ibid.), so the point is made regarding the *mishkan* that "Moshe was not able to enter the tent of the testimony because the cloud resided thereupon" (Shemot 40:35). Only thereafter does it state at the beginning of Va-Yikra that "the Lord called to Moshe and spoke to him."

Hirsch and Ramban are in agreement with one another, with Hirsch also stipulating the parallelism between the one-time revelation at Sinai and the ongoing revelation through the medium of the *mishkan*.

In fact, this point was made before Ramban by Yehudah ha-Levi (in the *Kuzari*), who compares the centrality of the *mishkan* within the Israelite camp to the centrality of the heart to the human body.

ಱ PART THREE: THE LOGISTICS

Following Nehama's example, here is a diagram of the campsite. How many of the following questions can you answer based upon the information it provides? Any reasonable explanation – no matter how speculative – is acceptable, providing it is logical and textually compatible.

Dan
North
157,600

<table>
<tr>
<td>

Ephraim
West
108,100

</td>
<td>

Yehudah
East
186,400

</td>
</tr>
</table>

Re'uven
South
151,450

Question 1: Why was the *mishkan* populated most heavily on its eastern flank?

Question 2: Why was it populated most lightly on the west?

Question 3: Why was the flag of Yehudah at the lead when they traveled and that of Dan at the rear?

Question 4: Why did the flag of Reuven join with Yehudah to lead the *mishkan* in travel, while that of Ephraim joined Dan in bringing up the rear?

Answer 1: Since their course of travel through the wilderness was primarily eastward, it made sense to have the most populous tribes encamped on that side to afford protection.

Answer 2: Since the west faced territory they had already passed through safely, it was the direction which required least protection. Therefore, it was guarded by the least populous tribes.

Answer 3: Yehudah and Dan were the largest flags as well as the most competent tribes militarily (as evinced both by the blessings they received from Yaakov and Moshe as well as the roles they played in the time of the *shoftim* and early monarchy). Therefore, one of them led and the other brought up the rear.

Answer 4: It makes logistical sense for Reuven, the smaller flag adjacent to Yehudah, to join it at the front rather than trouble Ephraim to "leapfrog" over the *mishkan*, which was interposed between them in the line of march.

194

◎ PART FOUR: THE MORAL IS...

Like Nehama, our task is to find religious, moral and ethical significance in textual and exegetical details. I would submit that in the aforementioned "table of organization" – as we have interpreted it – there resides such significance.

If we are correct in our assumption (based, essentially, on the approach of Rashbam outlined in Part One) that the arrangements by tribes and flags were meant to facilitate the impending journey and conquest, then we see that the Israelites exerted every effort to meet the anticipated challenges with their own human capacities rather than rely, exclusively, on divine intervention.

Although they were promised that intervention and had witnessed its manifestations in the past, they did not simply sprawl aimlessly about the *mishkan* and march towards the Land of Israel in arbitrary sequence. Rather, God instructed them to calculate their dispositions to play to their actual strengths and compensate for their actual weaknesses.

Like Nehama, again, we might conclude by drawing a parallel from the strategic organization of the Israel Defence Forces as a contemporary instance of *ein somekhim al ha-nes* – one does not rely exclusively on divine intervention.

NASO

What Does One Thing Have to Do with the Next?

CASSUTO ON CONNECTING THE TEXTUAL "DOTS"

✍ PREFACE

One of Nehama's many estimable qualities was her indefatigable quest for truth. In that quest, she knew no restrictions save for truth itself. In an earlier unit (Behar), we noted her indebtedness to Martin Buber for his German translation of the Torah as well as for his insights into Biblical literature. We pointed out (there) that Nehama acknowledged that indebtedness even at risk to her reputation.

In that same context, we took note of Moshe David (Umberto) Cassuto, a modern Orthodox Biblical scholar whose work Nehama appreciated and acknowledged. Born in Florence, Italy, in 1883, Cassuto was a keen student of the ancient Near East and pioneered the study of Canaanite literature and culture that is associated with the name of the ancient city of Ugarit. Cassuto wrote extensively on the relationship between Biblical and Canaanite literature and also composed commentaries on Bereishit and Shemot. He subsequently moved to Israel and died in Jerusalem in 1951.

✍ PART ONE: CASSUTO ON JUXTAPOSITION

The beginning of this week's *sidrah* presents an ostensibly haphazard structure comprising a jumble of subjects with no clear connection between them. The chapters dealing with the arrangement and composition of the camp of Israel (2:1–5:4) are followed by the treatment of the guilt offering (5:5–8), to which are joined two verses (9, 10) concerning the priestly portions (*matnot kehunah*). Then, we are introduced to the suspected adulteress (*sotah*; 5:11–31), followed by the *nazir* (6:1–21), after which the formula for the priestly blessing is appended (6:22–27).

Since it is the nature of commentary to abhor the random, exegetes from Rashi down to this century have endeavored to impose order on an otherwise random sequence.

Here is what Cassuto had to say about the connection between the arrangements of the camp and the guilt offering:

> These apparently unconnected items are actually linked to each other in accordance with the Bible's own principles of order and arrangement. At the end of the chapters treating the Israelite camp, it is recorded that the Israelites were commanded to expel lepers from the camp (5:1). The very mention of the word leper recalls the guilt offering ('asham) he has to bring on the day of his purification (Va-Yikra 14:12), and this accounts for the introduction of the 'asham at this juncture.

The remaining items in the *sidrah*, according to Cassuto, are also linked; this time by linguistic associations. The word *ma'al* (trespass) links *'asham* (5:6) and *sotah* (5:12), while the term *peri'at rosh* (uncovering the head/letting hair grow) links *sotah* (5:18) and *nazir* (6:5). As presented by Cassuto, subject matter in the Bible is often arranged by a process of thought or word association.

ᔥ PART TWO: THE MIDRASH

The Midrash, however, takes a different approach:

> "For them that honor Me, I will honor, and them that despise Me shall be lightly esteemed" (1 Shemuel 2:30). Who were those who honored God? The proselytes.... Who were those who despised God? Those who worshipped the golden calf. How did God repay them? He smote them with leprosy and venereal disease and expelled them from the camp. How did God honor the proselytes in return? He inserted the chapter warning us to look after them after the one dealing with expelling the lepers from camp.
>
> From this, we learn that God repels the sinners of Israel while befriending the proselytes who seek Him. They are protected by the same laws as the Israelite, and whoever takes from them by

violence is dealt with just as if he had taken from an Israelite (*Bemidbar Rabbah* 8:3).

According to this Midrash, then, the link between lepers and stealing from a *ger* is formed by way of contrast, an alternative method of organization.

∞ PART THREE: RASHI

While we have found frequent reference in the commentaries to *gerim*, it is not at all clear where they appear in the text of the *sidrah*. The pertinent verses (5:5–8) contain nary a hint of proselytes. However, if we start with the oft-repeated assumption that the Torah never repeats itself unnecessarily, the reappearance of the details of robbery or abuse of trust (that were enumerated in Va-Yikra 5:20–26) in Bemidbar 5 is meant to add something new to our understanding of those laws.

As Rashi comments (5:6):

> The Torah repeats here the laws stated in Va-Yikra pertaining to robbery with violence, perjury, and trespass against God, in order to introduce two new elements: (1) the element of confession (*vidduy*), teaching us that the offender is only obliged to pay a fine of a fifth, and a guilt offering – on the evidence of witnesses – if he himself admits the wrongdoing; (2) something that was taken unjustly from a *ger* – who dies without leaving an heir – is restored to the *kohanim*.

While the verse in question (5:8) makes no explicit reference to a proselyte, the words "If the man has no kinsman" are an implicit reference. As the *Sifrei* explains (*ad loc.*):

> Is there anyone is Israel who has no next of kin; no brother, nephew or distant relation going back to Yaakov? This can only refer, therefore, to a *ger* who dies leaving no heirs.

Note: Go back to Va-Yikra 25:26. Why can't we ask the same question there?

✌ PART FOUR: WHY GOD LOVES *GERIM*

Hazal, in *Bemidbar Rabbah* (op. cit.), offered the following rationale to account for why God bestows His love so bounteously upon the *ger*.

> Why does God love the righteous? Because they have no hereditary or family title.... If a man wants to become a priest or a Levite he cannot, because his father was not.... But if one wants to become a righteous man, even if he is a gentile, he can, as there is no family monopoly on it. That is why it states: "Those that fear the Lord, bless the Lord" (Tehillim 135:20), and not "the house of those who fear the Lord."
>
> Proselytes are what they are by virtue of no family title, but they have simply come to love God of their own free will. He therefore responds by loving them. As it is written: "The Lord loves the righteous. The Lord protects the *gerim*" (Tehillim 146:8–9).

The treatment of proselytes as a separate category in the laws of theft implies that there is also a significant moral principle regarding theft from a proselyte: It is the equivalent of stealing from God Himself.

BEHA'ALOTEKHA

Freedom from Responsibility?

NEHAMA AND SHADAL ON "GRUMBLING" AND "HANKERING"

✺ PREFACE

Discussing the Israelites, Nehama wrote:

> The secret of their longings was to shake off the awesome and historic implications of the freedom granted them: "He only is a free man who occupies himself with the Torah" (Avot 6:2). They wished to revert to Egyptian serfdom, which was trammeled by no Torah or mitzvot (*Studies in the Weekly Sidra,* first series, 5715, #32).

Unlike popular American culture, which regards freedom as license, Judaism first posits man's obligations and then defines freedom as the ability to fulfill those responsibilities. In this week's *sidrah,* we shall have an opportunity to reiterate some of the conclusions we have previously stipulated in this regard[1] and to see how they operate, in reality, with regard to the activities of the Israelites during their journeys.

✺ PART ONE: I'LL HAVE FISH, PLEASE

We have become accustomed to the ingratitude that the Israelites demonstrated towards God just about every time they encountered an obstacle (see, for instance, Shemot 14–15). They quickly became demoralized and grumbled about returning to Egypt. Note here, in particular, their "nostalgic" reference to the menu they were accustomed to in Egypt (Bemidbar 11:6):

---

[1] See our study on Behar, "Finding Freedom in Servitude."

We recall the fish that we ate in Egypt *hinam*; the cucumbers, the melons, the leeks, the onions, and the garlic.

In order to ascertain the precise meaning of the word *hinam*, let us compare the commentators:

Rashi (quoting the Sifrei): How can you say the Egyptians gave them fish [for free]? Surely it says (Shemot 5:18) "and straw shall not be given to them;" if they wouldn't give them straw free of charge, would they give them fish!?

Ibn Ezra: Cheaply, as though it were free.

Ramban: Simply, the Egyptian fishermen enslaved them to haul in the nets in which they caught fish, and they would give them some of the catch – as is the custom of all fishermen.

S.D. Luzzatto (Shadal): The word *hinam* implies nothing less than "free of charge." The Egyptians supported the Israelites by providing them with cheap items of food, such as fish and cucumbers, which were plentiful in Egypt. Herodotus informs us that on one of the Egyptian pyramids there was an inscription stating that the king who erected it expended 1,600 measures of garlic and onions on food for the workmen. Herodotus further states that the Egyptians did not themselves eat fish and it was therefore understandable why they gave it to the Israelites.

To characterize the respective interpretations of *hinam*: Shadal takes it literally; Ibn Ezra treats it as a form of hyperbole (exaggeration); and Ramban equivocates somewhat by allowing that while it was free of charge, they paid for it (dearly!) by their slave labor.

৪৩ PART TWO: FREE FROM, OR FREE TO?

Rashi, however, rejects the literal – and, probably, the hyperbolic – interpretations. Instead, he says: *hinam min ha-mitzvot*, free of [the responsibility of] mitzvot. It is this interpretation that will lead us back to our earlier discussion (see Preface) of the Jewish concept of freedom. According to this interpretation, the Israelites complained not so much about the changes in their menu as the drastic alterations in their lifestyle.

Here is how Nehama presented the issue:

> Was it really and truly the lack of cucumbers and onions and garlic in their diet that was the decisive factor leading to their grumbling and rebellion? Perhaps this was merely the outward form their dissatisfaction took? Their grumbling was prompted by rebellion against responsibilities [such as the] the *mitzvot*, the rites and duties the Torah imposed on them; a revolt against the shackles of civilization, bringing wild and rebellious nature to heel; against order and regulation beginning with the regime of the camp (Devarim 23:14), the elementary rules of hygiene, and ending with dietary, Shabbat, and festival restrictions, laws of equity and brotherhood. And what was hardest to bear – the prohibitions against immoral and forbidden sexual relations and the stern penalties involved.
>
> Since it is human nature to suppress rather than proclaim one's hankerings after these things, they disguised their real inclinations in the garb of cucumbers and onions and various items of food abundant in Egypt. "Yonder," in the world of slavery, persecution and oppression, they received fish "free." What is meant by free? Free from the mitzvot (*Studies in the Weekly Sidra, op. cit.*).

A comparison between Rashi's interpretation of 11:10 (beginning with: "Our Sages said") and Nehama's presentation indicates that they intersect.

The verse says that Moshe heard the people crying "by their families." On the assumption that only the fact of their crying matters – and not its location or circumstances – what do the words "by their families" signify? Rashi (citing *Yoma* 75a) says:

> Our Sages said: "By their families" implies that they complained about family matters; i.e., the forbidden sexual relationships.

Note: Nehama states that "it is human nature to suppress rather than proclaim one's hankerings after these things" (i.e. sexual proclivities) and that the people, therefore, disguised their true objectives. What would she think of the license that society grants today to the public discussion – and display! – of even the most intimate affairs?

℘ Part Three: The Grumbling

The term "grumbling," which we have used here several times, comes from Tehillim 106, a psalm that contains several fascinating poetic versions of

Jewish history including – as one would expect – the exodus from Egypt and the events that followed thereupon.

Examining the psalm – beginning with verse 7 ("our ancestors in Egypt") and following – we find that verse 14 ("they tested God") and 15 ("He granted their request") clearly correspond to this week's *sidrah*,[2] while verse 25 seems to summarize the many instances in which the Israelites displayed their ingratitude towards God, to wit: "They grumbled (*va-yeragnu*) in their tents and ignored the voice of God."

Not all instances of grumbling were alike. If we were to compare the grumbling in Bemidbar 11:4–6 with that related in Shemot 14:11–12 and 15:22–25, we would find that "God's anger was kindled" here and not there. Grumbling is more understandable – and, arguably, tolerable – when it comes from recently freed slaves who are still under threat of being retaken than when it comes from people who are unthreatened and who have already savored freedom.

Similarly, if we compare Moshe's reactions to the grumbling here and there, we would see a fundamental difference, too. In Shemot, Moshe is optimistic and inclined to either let things work themselves out or to rely on God to resolve them. By the time we reach Bemidbar, however, he has grown pessimistic and correspondingly short-tempered.[3]

---

[2] Verse 13: "How quickly they forgot His deeds; they did not await His advice," appears to relate to the episode of the golden calf, which begins when the people grew impatient and chose not to wait until Moshe's return. On the other hand, the episode of the golden calf is referred to explicitly beginning with verse 20!

[3] The Israelite behavior in the cases of the *egel ha-zahav* and the *kivrot ha-ta'avah* is compared and contrasted by Rabbi Joseph B. Soloveitchik in "Teaching with Clarity and Empathy," in *Reflections of the Rav* (Jerusalem, 1979), 150ff.

In a fortuitous coincidence that we have already noted (see the Preface to Tazria), Nehama Leibowitz and Joseph Soloveitchik attended the University of Berlin at the same time, in the early 1930s.

SHELAH LEKHA

"Man is Led on the Path He Wishes to Follow"[1]

NEHAMA'S *AHAVAT HA-ARETZ* AND THE CALUMNY OF THE *MERAGLIM*

✍ PREFACE

Nehama's love for *Eretz Yisrael* was the centerpiece of her life. Once she "ascended," she never contemplated leaving. No offer, however lucrative, could dissuade her; she was totally committed to *yishuv ha-aretz* and would brook no "calumny" against the land or its inhabitants.

The operative word in this week's *sidrah* is not *meraglim*, spies, but *anashim*, men, and their task is described as *latur*, to explore, and not to spy out the land that they were promised. In spite of this, the episode has come down to us, through rabbinical tradition, as *het ha-meraglim*: the blunder of the spies. The difference between the intent with which the twelve were dispatched (as "scouts") and the function they actually served (as "spies") is the focus of our study.[2]

✍ PART ONE: THE PLAN AND ITS EXECUTION

Moshe poses six questions to the scouts:

(1) Are its inhabitants strong or weak?

(2) Are they few or many?

(3) Is the land good or bad?

(4) Do they dwell in tent camps or in fortified cities?

---

[1] *Be-derekh she-adam rotzeh lelekh bah – molikhim 'oto.* Cf. Talmud *Makkot* 10b, *inter alia.*
[2] Nehama herself devoted a special study to the story of the spies. It was published in *Tokhniyot u-Tekhanim,* edited by Hayyim Hamiel, 61ff., Jerusalem: 1983.

(5) Is the land fat or lean?

(6) Are there trees?

The answers they report are:

(A) The land is flowing with milk and honey.

(B) The inhabitants are strong.

(C) The cities are walled.

(D) There are giants in the land.

(E) The land consumes its inhabitants.

(F) All its inhabitants are people of stature.

ᔕᔕ PART TWO: AN ANALYSIS

The answers are given in three installments: verses 27, 28, immediately upon their return; v. 30, in reply to Caleb's words of encouragement; v. 32, in an address to all the people.

A close reading reveals the characteristics that distinguish their words on these three different occasions. The first installment (items A-B-C-D) addresses the questions that Moshe posed, providing information about the land, its inhabitants, and their dwellings. Their reply to Caleb's encouragement, "We will overcome," is judgmental: "They are stronger than we." Their third declaration: "The land consumes its inhabitants and all the people we saw in it are men of stature," was unsolicited.

While the spies clearly exceeded their instructions and possibly their competence, how do their comments combine to culminate in sin and rebellion against God?

They began with an objective report, moved to a subjective analysis, and ended up by discarding all pretense of objectivity. Indeed, if we revisit their opening statement in light of their conclusion, it appears – in retrospect – that even their positive observations on the land are outweighed by their insistence on the indomitable nature of the inhabitants and their formidable cities.

⁊ PART THREE: *MASHAL LE-MAH HA-DAVAR DOMEH?:* A PARABLE

According to R. Yitzhak Arama (Spain and Italy, 1420–1494; author of *Akeidat Yitzhak*), therein lies their crime:

> It can be compared to a man who says to his agent: Go to the warehouse and have a look at a garment the merchant has in stock. Examine it carefully for the quality of the wool and linen, for size, appearance and price, and report to me, as I wish to purchase it. If the agent returns and says: I had a look at it and the wool is pure, it is long and wide, green and red in color, and the price is a hundred gold pieces – he has carried out his mission properly. However, if he said: I had a look at it; the wool is pure, it is long and wide, but it is red and green in color and very expensively priced at one hundred gold pieces – then he has exceeded the bounds of his mission and become, instead, an adviser.

In Arama's parable, the key word that distinguishes the second report from the first is: "But," and in the report delivered to Moshe, its equivalent is the word *'efes* in verse 28. It transformed them from "scouts" presenting an objective account, to "spies" who gratuitously offered an (incorrect!) opinion.

⁊ PART FOUR: AN OFFENSE AGAINST GOD

We have seen, above, how the spies exceeded their instructions and, by editorializing rather than reporting, they betrayed the national trust which was invested in them. While that makes them traitors to their nation, how does it constitute a sin against God?

According to the Talmud (cited by Rashi), that is implied in their response to Calev: "We are unable to go up against that people, for they are stronger *mi-mennu,*" which can either mean "than we," or: "than He."

As Nehama explains:

> In verse 29, they had already made the point that their cities were heavily fortified and that the people were strong; a fact that Caleb had not denied. He merely encouraged the people by telling them that in spite of these obstacles they were well able to overcome them. Caleb does not explain how they were going to achieve this, and by whose aid, but, presumably, implies that they should rely on

divine help. It was this trust in God that the spies were repudiating....

As is often the case, the homiletical and literal meaning of the text do not contradict, but rather complement each other, revealing different levels and shades of meaning (*Studies in the Weekly Sidra*, first series, 5715, #33).

✎ EPILOGUE: SPURNING THE LAND

The spies were guilty not only of treachery towards the Israelite nation and the repudiation of divine Providence; they also committed the unpardonable blunder of spurning the Promised Land. As Arama sums up:

It is this repudiation, this spurning of *eretz Yisrael*, which is responsible for our tribulations and exile, for our being a reproach to our neighbors and a scorn and derision to them that are round about us.[3]

---

[3] The slander is also the subject of an essay by Rabbi Joseph B. Soloveitchik, "The Singularity of the Land of Israel," in *Reflections of the Rav* (Jerusalem: 1979), 117ff.

KORAH

The One versus the Many

MALBIM AND NEHAMA ON *KORAH VA-'ADATO*

✍ PREFACE: ONLY A DIFFERENCE OF OPINION?

Nehama explains the "psychology" of Korah's camp as follows:

> They interpreted the mission of holiness, the role of "chosen people" with which they had been charged by God, in the sense of conferring on them superiority and privilege, rather than as constituting a call to shoulder extra duties and responsibilities (*Studies in the Weekly Sidra*, first series, 5715, #34).

The Mishnah (*Avot* 5:17) characterizes the disputes between Beit Hillel and Beit Shammai as *mahloket le-shem shamayim*, a controversy pursued in a heavenly cause, while it personifies its converse, a *mahloket she-lo le-shem shamayim*, as that of *Korah va'adato*, Korah and his congregation.

There is a marked disparity between the ways the two characterizations are formulated. The first names the two disputants (Hillel and Shammai), while the second appears to name only one (Korah). In other words, why does the Mishnah not refer to the latter as "the controversy of Korah and Moshe"?

✍ PART ONE: A DISTINCTION

Malbim (Russia, 1809–1879) shares with us an interesting insight into this distinction:

> Our Sages wished to point out that in a holy or heavenly cause both sides are, in fact, united by one purpose: to further unselfish, divine ends. In a controversy prompted for unholy ends, however,

for personal advancement and the like, then even those who have come together on one side are not really united, but are governed by their own calculations of what they stand to gain, and are ready to cut each others' throats if it so serves their interests.

In reply to the question we posed in the Preface, the Mishnah utilizes the phrase: "The controversy of Korah and his congregation" because, according to Malbim's explanation, this names the two parties! Korah and his confederates were "fair weather" friends whose own internal differences overshadowed their makeshift common purpose.

As Nehama elaborates:

> Korah's followers were simply a band of malcontents, each harboring his own personal grievances against authority; animated by individual pride and ambition, united to overthrow Moshe and Aharon, and hoping thereby to attain their individual desires.
>
> What would really happen, however, would be that they would quarrel amongst themselves, as each one strove to attain his selfish ambitions (*Studies in the Weekly Sidra, op. cit.*).

✄ PART TWO: *IS* THE CONGREGATION, OR *ARE* THE CONGREGATION?

If we examine the text of their complaint (16:3), we can spot an interesting anomaly:

> You take too much on yourselves, seeing that the entire congregation *are* holy, every one of them, and the Lord is among them; why do you exalt yourselves over the Lord's congregation?

The singular noun *'eidah* (congregation) is treated here as a plural: *kedoshim* (*are* holy).

An explanation for this aberration resides in the answer we provided to the previous question, in the distinction between people united in one unselfish purpose and those who merely make common cause for individual, selfish goals. In the eyes of Korah's confederates, the people of Israel were individuals and, from their warped perspective, the assertion of their selfish ambitions surely outweighed their group feelings. Whereas God had challenged the Jewish people to become holy (Va-Yikra 19:2), they blithely assert holiness as a preexisting condition, one entirely unsubstantiated by the events described in the *sedarim* of the last two weeks!

209

✖ PART THREE: IT'S THE WAY THAT YOU SAY IT!

Following yet another of Nehama's "*trick-im*," we shall compare and contrast the dialogue of Moshe and Korah. A close reading of their verbal give-and-take reveals a kind of symmetry:

Moshe said:	They said:
1. Is it too much (*rav lakhem*) for you (7)	1. Is it too much (*rav lakhem*) for you? (3)
2. It is not enough (*ha-me'at*) for you (9)	2. It is not enough (*ha-me'at*, 13)
3. Do you seek priesthood, too? (10)	3. Do you seek domination over us? (13)

Following Nehama, again, by being concise, we may characterize the symmetry between their respective remarks as a sign of the Korahites' impudence and mockery. According to Yitzhak Arama, this impudence is exacerbated by Datan and Aviram's use of *ha-me'at* (v. 13) to belittle Moshe's efforts to lead them out of Egypt. In spite of his oft-repeated promise that God was bringing them into a "land flowing with milk and honey," from their warped perspective, the "land of milk and honey" was Egypt.

✖ PART FOUR: THE STRAW THAT BROKE....

Moshe began to deal with them with patience and tolerance. After Datan and Aviram decline his invitation to join him, however (ostensibly for a discussion of their complaints, cf. vv. 14–15), he becomes angry, whereas he had not been angered either by their earlier comments or – according to Arama – by their tone of mockery. What brought about this drastic change?

The Midrash *Tanhuma* explains:

> To what can this be compared? To one who debates and argues with his colleague. If his colleague replies to him – he is pleased; if he does not reply – he is exceedingly displeased.

And Nehama elaborates:

> There is no greater annoyance than when one party to a dispute refuses to sit down and talk things out with the other side. In such

a situation lies little hope of a peaceful settlement. It was therefore only at this point that Moshe became really angry (*op. cit.*).

∞ PART FIVE: ALL FOR ONE…?

When God announces His plan to destroy the people, Moshe counters with: "If one man sins, will You take Your anger out on the entire congregation?" (v. 22). This response must be compared and contrasted to other incidents narrated either in the Torah or in the Prophets in which God displays a like tendency towards "collective punishment." First, at the golden calf (Shemot 32:11), then the improprieties with the Midianite women (Bemidbar 25:11), and later, the theft of the spoils of Jericho by Akhan (Yehoshua 22:20). (God's negotiation with Avraham over the fate of Sedom (Bereishit 18) also implies this tendency.)

This raises a thoughtful question: Given that God had already indicated at the golden calf that he would hold an entire people responsible for the sins of a few, why does Moshe appear to be surprised by it here? Perhaps it isn't as much his surprise as his consternation that an argument *ad hominem* – i.e., directed at him personally – could serve as the cause for national catastrophe. As "the most humble person on the face of the earth," Moshe was reluctant (or unable) to see himself as the trigger for collective devastation.

As a result, God has to explain to him (v. 30) that His anger is provoked by the people's callous attitude towards Him, and not (only) by their treatment of Moshe.

HUKKAT

Fighting Fiery with Fiery

PESHAT AND *DERASH* AND THE *NEHASH HA-NEHOSHET*

℘ PREFACE: GRATITUDE AND INGRATITUDE

In an earlier discussion of *mashal* (parable),[1] we noted the inclination of the Midrash to compare the relationship of the Israelites and God to that of a child who fails to show his father proper gratitude for the care he exercises in keeping him safe and secure. By dint of a sharp linguistic insight, Nehama will strike a similar theme in this week's *sidrah,* apropos of the incident involving the *nehashim ha-serafim*, the "fiery" serpents:

> It was not therefore the attack of the serpents, but rather their absence during the whole of their wanderings till then, that constituted the miracle![2]

℘ PART ONE: THE CURRENT CRISIS

In Part One of our lesson on the *sidrah* of Beha'alotekha we noted:

> We have become accustomed to the ingratitude that the Israelites demonstrated towards God just about every time they encountered an obstacle. They quickly became demoralized and grumbled about returning to Egypt.

Here, too, the people grow "short-tempered" and reiterate the familiar complaint: "Why did you bring us out of Egypt to die in the wilderness?" (Bemidbar 21:5). This time, however, there is a subtle change. While the first

---

[1] See Beshallah, Part Three.
[2] See *infra.*

two complaints were formulated in the grammatical singular [*he'elitanu*, Shemot 14:11, Bemidbar 16:13], the current complaint is in the plural [*he'elitunu*]. Initially, the people addressed Moshe alone; now they have included God in their complaint.

As Rashi says (citing the Midrash *Tanhuma*): "They equated the servant with his Master.... They are both alike."

ଛ PART TWO: CAUSE AND EFFECT

The full text of the *Tanhuma* cited by Rashi adds a phrase to that which we have just quoted. Implying a direct causal relationship between the consecutive verses, it says: "Right away, God dispatched fiery serpents among the people and they bit the people." This is highly reminiscent of another Midrash that Rashi cited (and that we used) to the episode of Amalek (Shemot 17:8). That Midrash criticized the Israelites for responding to the attack by Amalek by questioning God's Providence, and insinuated that the attack itself was a direct and equivalent result.

The Midrash says:

> I [the Lord] am always among you and ready to serve your needs, yet you say: "Is the Lord among us or not?" By your lives! A dog will come and bite you, and then you will cry to Me and know where I am.

> This can be compared to the case of a man who carried his son on his shoulders and went on a journey. The son caught sight of something alongside the road and asked his father to pick it up – and he did, two or three times.

> Then they met someone along the way and the son asked him: Have you seen my father? The father replied: You don't know where I am? Whereupon he threw him down and a dog came and bit him.

Similarly, in our *sidrah*, after the Jews questioned God's ability to provide for them, they were attacked and bitten by the fiery serpents.

❧ PART THREE: A FINE DISTINCTION

Fine linguistic distinctions, as we have repeatedly observed, are grist for the mills of exegesis. By comparing the verb meaning "to dispatch" that is used regarding the serpents in 21:6, with the verb used in 13:3 (last week's *sidrah*) regarding the "spies," we may note such a distinction. Whereas Moshe's action vis-à-vis the spies is designated: *va-yishlah*, God's action with the serpents is *va-yeshallah*. Whereas *va-yishlah* is in the *kal* form and its meaning is always: "sent," *va-yeshallah* is in the *hiph'il* form and it means "to release, to set free."

That distinction is borne out in the following verses as well:

Bereishit 32:4   Yaakov sent messengers before him
   "   37:14   [Yaakov] sent [Yosef] from the Hebron valley
Shemot 5:1   God said [to Pharaoh]: release My people
   "   13:17   And it came to pass when Pharaoh released the people
Devarim 22:7   You shall surely release the mother and keep the young

Applying this distinction to our verse (21:6), we note that it does *not* say "God *sent* the serpents," but "God *released* the serpents." "Released" implies that the serpents were already there but had been restrained by God prior to this moment. Indeed, this is what the Torah says (Devarim 8:15): "[God] led you through the great and awesome wilderness of snake, fiery serpent and scorpion...."

In this very vein, Nehama writes:

> If the serpents had not bitten them until now, it was only thanks to Divine Providence which had been watching over them, leading them through that great and terrible wilderness and not allowing the serpents to touch them, just as He did not allow the drought to overcome them with thirst but drew them out water from the rock.
>
> However, since the Children of Israel had spurned the Almighty's supernatural intervention, not wishing to live on the bread He provided – the manna – but aspiring to lead a more normal "natural" existence, the Lord let things go their ordinary, normal, way. He allowed the serpents to behave in their natural manner, in the great and terrible wilderness, which was to bite anyone crossing their path.

It was not therefore the attack of the serpents, but rather their absence during the whole of their wanderings till then, that constituted the miracle (*Studies in the Weekly Sidra*, first series, 5715, #35)!

Note: Read the following verses and explain whether they support or contradict the distinction we have drawn: Bereishit 8:8 ("[Noah] released the dove") and Tehillim 78:49 ("He let His anger loose upon them," which you may recognize from the Haggadah).

&) PART FOUR: FIGHTING "FIERY" WITH "FIERY"

The function of the copper snake has provoked much curiosity. The Mishnah (*Rosh Ha-Shanah* 3:5) asks rhetorically:

> Could a [copper] serpent give life or cause death? Rather it teaches us that if the Israelites looked heavenward and subjugated their hearts to their Father in heaven – they were cured. Otherwise they pined away.

The Zohar (Shelah, 175) similarly suggests:

> Whenever a victim gazed upon the likeness of the serpent he became filled with awe and prayed to God, knowing that this was a punishment he deserved. As long as a child sees the father's strap, he fears his father.... Here they saw the strap with which they had been beaten and this led them to redemption.

And Rabbi S. R. Hirsch explains:

> Every victim of the serpents' venom had to concentrate his attention on the image of the brazen serpent to enable him to realize that even after God had delivered him from the serpents, there lay ahead of him fresh dangers.... Nothing is more calculated to make man more satisfied with his lot than the knowledge of the chasm that ever yawns beneath him....

Note: The Mishnah we just cited gives a similar explanation for the raising of Moshe's hands during the battle with Amalek (Shemot 17:11). In what ways are the two cases similar?

Speaking of linguistic distinctions, compare Bemidbar 21:8 with 21:9. Can you suggest a reason for the change from the verb *ve-ra'ah* to *ve-hibit*? What distinction separates them?

BALAK

Prophets and Sorcerers;
Curses, Blessings and Discrepancies

A CLOSE LOOK AT BIL'AM AND A CLOSE READING OF HIS TEXT

℘ PREFACE

In this week's *sidrah,* we encounter Bil'am, one of the most formidable characters in the Torah. On the one hand, his prophetic abilities are recognized by the Midrash as equal to those of Moshe himself:

> Bil'am possessed three characteristics that Moshe did not possess: He knew who was speaking with him; when God would speak with him; and he could converse with God whenever he pleased (*Bemidbar Rabbah* 14:20).

On the other hand, however, he is ubiquitously referred to as *bil'am ha-rasha'*, Bil'am the wicked, and is counted among the "four commoners [who] have no share in the world-to-come" (Mishnah *Sanhedrin* 10:2).

Was Bil'am a genuine prophet or a nefarious sorcerer? In either case, seeing how ineffectual were his attempts to hurl imprecations at the Israelite nation, how much stock should we put in his blessings?

℘ PART ONE: ...AND SOME HAVE PROPHECY THRUST UPON THEM

Nehama wrote:

> The prophets of Israel themselves do not run after prophecy. On the contrary, a glance at Exodus 3–4 or Jeremiah 1 reminds us that they objected, as a rule, to this sudden imposition of responsibility

> from on high (*Studies in the Weekly Sidra,* first series, 5715/1955, #36).

Following the leads Nehama has provided, we are commended to compare the prophetic initiations of Moshe and Yirmiyahu with that of Bil'am.

Moshe's initial response to God's summons to him to prophesy was a clear demurral: "Please, God, send anyone [but me]" (Shemot 4:13). Yirmiyahu, too, demurred, declaring: "I know not how to speak, for I am [too] young" (1:6), even as Yesha'ayahu before him had protested his own election, saying: "Woe unto me, I am undone; for I am a man of unclean lips, dwelling among a people of unclean lips" (6:5).

Indeed, the standard description of the manner in which Israelite prophets received their prophecies underscores their passivity: "The word of the Lord *came unto* Hoshea" (1:1); "… *came unto* Yoel" (1:1); "… *came* expressly *unto* Yehezkel" (1:3). Contrast this to Bil'am, who makes multifarious preparations (seven altars, seven bullocks and seven rams) to receive the divine word and whose approach to prophecy is aptly described as "*going to* meet with enchantments" (Bemidbar 24:1).

Nehama characterizes the distinction between them as follows:

> As Nahmanides observed in respect of sacrifices, the person bringing them wishes, through their medium, to achieve closer communion with God, elevating human nature to a Divine level, whilst Balaam wanted to mould, as it were, the Divine will to his own nefarious ends, bringing the Divine down to mortal level (*ibid.*).

The alacrity with which Bil'am pursued his "calling" is the boldest indication that he was not seeking to enlist in the same corps of divine messengers into which Israelite prophets were unwillingly drafted.

℘ Part Two: All for One (or Not?)

On several occasions, we have looked at examples of how Rashi deals with parallel or repetitive passages and how he reconciles substantial differences between them.[1] In this week's *sidrah*, we have the opportunity to see how he treats imperfect parallels and what conclusions he draws from them.

Twice the Torah narrates encounters between Bil'am and his Moabite patron Balak. In one case it states:

> [Bil'am] returned to [Balak] while he stood alongside his sacrifice, along with *all* the Moabite princes (23:6).

The second time, however, it states somewhat differently:

> [Bil'am] came to [Balak] while he stood alongside his sacrifice, with Moabite princes in his company (23:17).

Is the absence of the qualifying adjective "all" in the second sentence a stylistic variant with no actual significance or is it an indication that we are to seek a distinction between the two circumstances?

Rashi, maintaining what some modern scholars have called the "omni-significance" of the Torah text, finds in favor of the latter proposition, commenting:

> "With Moabite princes in his company": Earlier it stated: "along with all the Moabite princes." When [the princes] saw that he was hopeless, some of them abandoned him, leaving behind only a portion of their company.

Nehama wryly notes:

> This is a well-known phenomenon: Initially everyone stands by, ready to participate in the great "happening." The sorcerer will curse the enemy and verbally subjugate him and they will share in the victory. When the first setback occurs, however, when things don't work out exactly as anticipated, "some of them abandoned him." They are no longer committed to his wickedness; it is no longer worthwhile (*Rashi's Commentary on the Torah*, 288).

---

[1] See our study of Hayyei Sarah in general and Part Four in particular.

∾ PART THREE: MORE (OR LESS) ALL

Two similar verses in Bereishit contain the identical discrepancy we have just described. The first records a unanimous opinion, while the second omits the unanimity:

- The matter pleased Pharaoh and pleased *all* his servants (41:37).

- The word spread through Pharaoh's palace that Yosef's brothers had arrived, pleasing Pharaoh and his servants (45:16).

This time, however, Rashi provides no explanation for the discrepancy, leaving it to us to figure out whether he regarded it as noteworthy at all.

At first glance, it appears that the two verses in Bereishit are describing dissimilar situations. The first describes the reaction to Yosef's initial interpretation of Pharaoh's dream and, in particular, his recommendation to store grain away against the prospective famine. The second verse, however, relates explicitly to the news of the arrival of Yosef's brothers. While we would expect all of Pharaoh's advisers to be present at the first instance and their unanimity is significant, not all of his servants necessarily were present when the news of Yosef's brothers circulated, nor would their unanimous greeting of that news be significant.

On the other hand, applying the psychological insight provided by Rashi and Nehama in the case of the Moabite princes, we might yet arrive at a similar conclusion vis-à-vis the Egyptian courtiers. Namely, that while their initial reaction was unanimously favorable, subsequent events caused some of them to recant. Indeed, just such an interpretation appears in the Yemenite *Midrash ha-Gadol:*

> "Pleasing... his servants": But not all his servants. They said: He is but one and yet he was able to diminish our stature; they are ten – how much more so! To wit: "The Egyptians rejoiced at their exodus" (Tehillim 105:38); they rejoiced at their exodus, but not at their arrival.

∾ PART FOUR: UNANIMITY VS. DISCORD

The propensity of Sefer Devarim to reflect on episodes and events that are described earlier in the Torah is well known. In its reflections on two such episodes, the spies and the revelation at Mt. Sinai, Rashi finds a "discrepancy" comparable to that which we have been illustrating.

- You all approached me and said: Let us send men before us to spy out the land.... (Devarim 1:22).

- When you heard the voice from within the darkness while the mountain was ablaze, all the chiefs of your tribes and your elders approached me, saying... You approach [God] and listen on our behalf... (*op. cit.,* 5:20ff).

In both cases, Moshe is approached and petitioned for a specific, strategic purpose; yet in the first case the approach is made by "you all," while in the second case it is made by "all the heads...." Is this, too, just stylistic, or is it significant? Rashi comments:

> "You all approached me": In utter confusion (*'irbuviyah*), while later on it states: "All the chiefs... approached me." The [latter] approach was proper; the young deferred to the elders, and the elders to the chiefs. Here, however, "you all approached" in utter confusion; the young shoving their elders and the elders shoving the chiefs.

Rashi's distinction, while not explicit in the texts of the specific verses we have cited, is borne out by the larger contexts in which they appear. The theophany at Sinai inspires a deep appreciation of the need for order and propriety, leading to God's wistful: "If only this emotion of awe would last forever" (op. cit., 5:26), while the approaching conflict with the Canaanites induces anxiety and bedlam, as reflected in: "You refused to proceed, rebelling against God, and grumbled in your tents" (*op. cit.,* 1:26–27).

PINHAS

The Danger Inherent in Zealotry

RAV KOOK AND THE NETZIV ON VIGILANTISM

õ Preface

As related at the close of last week's *sidrah*, Pinhas stepped into the breach that was created by the lascivious Midianites (see below, Part Four) by slaying the Midianite princess, Kozbi, and the Israelite prince, Zimri. Although he acted without consulting with Moshe or Aharon and without what we would call "due process of law," he was rewarded with "eternal priesthood." Nehama, ever sensitive to even the faintest hint of injustice, attempts to rationalize the events. Her point, as we shall shortly characterize it, is:

> Anyone who can be suspected of an ulterior, selfish motive will be; and only someone whose record is one of unlimited and unblemished tolerance may dare to act to the contrary (*infra*).

õ PART ONE: IS VIGILANTISM TO BE REWARDED?

Given the conventional antagonism towards "taking the law into one's own hands," how can the Torah be tolerant of vigilantism, let alone reward it? The Talmud Yerushalmi (*Sanhedrin* 9:7) states that Moshe and the elders disapproved of Pinhas's action and even sought his excommunication. Clearly, it implies, they were worried about the precedent it might set.

If that is the case, why was he rewarded? The decision, says the Talmud, was made by *ruah ha-kodesh*, which declared that his intentions were pure and his motives noble: "Because he was zealous for his God and atoned for the children of Israel" (25:13). This implies that every act of vigilantism should be viewed critically, and that only divine intercession – something upon which we cannot rely today! – can actually determine what someone's motives really were. The moral is: before acting as a vigilante, consider that you are probably going to be "misunderstood" and judged harshly. Is it still worth it?

ଚ PART TWO: AH, THERE'S THE RUB!

God Himself says: "And I did not consume the children of Israel in my zeal" (25:11). Pinhas was correct in acting as he did, for without his intercession the Jews would have been punished sorely. When confronted with the dilemma of taking unilateral action and risking condemnation or suffering the disastrous consequences of inaction, what guidelines are available?

The answer comes to us by way of the Talmud (*Berakhot* 28b), which identifies Shemuel ha-Katan as the sage who authored *birkhat ha-minim*, the prayer against heretics found in the *amidah* (the *Shemoneh Esreh*). Ironically, however, in *Pirkei Avot* (4:19), the motto of Shemuel ha-Katan is: "Do not rejoice when your enemy falls, nor delight in his stumbling." How could such a man be responsible for a prayer which "breathes vengeance on those treacherous to their people"?

Rav Kook, in his commentary on the *siddur* (*Olat Re'iyah*) provides an explanation, which Nehama renders:

> Whilst any sage distinguished for his piety and learning is capable of formulating prayers breathing sentiments of mercy and love, such a prayer as this one, so full of hate and condemnation, is bound to rouse the private feelings of animosity and spite on the part of the author against the enemies and persecutors of his people. Such a prayer must therefore originate with one noted for the holiness and purity of character and entire lack of the passion of hatred.
>
> Such a man was Shemuel haKatan. One could be sure that he was dominated by completely unselfish considerations and inspired by the purest of motives, and had removed from his heart all private feelings of hatred for the persecutors of his people (*Studies in the Weekly Sidra,* first series, 5715, #37).

In Nehama's words (above): "Anyone who can be suspected of an ulterior, selfish motive will be, and only someone whose record is one of unlimited and unblemished tolerance may dare to act to the contrary."

❧ PART THREE: WHAT IS A "COVENANT OF PEACE"?

Just what did the *berit shalom* afford Pinhas? According to Abrabanel, it guaranteed him divine protection against the next-of-kin of Zimri who were bound, otherwise, to seek retribution for his death. According to the Netziv (Naftali Tzvi Yehudah Berlin, 1817–1893; author of *Ha'amek Davar*), however, it is not protection against an external threat, but an internal one: the threat of demoralization which could result from the unilateral taking of a human life.

In Nehama's words:

> In reward for turning away the wrath of the Holy One, blessed be He, He blessed him with the attribute of peace, that he should not be quick tempered or angry. Since it was only natural that such a deed as Pinhas' should leave in his heart an intense emotional unrest afterward, the divine blessing was designed to meet this situation and promised peace and tranquility of soul (*ibid.*).

The Netziv's explanation is reminiscent of one that the Sefat Emet (Yehudah Leib Alter of Gur; Poland, 1847–1905) provided for the behavior of Yaakov Avinu. According to the Midrash, before Yaakov entered his father's presence to seek his brother's blessing, he recited the prayer: "Lord, spare my soul from the language of falsehood, from speaking distortions" (Tehillim 120:2). The Sefat Emet asks: Yaakov was preparing to utter a complete fabrication. How could he pray to be spared from falsehood?

He answers: He was not concerned about the falsehood he was about to tell his father; he had already deliberated over that and decided it was necessary and justified. Yaakov's concern was whether after having told one falsehood he would become a habitual liar, and he prayed to be spared from this possibility.

❧ PART FOUR: THE BIGGER THEY ARE...

For what reason does the Torah record the identities of Pinhas's two victims? According to Rashi, Zimri is identified: "to sing Pinhas's praises. In spite of the fact that Zimri was a prince, Pinhas did not refrain from his act of zeal on behalf of God." And Kozbi is identified: "To tell us the extent of the Midianite hatred; they went so far as to prostitute a king's daughter in order to trick the Israelites into sin."

If their identities are important enough to be listed – unlike, for instance, that of the "gatherer of sticks" in Bemidbar 15:32 – why were they not named in the original narrative (in last week's *sidrah*)? Why "withhold" their identities until this week's reiteration?

Last week they were indistinguishable from the general licentiousness that afflicted the Israelites, and their individual identities were of no particular consequence. This week, however, they are the specific objects of Pinhas's actions and the more we know about their status the more we are in awe of him for their execution.

Speaking of that licentiousness, the Talmud describes the intrigue with which the Midianites set their women up as lures for the Israelites, and the guile that the Midianite women exercised in order to snare the Israelites into both licentiousness and idolatry:

> She said to him: Will you drink a cup of wine? As soon as he had
> drunk it, the evil inclination burned within him and he said to her:
> Yield to me! She then took an idol out of her bosom and said to
> him: Worship this! He said to her: Am I not a Jew? She said: What
> do you care?... Moreover, I will not submit to you until you
> repudiate the law of Moshe your teacher (*Sanhedrin* 106b).

Where does the Talmudic Aggadah find the connection between Midianite licentiousness and idolatry? Probably in Hoshea 9:10: "They went to *ba'al pe'or* and separated themselves unto that shame (i.e., the licentiousness), and their abominations (i.e., idolatry) were like that which they loved."

Note: In the commentaries of Rashi cited just above, we saw that he gave a different reason for the identification of Kozbi from the one he had previously given for Zimri.

The Gur 'Aryeh asks: Why could they not have both been identified "to sing the praises of Pinhas"? Find an answer to this in Rashi's own words!

MATTOT

The First Halutzim

MOSHE AND THE TWO-AND-ONE-HALF TRIBES NEGOTIATE

➣ PREFACE

Nehama Leibowitz, whose *'ahavat ha-'aretz* was noted earlier,[1] opens the study of this week's *sidrah* with the following words:

> This week's *sidrah* discusses, among other things, a highly topical issue touching on the problem, or dilemma, of the choice of a career – personal advancement – or the fulfillment of a mission that has faced and continues to face Jewish youth, especially those intent on discharging the cardinal mitzvah of settlement in the Land of Israel.
>
> We find the utilization of the term *halutzim* applied to the "armed men" of the two and a half tribes who agreed to help their brethren conquer the Holy Land. That term has already entered the everyday vocabulary of Jews the world over and has come to represent the pioneer who deliberately forsakes all considerations of career for the mission of building, with his own hands, the future of his people in *'Eretz Yisrael*. It is now a platitude to say that the State of Israel was built up by generations of such *halutzim* (*Studies in the Weekly Sidra,* first series, 5715 #38).

➣ PART ONE: THE DILEMMA

The Torah introduces the episode involving the tribes of Reuven and Gad with the observation (32:1) that they had considerable livestock (*mikneh*) and that the Land of Gilead was suitable for livestock. This indicates that their

---

[1] Cf. the *sidrah* of Shelah Lekha.

motivation was primarily materialistic; their principal consideration was their cattle. In a sense, the word *mikneh* serves as an envelope for the verse; the world of Reuven and Gad began and ended with their livestock.

The challenge to Moshe's authority by the two and one-half tribes differs from the previous challenges that we have encountered in Sefer Bemidbar. Whereas the previous complaints were about something the people claimed to be missing and for which they yearned, here their complaint is that their situation is so good that they do not want to change it.

ஐ PART TWO: "THEY SAID" AND "THEY SAID" AGAIN; HOW MANY REQUESTS DID THEY MAKE?

Their initial approach to Moshe is detailed in vv. 3–5 and he responds in vv. 6–15. They approach, again, in vv. 16–19, and Moshe responds in vv. 20–24. They acquiesce in vv. 25–27, Moshe delivers their final instructions in vv. 28–30, and in v. 31 they render their final affirmation of the arrangements.

A close reading of the transcript of their conversation reveals that Moshe speaks much more than they do, primarily because, in his response, he delivers a history lesson (vv. 10–15), which he feels is relevant.

A breakdown of the conversation also indicates a significant difference between what they say to Moshe in vv. 2–4 and what they say in v. 5. In vv. 2–4 they are merely describing their situation, whereas in v. 5 they actually make a request.

Since their initial approach (2–5) is uninterrupted, however, why does v. 5 begin, again, with the verb *va-yomru* (they said)? Ordinarily, when this happens, we assume a pause took place in the action. In this case, then, we can imagine that after describing their circumstances, they looked to Moshe to see if he would anticipate their request and save them the trouble (and embarrassment?) of having to come right out and say it. When he didn't appear to be picking up on their hint, they spelled it out.

There is also a difference between the requests they make the first time and the second. The second time they are prepared to make their original request contingent upon their service to their brothers in conquering the land. They still want the Land of Gilead to be apportioned to them and will forego a share in Israel, proper, but they now indicate a willingness to share directly in the military burden.

◈ PART THREE: MOSHE MEETS THE CHALLENGE

Although their response seems to meet the conditions Moshe set, he did not adopt their recommendations wholesale.

Compare – closely! – their offer (vv. 16–19) with Moshe's revised formulation (20–24); there are striking differences between them. They refer (twice) to their allegiance to "the children of Israel," while Moshe refers (six times!) to their allegiance to "the Lord."

Nehama says:

> The two and a half tribes saw it in the light of a purely mercenary agreement between themselves and the rest of Israel. They would contribute their share in helping to conquer the land and, in return, would be allotted the region they desired.
>
> Not so Moshe. He stated everything in terms of responsibility to and dependence upon God who alone drives out the enemy and apportions the land (*op. cit.*).

A comparison between v. 16 and v. 24 discloses yet another difference, one remarked upon by Rashi on v. 16. They (typically!) mention their livestock first and their children second; Moshe instructs them to reverse the priority and build secure residences for their children before building pens for their cattle.

Note: A final observation leaves us on a cautionary note: Why do they add the words: "as my lord commands" to their final agreement (v. 25)? The answer is that it intimates that their acquiescence was only under duress!

MAS'EI

From Words to Sentences to Shakespeare

NEHAMA CITES *HAMLET* TO EXPLAIN THE SEQUENCE

⁊ PREFACE

Although a consideration of Rashi's grasp of Hebrew grammar is critical for a proper understanding, let alone evaluation, of his exegetical endeavors, Nehama was aware of just how abstruse a subject that could be.[1] We, too, have avoided confronting it head on, but, as the rabbinic adage goes: *patur b'lo k'lum, e-efshar*; one cannot exempt oneself from it entirely. While we have previously discussed aspects of Rashi's knowledge of Biblical Hebrew,[2] this week's *sidrah* provides an opportunity to refine and extend that discussion.

Furthermore, in the *sidrah* of Aharei Mot (Part Four), we highlighted Nehama's appreciation of the way Rashi reconciles Biblical verses that appear to contradict one another. In this week's *sidrah*, we shall take a similar occasion and opportunity to note the holistic way in which Rashi treats the Written and Oral Laws.

⁊ PART ONE: A LESSON IN LEXICOGRAPHY

The DNA, so to speak, of Hebrew – as of all Semitic languages (such as Aramaic and Arabic) – is the verbal root (*shoresh*) of three letters (i.e., tri-literal), from which most words in Hebrew derive.[3]

---

[1] "This is not the place to consider Rashi's grasp of Hebrew grammar" (*Rashi's Commentary on the Torah*, 26).

[2] See the unit on Tetzaveh and Part Five of Hayyei Sarah.

[3] Exceptions include words borrowed from non-Semitic languages (e.g., Egyptian, Persian) as well as Hebrew words whose verbal roots have four letters.

This recognition, however, was late in arriving. The "discovery" of tri-literalism is generally credited to the North African grammarian, Yehudah Hayyuj (tenth and eleventh centuries) and his Spanish disciple, Yonah Ibn Jannah. Rashi, who lived in northern France (1040–1105), was unaware of their work and would have been unable, in any event, to use it because they wrote in Arabic. In contrast, Avraham Ibn Ezra (1092–1167, Spain) knew Arabic, had detailed knowledge of their works, and made extensive use of them in his own commentaries.

The most significant consequence of Rashi's unawareness is his acceptance of the proposition that verbs can derive from roots of only two letters (bi-literal) or even of a single letter (mono-literal). If a comparison between two words can be made if they share only two root letters or only one – rather than three – the odds in favor of their comparison rise considerably. Rashi, then, was able to compare many Biblical words to one another because they shared one or two root letters, while Ibn Ezra rejected those same comparisons because they failed to match on all three points of comparison.

ಬ PART TWO: INHERIT THE WHAT?

One example will have to suffice. In Modern Hebrew, we regard the root of the verb "to give" as *n-t-n*. Rashi thought it was the single letter *t*,[4] because that is the only letter that appears throughout all the verb's conjugations. (The initial *n* falls out in the imperfect [future] while the final *n* falls out in the perfect [past].) Hayyuj, et al., recognized that a "fallen" letter could remain "radical" (i.e., part of the root) if it left behind a trace of its presence (in this case, the *daggesh* in *natatti* [perfect] and *etten* [imperfect]).

A comparable example exists in the text of this week's *sidrah*. Look at the following verses:

> *horashtem* the inhabitants of the land before you (33:52);

> *horashtem* the land and inhabit it (33:53).

---

[4] In this respect, Rashi was following the lead of the tenth-century Spanish poet-grammarian, Menahem ben Saruk, who had compiled a Biblical dictionary (in Hebrew), called the *Mahberet,* which Rashi used. Cf. the *Mahberet* of Menahem (ed. Phillipowski, 1854), 156.

On the appearance of a similar term in last week's *sidrah*: "The children of Makhir... went to Gilead and *yoresh* the indigenous Amorites" (32:39), Rashi made the following observation:

> *Yoresh*: following Targum, to expel. The word *r-sh* serves two definitions: inheritance and expulsion.

Consistent with this identification, Rashi explains that to perform the act of *horashtem* on human beings is to expel them (*gerashtem*), and to perform it on a land is to expel its inhabitants.

A similar sighting of this ostensible root is reported by Rashi in Bereishit 45:11, where Yosef tells Yaakov:

> I shall sustain you there [i.e., in Egypt] because five years remain to the famine, lest you and your household and all that is yours *tivaresh*.

Rashi comments:

> [Following Targum:] Lest you be impoverished, as in "[God] impoverishes [*morish*] and enriches [*ma'ashir*]" (1 Shemuel 2:7).

Nehama notes:

> A contemporary reader..., who is trained to recognize that Hebrew verbs have seven conjugations, will surely say that one may not confuse them [as Rashi appears to do]... Moreover, these are not merely different conjugations, but different verbal roots... inheritance deriving from *y-r-sh* and impoverishment from *r-u-sh*....[5]
>
> We should not, however, ignore the proof text Rashi cited of "God impoverishes and enriches," since even contemporary linguists recognize the affinity that these roots have for one another...(*Rashi's Commentary on the Torah*, 25).

❧ PART THREE: ONCE AGAIN INTO THE BREACH

As noted in the Preface, we have given prior consideration to Rashi's attempts to harmonize the Written and the Oral Laws. In this week's *sidrah*, we find the following ostensible discrepancy:

---

[5] In the *Mahberet,* all these examples are listed together under the ostensible verbal root: *r-sh* (ed. Phillipowski, 166–167).

These cities shall be for their residence and their grounds shall be for their cattle, their property and all their livestock. The grounds [shall be measured]... from the city wall outward a circumference of one thousand cubits. You shall measure outside the city two thousand cubits southward... eastward... westward... and northward, with the city at the center. These shall be the grounds of the Levites (35:3–5).

Were the grounds allocated to the *leviyim* to consist of a circumference of one thousand cubits or of two thousand cubits? Rashi's comment (35:4) again serves to reconcile the ostensible discrepancy:

"A circumference of one thousand cubits": Yet later it states, "two thousand cubits." How can this be? The circumference was to be two thousand; the inner thousand for [domestic] grounds, and the outer thousand for fields and vineyards.

Nehama notes that, in this instance, the estimation was based upon the Torah's stipulation that the grounds be utilized for cattle, property and livestock – seemingly excluding agricultural use:

[Yet] it is impossible to raise sheep and cattle without room for pasture! This accounts for the larger of the two measurements (v. 5): "Two thousand cubits" [are divided into] one thousand inner, which are adjacent to "the city wall outward," for grounds and one thousand outer for fields and vineyards (*ibid.*, p. 275).

○○ PART FOUR: ALL'S WELL THAT ENDS WELL

In our unit on Noah, we dealt with Rashi's treatment of sequences that appear to have been altered. One illustration we provided there[6] consisted of a subject from this week's *sidrah*: the daughters of Tzelafhad. Three verses in the Torah list the names of his five daughters. In two of them (Bemidbar 26:33 and 27:1), the list is: Mahlah, Noah, Haglah, Milkah, Tirtzah. In the third (Bemidbar 36:11), however, the order varies: Mahlah, Tirtzah, Noah, Haglah, Milkah. Rashi believes they were, essentially, "equal to one another;" that the third verse marks their order by age while the sequence in the first two verses is dictated by the order of "their wisdom."

---

[6] Noah, Part Three.

Nehama records the observation by the noted sixteenth-century super-commentator on Rashi, R. Eliyahu Mizrahi, who asks: In what respect were they "equal to one another?" His reply:

> That the older in years would respect the one who was greater in wisdom, while the one who was greater in wisdom would [yet] respect the one older in years.

She then offers the following elaboration:

> The reader may think that the interpreter is burdening the change in sequence with a significance it really lacks. That is not the case. Perhaps we can endear the exegetical approach to the contemporary consciousness by citing a detail from the Shakespearean play, *Hamlet*. The king, who murdered his brother, and the queen summon the two wicked courtiers, Rosencrantz and Guildenstern, and induce them to spy on Hamlet, their erstwhile boon companion, and reveal to them his secrets. Their request concludes as follows (Act II, scene 2, ll. 33–34):
>
> KING: Thanks, Rosencrantz and gentle Guildenstern.
>
> QUEEN: Thanks, Guildenstern and gentle Rosencrantz.
>
> This informs us that they are regarded equally by both the king and queen; neither one is given preference lest they become jealous of one another; so that they may devote themselves wholeheartedly to the dastardly plot (*ibid.*, 221).

Devarim

DEVARIM

Tough Words

RASHI'S INCLINATION TO INDICTMENT

✂ PREFACE

Nehama wrote:

> In our *parashah*, Moshe Rabbeinu turns to the generation that will
> enter the land that now stands to cross the Jordan and conquer the
> land – a situation that resembles that of its parents, the generation
> of the exodus, thirty-eight years earlier.... At that critical moment,
> on the eve of the conquest, the Israelites committed a deed that
> delayed their entry into the land by thirty-eight years....
>
> Now they need only to learn their lesson and not to deteriorate
> as their parents, lest their entry into the land be delayed [further]....
>
> Just how much Moshe wanted, in this *parashah*, to warn the
> second generation to learn from its parents' mistakes, will become
> clear...(*Iyyunim be-Sefer Devarim*, Jerusalem: 1994, 9–11 *passim*).

It is clear from Rashi's commentary at the opening of Sefer Devarim that
he regards the book as Moshe's admonition of the Israelites on account of
the many faults and foibles they displayed throughout his forty-year
leadership. In this lesson, we shall see that this tendency to view Moshe's
words as critical led Rashi to interpretations that appear to run counter to
the *peshat*.

✂ PART ONE: *SHEVAH* OR *GENAY?*

In chapter 1, vv. 12–17, Moshe proposes to appoint a leadership cadre to
assist him to administer the affairs of Israel. In verse 14, we find the people's
response. The question: Is their response favorable or unfavorable?

According to the strict *peshat*, it is entirely favorable. In v. 13, Moshe makes the proposal, in v. 14, the people appear to give their approbation and, finally, in v. 15, Moshe implements it.

Rashi, however, treats v. 14 as still another indictment. Moshe accuses the people of favoring the proposal for selfish interests – to benefit from the susceptibility of many judges to bribery.

Note: This discussion is reminiscent of Rashi's commentary on the verse "Noah was a righteous and steadfast man *in his era*" (Bereishit 6:9). There are two distinct ways in which the underlined phrase can be understood: One is characterized as *shevah*, admirable, while the other is *genay*, shameful.

❧ PART TWO: SETTING THE TONE

Why did Rashi prefer an interpretation that discredits Israel over a more straightforward one that would reflect well on the people? Because Rashi set a distinctly disparaging tone from the outset. Instead of the first several verses being a noncommittal narrative introduction stating the time and place of Moshe's valedictory, Rashi turns them into a list of specific charges brought against the people on account of their recalcitrant behavior. Indeed, Rashi uses a particular pejorative word in his very first sentence (and, again, in the continuation of verse 1, as well as in verses 3 and 4). The word is: *tokhehot*, [words of] rebuke.[1]

Here, Rashi seems to be in blatant disregard of the *peshat* in his commentary to the very first verse. Rather than seeing the several place names appearing there as features of the natural geography of the wilderness of Sinai, Rashi interprets them as signs or symbols of the spiritual wilderness that characterized Israel's quarrelsome and confrontational relationship with Moshe and with God.

❧ PART THREE: I SPY?

We next encounter the first reiteration of an earlier episode, that of the *meraglim* (spies). It is advisable to compare Moshe's "first person" narrative here with the Torah's "third person" account that was rendered in Bemidbar, chapter 13.

---

[1] See Behukotay regarding rebuke in general.

According to Bemidbar, the plan to spy out the land was initiated by God who instructs Moshe, "send men to survey the land" (13:2). According to Devarim, however, it was the people who approached Moshe [*va-tikrevun 'eilay*] with the unanimous proposition [*kulkhem*] of "let us send men before us to investigate the land" (1:22).

So whose initiative was it?[2] We may reason as follows: If the initiative belonged to God, He could not have held the people responsible for its consequences. Therefore, it would appear that the initiative was their own and God (merely) gave it His consent.

If the initiative was fraught with potential disaster, however, why does God instruct Moshe to adopt it? Should this factor not mitigate on their behalf? If we are correct in asserting that the initiative lay with the people and that Moshe sought approval from God, then God's reply is affirmative, albeit heavily tinged with caution. Here, we would do well to examine minutely the text of Bemidbar 13:2: "Send *you* men…" (*shelah lekha 'anashim*). God seems to be saying to Moshe: "If *you* want to send them, go ahead," implying that while He was not forbidding it, neither was He recommending it. By electing to exercise his own discretion in the matter, Moshe was also accepting its consequences without mitigation.

✂ PART FOUR: UNANIMITY ISN'T ALL IT'S CRACKED UP TO BE

In his commentary to the aforementioned description of the proposition as "unanimous" [*kulkhem*], Rashi raises the ugly specter of Moshe succumbing to a confrontation with a mob. He says:

> You all approached me: In turmoil (*be-'irbuviah*); children shoving their elders and the elders shoving the leaders.

Here, we see Rashi, once again (see Part Two), taking a pejorative perspective on something that could be interpreted favorably just as well. Rashi, however, claims textual justification, based upon a comparison with Devarim 5:20ff.:

---

[2] In a case where the details of the two accounts do not match, we face a significant methodological question: To which account should we give greater credence? We have addressed this question in Part Four of Hayyei Sarah, entitled: "Correlating an Event and Its Report."

When you heard the sound from amidst the darkness while the mountain was ablaze, all the leaders and elders of all your tribes approached me (*va-tikrevun 'eilay*) and said: Behold, God has manifested to us His grandeur and majesty.... Why should we face the prospect of death by means of this great blaze.... Draw you near and listen to whatever God says, and instruct us....

In both cases, we find the identical intimation of a unanimous approach. In what does the difference reside? According to Rashi, in the distinction between *kulkhem* (all of you), implying turmoil, and *kol rashei shivteikhem ve-zikneikhem* (the leaders and elders of all your tribes), implying an orderly approach. To quote Rashi (1:22):

That approach (5:20) was proper (*hogenet*). Children deferred to their elders and sent them ahead, and the elders deferred to the leaders and sent them ahead.[3]

---

[3] We made brief reference to this point earlier (Balak, Part Four) in the context of examining repeated narratives that are distinguished by either the presence or absence of unanimity.

VA-ET'HANAN

Answering a "Wise Guy"

NEHAMA AND THE *ARBA'AH BANIM*

∞ PREFACE

We are all familiar with that section of the Haggadah of *Pesah* that features the *'arba'ah banim*.[1] Here, we shall first look at the textual underpinnings of the entire notion of "four children" and then narrow our focus on the one who appears in this week's *sidrah*. Nehama's thoughts on and interpretations of these passages have been collated and published as *Studies on the Haggadah from the Teachings of Nechama Leibowitz,* edited by Yitshak Reiner and Shmuel Peerless (Jerusalem: Urim Publications, 2002).

∞ PART ONE: WHO KNOWS FOUR?

The designations of the "four children" – i.e., wise, wicked, simple and unable to question – do not originate in the Torah; they are deduced (in the *Mekhilta*) from the evidence provided by four different verses that were selected on account of a common concern for responding to children:

1. Shemot 12:26: Whenever your children shall tell you: What is this service to you?

2. Shemot 13:8: You shall tell your child on that day...

3. Shemot 13:14: Should your child ask you tomorrow: What is this?

---

[1] In deference to current sensitivity to gender-biased language, I will use the phrase "four children" rather than "four sons" throughout this essay.

4. Devarim 6:20–21: When your child asks you tomorrow: What are these testimonies, statutes and legislations…? Tell your child….[2]

Note: Superficially, Devarim 6:21 seems identical with Shemot 13:8. Both describe a parent telling a child; the difference, however, is that Devarim 6:21 is preceded by the posing of an actual question (in 6:20 – our focus), while the verse in Shemot is not.

The division into four distinct typologies, however, derives not from obvious differences between them but from nuances of language and style. Other than plural (*beneikhem*, #1) and singular (*binkha*, #2,3,4), there is no obvious difference in the references to the children. There are, however, the following subtleties:

1. One child doesn't ask; he tells. This implies assertiveness and aggressiveness inconsistent with normative behavior. Hence, this is the "wicked" child.

2. Another child neither asks nor tells. Hence, this is the one incapable of questioning.

3. A third child's question is simplicity itself: "What is this?" Hence, this is the simple child.

4. The reference in the fourth child's question to "testimonies, statutes and legislation" implies that this is the wise (i.e., righteous) child.

✆ PART TWO: WHAT WAS THE QUESTION, AGAIN?

As noted by the Haggadah, the wicked child seems to exclude himself from the *Pesah* proceedings through his use of the word *lakhem* (you – masculine plural), implying otherness or alienation. To wit:

> *Lakhem ve-lo lo:* [What is this service] to you, rather than to him. Since he excluded himself from the rule, he has committed heresy (*kafar be-'ikkar*).

The problem is that the so-called wise child uses a similar phrase, asking: "What are these testimonies, statutes… that the Lord our God has

---

[2] For a table listing these verses alongside the text of the *Mekhilta*, see *Haggadat Nehama* (Jerusalem: Urim, 2003), 45.

commanded you (*etkhem*)?" Why does no comparable opprobrium attach to him?

The use of *etkhem* (which may, itself, be stylistic) is counterbalanced by the wise child's acknowledgement of the *Pesah* laws as emanating from God, as opposed to the wicked child who pointedly makes no such admission.

Note: Nehama was aware that the Talmud Yerushalmi and some editions of the Mekhilta preserve a different version of the wise child's question, in which the key objective word is *'otanu* (us), rather than *'etkhem* (you). She dismissed this evidence, however, since no matter how germane it may be to the text of the Haggadah, it is of no consequence in an examination of the text of the Torah.

෨ PART THREE: THE ANSWER – PLEASE!

The vindication of the "wise child" on account of the reference to God is restricted by R. Yitzhak Arama, author of *Akeidat Yitzhak*. Stipulating that "acknowledgement of God does not necessarily constitute acceptance of mitzvot," he offers a similar answer that revolves about a verse in Yehoshua.

In Yehoshua, the tribes of Reuven, Gad and Menashe are confronted over their construction of an altar in Trans-Jordan. In order to dispel the criticism of their brother tribes, they seek to justify their actions as follows:

> Have we not done so on account of anxiety over a matter, saying:
> In time to come, your children will say to ours, what have you to
> do with the Lord, God of Israel? (22:24)

In other words, they maintain that the altar is intended to bolster their relationship with God rather than diminish it.

When we read this verse carefully, we note that it has something in common with the verses under consideration here. In fact, it has two striking affinities for our verse:

1. The concern with responding to children (see Part One), which is the common denominator of all four verses;

2. The specific use of the phrase *mah… lakhem* (what is … to you?).

According to Arama, this telltale phrase, which indicates "skepticism and condemnation" (*'ir'ur ve-kintur*), is what taints the question of the wicked child and distinguishes that child from the one who is wise.

✂ PART FOUR: IS EXCLUSION HERETICAL?

Earlier (Part Two), we cited the Haggadah's evaluation of the question of the wicked child: "Since he excluded himself from the rule, he has committed heresy (*kafar be-'ikkar*)." To that, we now add its concluding phrase: "Had he been there [in Egypt], he would not have been redeemed."

The immoderate language of the Haggadah requires examination. Why is his self-exclusion from the rituals of *Pesah* deemed heresy? Why would he have forfeited his right to redemption?

In the *sidrah* of Bo,[3] we discussed the *korban Pesah* in some detail. In particular, we juxtaposed it with the Egyptian abhorrence (*to'avat mitzrayim*) towards eating the flesh of sheep and cattle, and cited Moshe's concern over sacrificing to God while still in Egypt:

> It would not be proper because the Egyptians regard our sacrifices to the Lord as abominations. Could we break an Egyptian taboo before their very eyes without their stoning us? (Shemot 8:22)

While our conclusions there were limited to the ritual details of the sacrifice (e.g., why only sheep or goats? Why roasted whole?), here we can extrapolate from those details a point of principle: Participation in the original *korban Pesah* constituted the rejection of [Egyptian] superstition and idolatry. Therefore, anyone who had excluded himself from its performance on account of its inherent danger was thereby giving notice that he was in greater fear of the deities of Egypt than of the God of Israel.

Such a person is, by definition, a heretic and, in valid historical hindsight, would surely have forfeited his right to be redeemed from slavery.

---

[3] Part Four.

EKEV

The Land of Israel: A Mixed Blessing

RASHI'S USE OF *MASHAL*; EXPLAINING THE *SHEMA'*

✥ PREFACE

The centrality of the Land of Israel, a viewpoint steadfastly maintained by Nehama,[1] is underscored by Rashi in his commentary on the very first verse in the Torah. Citing the *Midrash Tanhuma,* he asks, rhetorically, why the Torah begins with the description of creation, rather than with an actual mitzvah. The answer is that God's authorship of creation entitles Him to distribute the Earth as He chooses and that entitlement upholds Israel's right to possess its land. In this week's *sidrah*, we will examine the correlative question of what circumstances can cause the people of Israel to lose the right to their land and suffer exile.

✥ PART ONE: THE LAND – A SOURCE OF PROSPERITY

This week's *sidrah* is positively overflowing with references to the Land of Israel and the bounty it can provide. It begins:

> In consequence (Ekev) of your obedience to and observance of these laws... [God] will love you, bless you and increase you, blessing your children and the produce of the land... that He vouchsafed your ancestors to deliver to you (7:12–13).

In continuation, the Torah describes the physical geography of the Land of Israel and mentions – by name – its seven special agricultural species. From these conditions, it concludes: "Eat to satiety and bless the Lord, your God, for the good land He has given you. Beware lest you forget the Lord,

---

[1] See our Prefaces to Shelah Lekha and Mattot.

your God, and fail to keep His commandments...." (8:7ff.). If, on the other hand, the people eat to satiety, etc., but credit it all to their own prowess and neglect God's role, then they are threatened with expulsion (8:17ff.).

Later yet, the *sidrah* refers to the land's unique climate as a further cause for enlightened dependence upon God:

> The land that you are approaching to occupy is unlike the land of Egypt that you have left, which could be sown and irrigated [easily] by foot like a vegetable garden.... It is comprised of hills and valleys that drink in the precipitation from heaven. It is a land that the Lord, your God, inquires of; His eyes are constantly upon it, from year's start to year's end (11:10–12).

൭ PART TWO: NOW HEAR THIS!

The most significant and memorable references to the Land in this week's *sidrah* occur in the section that is known, traditionally, as the second – or middle – portion of Shema'.

> It shall come to pass if you listen attentively to My mitzvot that I am commanding to you this day... I shall provide precipitation for your land at fixed times – early and late seasonal rains – and you shall gather in your grain, wine and oil. Beware lest your hearts be seduced to stray after alien deities and bow to them. God will be enraged with you; He will restrain heaven and there will be no rain, and the earth will not yield its produce. You will quickly be expelled from the good land.... (11:13–18)

Note, again, the stark alternatives: Be obedient, and the earth will be a source of bounty and blessing. Disobey, and it will be the cause of famine and devastation.

൭ PART THREE: WHAT DOES THIS REMIND YOU OF?

In stipulating and clarifying the conditions under which the people are susceptible to expulsion, Rashi resorts to a parable (*mashal*):

> "You will quickly be expelled": In addition to all the other privations, I will expel you from the land that has caused you to sin. This resembles the case of a king who dispatched his son to a party, instructing him not to eat to excess lest he return home

soiled. The son paid him no mind, ate and drank to excess and threw up over all the partygoers, who took him bodily and threw him out of the palace.

The king represents God. The son is Israel. The party is the Land of Israel. The instructions are to be cautious while enjoying its many advantages (see 8:7–11, cited in Part One). The overeating represents Israel's taking God and His blessings for granted leading, eventually, to their total disregard of Him in favor of idolatry. (Cf. Devarim 32:13–15.) The eviction from the palace represents their exile from the Land of Israel.

ᔐ PART FOUR: PARABLES AND BEGINNINGS – A QUESTION OF METHODOLOGY

Here we have touched – not accidentally – on a perennial "sore spot" in the history of understanding Rashi. If we go back to the beginning – literally – to Rashi early on in Bereishit (3:8), we recall that he formulated his approach to Aggadah as follows:

> There are many Aggadic *midrashim,* and our Sages have already arranged them appropriately in *Bereishit Rabba* and other anthologies. I [on the other hand] have come [to comment] only on the straightforward meaning of Scripture (*peshuto shel mikra'*) and those Aggadot that settle a scriptural problem, "as a word fitly spoken."

Rashi appears to be saying that he will utilize Aggadic *midrashim only* if they contribute to the resolution of a scriptural problem. How then do we account for the numerous instances in which Rashi cites an Aggadah *after* stipulating an interpretation that he designates the *peshat?* After studying the explanations of nearly a dozen super-commentators on Rashi, Nehama concludes that there are two schools of thought.

One school takes Rashi at face value and insists that if he cites an Aggadah, then it is in resolution of a problem unsolved by the *peshat.* This school labors to determine what the problem(s) is (are), what the *peshat* contributed to the resolution, and what was the "balance" of the problem(s) addressed by the Aggadah. The second school assumes that Rashi took himself at his word and that any interpretation he designated as *peshat* is the resolution of the problem. What then does the Aggadah accomplish? It magnifies Torah and adorns it [*lehagdil torah u-le-ha'adirah*] by adding a moral, ethical or spiritual dimension to the text.

Note: The subject of *shema'* is examined in great depth by Nehama's illustrious brother, Yesha'ayahu Leibowitz, in an essay entitled: "The Reading of Shema."[2] He focuses, *inter alia,* on the contrast between the unconditional ("categorical") nature of belief reflected in the first portion of *shema'* (Devarim 6:4ff.) and the belief reflected in the second portion, featured in our *sidrah* (11:13ff.), that appears to require sanctions.[3]

Another contemporary examination of *shema'* is by Norman Lamm, who observes, in a similar vein, that:

> The Shema has much to tell us about the tension between spirituality and law that lies at the very heart of the Jewish religious enterprise.[4]

---

[2] *Idem., Judaism, Human Values and the Jewish State* (Harvard: 1992), 37ff.

[3] We devoted a portion of an earlier unit (Tazria) to a comparison between the Leibowitz siblings.

It would not be untoward to repeat here an observation once made by Professor Uriel Simon, marveling at the perspicacity of the parents of these two remarkable siblings. They named their elder son Yesha'ayahu, as though they knew he would become a great *mokhiah* (chastiser) and thereafter named their daughter Nehama, as though to offer a note of consolation.

[4] *Idem. The Shema: Spirituality and Law in Judaism* (JPS: 1998), 6.

RE'EH

Rashi and Halakhah

HERMENEUTICS AND TARGUM ONKELOS

❧ PREFACE

Nehama observed that:

> The *parashah* of Re'eh is the first among the *parashiyot* of Devarim most of whose content comprises commandments and laws whose importance is all the greater on account of their imminent entry into the land (*Iyyunim be-Sefer Devarim*, Jerusalem: 1994, 121).

The large number of mitzvot (38) contained in this week's *sidrah* provides us with an opportunity to broaden the scope of our ongoing inquiry into Rashi's methodology by exploring his use of *Midreshei Halakhah*.

❧ PART ONE: INDENTURED HEBREW SERVITUDE

The Torah repeats the laws of *eved ivri*, the indentured Hebrew servant, which were introduced in the *sidrah* of Mishpatim. Essentially, if a Jewish man were to become so impoverished that he could not sustain himself and his family, his last resort was to "sell" himself into service to another Jew. This service would last for either six years or until the *yovel* (Jubilee year), at which point he was automatically liberated. The Torah also instructs the master to bestow gifts upon the departing servant in order to help us sustain the recollection of our own experience as servants. Should the servant decline his liberation, however, he has the option to extend his service "eternally." Such a servant has his ear pierced, on account of which he is called *nirtza'*.

Read the following phrases with Rashi. What possible renditions of the verses do his comments reflect, and what do his interpretations tell us about either the servant's release or extended service?

1. 15:14: "from your flocks, granary and wine press"

2. 15:17: "an eternal servant"

3. 15:17: "thus shall you do to your maidservant"

Note that in each of these three cases, Rashi advances a possible interpretation, rejects it, and substitutes a preferred understanding for the possibility he rejected.

1. The possibility is that the items enumerated in verse 14 are the *only* suitable gifts to give a departing servant, implying that in their absence the master is relieved of this obligation. Rashi's understanding, however, is that these are listed only as examples and that the principle, to give him gifts of significant value, must be observed in any case.

2. The possibility is that the extended period of service would last his entire life. Rashi's understanding, however, is that no servant can endure service beyond the *yovel*.[1]

3. The possibility is that the entire procedure of the extension of service, including the ear piercing, is conducted for a maidservant as well. However, Rashi's understanding is that the verse refers to the gift-giving, while only a male servant can become a *nirtza'*.

What enabled Rashi to determine the correct interpretation? In each case, he was persuaded by a particular form of Midrash, which we will now explore in greater detail.

೫ PART TWO: YOU MIGHT HAVE SAID...

The Midrash used by Rashi in each of the above cases follows the form: "*yakhol* X... (X is possible), *talmud lomar* Y (save for verse Y) [leading to conclusion Z]." This formula is unchanging. It always begins with the hypothetical answer (known as the *havah amina*, Aramaic for "one might have said"), rejects it on account of a textual proof, leading to the correct

---

[1] On this point, see our unit on Mishpatim.

understanding (known, in Hebrew, as the *maskanah*), which may be either stated explicitly or inferred implicitly.

A critical methodological question concerns the *havah amina*, the possibility to be rejected: Is it a "throwaway" (i.e., of no value in and of itself), or does it have any validity, per se?

In each and every case described above, the possibility that is raised and rejected is entirely credible, based upon either the literal sense of a word, or the context in which it appears:

1. If the Torah explicitly cites sheep, grain and wine, why not assume that is all it intends?

2. If the Torah intended for the *nirtza'* to serve only until *yovel*, why use *le-olam*, a word that literally means forever?

3. Why use the demonstrative pronoun *ken* unless it means to convey everything that it demonstrates?

Another methodological question follows therefrom: If both the *havah amina* and the *maskanah* are eminently credible, on what grounds does Rashi reject the former? Why should one explanation be any stronger than another explanation if they are both based upon logic and language?

This is the lesson we set out to examine here regarding Rashi and his use of *midreshei halakhah*.

❧ PART THREE: EXPLANATION BY WAY OF ILLUSTRATIONS

The answer, in brief, is that Rashi grants priority to any explanation that is provided by "tradition" over any explanation – however similar and cogent – that derives from a less authoritative source, including his own or another exegete's reasoning. Here is a passage from the Talmud and another from the Torah, with Rashi's accompanying commentaries, that illustrate and qualify this point.

A. Kiddushin 49a

> **Talmud:** R. Yehudah says: Whoever translates a verse literally is a charlatan and whoever adds to it blasphemes and reviles.

> **Rashi (ad loc.):** Translates literally: Omitting the additions made by our Targum [Onkelos]... such as [translating] *lo ta'aneh al riv* (Shemot 23:2) as "do not testify about an argument."
>
> Adds to it: Saying, if it is permissible to add [to the literal sense], then I shall add wherever I please.
>
> Blasphemes and reviles: Disparaging God by altering His intent. When Onkelos added, he didn't do so on his own recognizance; it was revealed at Sinai and forgotten until [the Men of the Great Assembly] restored it....

According to Rashi, Onkelos was able to violate R. Yehudah's proposition and add to the literal sense of a verse because he was not acting independently; rather, he was serving as a vehicle for the restoration of an original intent that was known to tradition and had subsequently been forgotten.

A pedagogical question arises, as well: Is it proper for Rashi to offer a mistaken interpretation even as a *havah amina* (hypothesis)? The answer is that the hypothetical interpretations of the three verses we are studying come with the recommendation of philology and logic and that gives Rashi license to propose them even though he knows, from the outset, that they are to be rejected.

Does Rashi ever overrule tradition in favor of a private interpretation? He appears to do so, although the jury is still out on the reliability of the passage in question. Here it is:

B. Bemidbar 26:23–24

The verses list the names of four families descended from the tribe of Yissakhar: Tola', Puvah, Yashuv and Shimron. Rashi compares these names to the list of the eponymous twelve tribes and their descendants in Bereishit 46:13: Tola', Puvah, Yov, Shimron. Spotting the difference, he says:

> Yashuv is Yov who is named among those who descended to Egypt, because all families were named for those who descended while those born subsequently did not have families named for them. The exceptions to this are the families of Ephraim and Menasheh, who were all born in Egypt, and Ard and Na'aman, children of Bela son of Binyamin.
>
> I found in the works of R. Moshe ha-Darshan that their [i.e., Ard's and Na'aman's] mother was pregnant with them when she

came to Egypt.... If this is an Aggadah, well and good; otherwise –
I would say that....

Here, Rashi proposes a solution based upon a passage he found in the
yesod (literary work) of Rabbi Moshe the Darshan, a well-known author and
compiler of Aggadah, who lived in Provence not long before Rashi. Rashi is
inclined to accept the explanation of pregnancy (itself reminiscent of the
legend concerning the birth of Yokheved, mother of Moshe) because it is
based upon the authority of Rabbi Moshe. He seems to be uncertain,
however, whether R. Moshe had received it as part of his tradition or had
said it entirely on his own authority. Therefore he qualifies his acceptance by
stipulating that "if this is an Aggadah," i.e. a part of tradition, then well and
good; if not, however, he has an original explanation he is willing to offer as
an alternative rather than leave the reader with an unanswered question.[2]

---

[2] For a methodological comparison between Rashi and Ibn Ezra in this matter, see
our unit on Terumah, Parts 3–4 in particular.

SHOF'TIM

When Justice is Blind or Otherwise Doesn't See

RASHI ON REPETITION AND REDUNDANCY

✍ PREFACE

Nehama notes:

> This week's sidrah, like others, takes its title from the first
> distinctive word, *shoftim*, judges, and deals, indeed, largely with
> matters concerning the judge and the judiciary (*Studies in the Weekly
> Sidrah,* first series, 43).

Two *sidrot* (alt: *sedarim*) of the Torah, Shof'tim and Mishpatim, bear
names that derive from the verbal root *sh-p-t,* which means to judge. Not
surprisingly, some of the contents of these two *sidrot* overlap as well. We
shall examine one verse in the current *sidrah* in great detail and contrast
Rashi's commentary here with the treatment he affords a nearly identical
verse in the earlier *sidrah.*

✍ PART ONE: O SAY, CAN YOU SEE...?

Compare Rashi's comments on the following related verses:

> **Shemot 23:8:** "Do not accept a bribe (*shohad*), because bribery will
> blind the sober (*pikkehim*) and distort the words of the righteous."

> **Rashi:** Even a Torah scholar who accepts a bribe will eventually
> lose his mind, forget his learning and his vision will dim.

> **Devarim 16:19:** Do not accept a bribe, because bribery will blind
> the eyes of the wise (*hakhamim*) and distort the words of the
> righteous.

> **Rashi:** Once [a judge] accepts a bribe, it is inevitable that he will incline towards the one [who bribed him] in order to acquit him.

In the verse from Shemot, Rashi treats blindness both metaphorically ("lose his mind") and literally ("vision will dim"), while in Devarim he offers only a metaphorical interpretation. We might have expected the opposite, because it is the verse in Devarim that explicitly mentions eyes. It is possible that Rashi was influenced less by the verb "to blind" (*ye'avver*), which appears in both verses as well as frequently throughout the Torah, and more by the unusual word *pikkehim*, which appears in its literal sense only once more in the entire Torah (Shemot 4:11).

Note: While on the subject of Rashi and metaphors in Mishpatim, look at Shemot 21:19: "If he [the victim] arises, goes out and about on his *mish'enet*, then the attacker is cleared and pays only his disability and medical expenses." Why does Rashi interpret *mish'enet* metaphorically (*burio*, well-being) rather than – literally – as a crutch?[1]

✍ PART TWO: SAY THAT AGAIN?

The Torah often repeats itself. Sometimes the repetitions are grouped together within textual proximity to one another like *peru u-revu*, be fruitful and multiply, in Bereishit 9:1 and 9:7, or *lo tonu*, the admonition against deceit, in Va-Yikra 25:14 and 25:17. Rashi, in each case, differentiates between the repetitious phrases, explaining that the first instance of *peru u-revu* was a blessing and the second, a commandment. He distinguishes between the iterations of *lo tonu* similarly, saying the first prohibits monetary cheating (e.g., overcharging), while the second prohibits verbal cheating (e.g., false advertising).

At other times, such as the instance we shall now cite, the repetitions are dispersed. Look at Devarim 1:17 and Devarim 16:19; the phrase reiterated there is the admonition to a judge of: *lo takir(u) panim*, not to grant preferential treatment or favoritism. According to Rashi, the first is an admonition [to the "authorities"] not to use favoritism in appointing judges. The second admonishes a judge not to show procedural favoritism to litigants by having one stand while the other is seated.

---

[1] For more about Rashi's use of metaphor, see Nitzavim.

Rashi does not treat both verses as unequivocal mandates for impartial rulings because such mandates already exist. Shemot 23:3 explicitly prohibits showing [unwarranted] respect to the indigent; Shemot 23:6 prohibits waiving his legal rights; and Va-Yikra 19:15 reiterates these admonitions while adding the directive to judge everyone with equity (*tzedek*). Since the subject of favoritism, per se, has already been covered by Torah legislation, Rashi is able to assign a more oblique meaning to the verses in Devarim.

Additionally, in imputing Devarim 1:17 to those who appoint judges rather than to the judges themselves, Rashi may have been reacting to the otherwise superfluous use of the word *mishpat* in that verse. Since the previous verse is explicitly addressed to "your judges" and includes the directive of equity, why repeat "judgment" in the next verse unless it refers, again, to a similar, albeit not identical, situation?

ᴘᴏ PART THREE: FROM FAVORITISM TO WITHHOLDING

The Torah has additional injunctions and admonitions in the administration of justice. One of them deals with withholding wages (*oshek*). The Torah states the prohibition in Va-Yikra 19:13: "Do not withhold from your neighbor" (*et rei'akha*), and reiterates it in Devarim 24:14: "Do not withhold from an afflicted and needy hired hand" (*sakhir 'ani ve-'evyon*). In this case, Rashi applies the first verse to withholding the wages of a hired hand, and the second to add another count to the indictment if the victim is also indigent.

Since the second verse explicitly mentions a hired hand [*sakhir*], what impels Rashi (again!) to overlook the context? On the assumption that the verse in Va-Yikra already refers to a hired hand, Rashi concludes that the verse in Devarim must be treating a separate, albeit similar, circumstance. Since it explicitly mentions an indigent worker, he infers that the verse in Va-Yikra had to be referring to one in better economic circumstances.

His determination that someone who withholds wages from such a worker commits a double crime is justified by the context. The very next verse (15) describes the downtrodden conditions of the poor worker, concluding: "Lest he call out to God on your account and you shall have sinned." Since it's obvious that you sin by withholding somebody's wages, why make it appear contingent on his complaint? Hence, Rashi assumes that the sin of withholding from an indigent worker is in addition to withholding from workers, in general.

◎ PART FOUR: TRUTH, JUSTICE, AND RASHI'S WAY

At other times, the repetitions are shaded in more subtle fashions. Take the case with which we began in Part One: Shemot 23:8 and Devarim 16:19, both of which prohibit taking bribes. On the former, Rashi says:

> A bribe do not accept [*shohad lo tikkah*] – even to rule truthfully ['*emet*].

On the latter, Rashi says:

> Do not accept a bribe [*lo tikkah shohad*] – even to rule equitably [*tzedek*].

Rashi's use of truth in one place and equity in the other, is, again, under the influence of the contexts. In Mishpatim, the admonition against bribery is preceded immediately by, "Keep far from falsehood" (*sheker*), hence the contrasting emphasis on truth. The verse in Shof'tim is surrounded by equity in both the previous verse [*ve-shaf'tu et ha-'am mishpat tzedek*] and the succeeding verse [*tzedek tzedek tirdof*], hence Rashi's preference here for equity.

The distinction is entirely one of style, not of content, as indicated by their combination in the concluding portion of Rashi's commentary to both verses:

"The words of the righteous: Equitable words (*devarim ha-mutzdakim*), truthful rulings (*divrei emet*)."

KI TETZE'

Propinquity; Supplying the Missing Links

SEMIKHUT PARASHIYOT

&ba; PREFACE

Nehama noted:

> The *parashah* of Ki Tetze' contains (according to the reckoning of
> Rambam) seventy-two mitzvot (commandments and prohibitions),
> making it the richest in mitzvot among all the *parashiyot* of the
> Torah (*Iyyunim be-Sefer Devarim,* Jerusalem: 1994, 201).

With such a large number of mitzvot, it is frequently difficult to
determine what dictates their sequence or juxtaposition in the Torah. On
occasion, Rashi uses *midrashim* to make this determination: Aggadic
midrashim, if the subject is narrative, and Halakhic *midrashim,* if the subject is
legal, as is the case in this week's *sidrah*.[1]

&ba; PART ONE: OUT OF CAPTIVITY

The *sidrah* begins with the laws of a captured concubine (*yefat to'ar,* 21:10–
14), continues with spousal jealousy and rivalry (*ahuvah/senu'ah,* v. 15–17),
then moves to the laws of the rebellious child (*sorer u-moreh,* v. 18–21).

While these seem like three entirely unrelated topics, a connection
between them can be established. Rashi (v. 11), for instance, views them as
successive stages in the deterioration of a marital relationship. If one weds a
captive – despite the Torah's implicit disapproval – she will cause friction in
the marriage and eventually the child of such a marriage will turn rebellious.

---

[1] We explored the question of sequence and juxtaposition in Naso, featuring the
approach of Moshe David (Umberto) Cassuto.

Indeed, we can extend the connection to the following verses, which require the prompt removal of the corpse of an executed criminal (v. 22–23) – a subject that does not appear, on the surface, to be related to what precedes it. Rashi, however, sees the continuation as an ongoing part of the previous scenario. If the parents of an incorrigible child do not deal with him in the fashion the Torah prescribes, but they show him misplaced mercy, he will end up committing a capital crime and be executed all the same.

❧ PART TWO: RETURNING A MISSING LINK

The Torah moves next to *hashavat aveidah*, the obligation to restore lost property (22:1–3). Can a link be established between this law and the fate of an executed criminal? While Rashi offers no explanation here, we can infer one from his previous remarks. The key to *hashavat aveidah*, Rashi notes, is to know when it is permissible to decline the opportunity to return a found item (*pe'amim she-atah mit'alem*, literally: occasions on which one may turn away) and when it is prohibited to decline. This offers a thematic link to the executed criminal whose parents – according to Rashi's explanation – didn't know when to turn away from his actions and when to turn him in.

What connects the restoration of property to the next law, helping overburdened animals [*hakem takim*, v. 4]? Two possible links exist. A topical one: both lost property and bearing the load deal with the treatment of domesticated animals. And a linguistic one: both feature the verb *'-l-m* in their respective prohibitions against making oneself ignorant or unaware of a situation.

Can any reasonable explanation connect the next law, which prohibits cross-dressing (v. 5)? This time it is Ibn Ezra who offers a link. He sets this prohibition squarely in the initial context of going to war and regards cross-dressing as a euphemism for the kind of licentiousness that is particularly pervasive during times of war.

❧ PART THREE: SOME LINKS ARE LINGUISTIC

The next law is the well-known *shiluah ha-ken* (v. 6–7), the requirement to dispatch the mother bird before taking her chicks. A possible linguistic link to what precedes it consists of the word *derekh* (road) that appears in the law of *hakem takim* as well. A conceivable thematic link is the care and treatment of animals. Admittedly, neither explanation can account for the laws of cross-dressing that intervene. (Although, the word *simlah* is also common to vv. 3 and 5!)

The law of the mother bird is followed by the requirement to place a parapet atop a new house (v. 8). Rashi again sees a progression, which he designates: *mitzvah goreret mitzvah* (one mitzvah draws out another). The reward for exercising care with the mother bird will be the opportunity to build a new house, followed by planting a new vineyard (v. 9), etc.

We may note an additional correspondence between laws of a new vineyard and those of a new house: both (along with a new wife) earn an exemption from military service (see 20:5–6).

ഇ PART FOUR: MATCHES AND MISMATCHES

Now read 22:9–12. Four apparently separate and unrelated laws are listed here:

1. prohibited mixtures of seeds while planting a new vineyard (*kil'ayim*);
2. prohibition against harnessing an ox and donkey to the same plow;
3. prohibition against wearing garments woven of wool and flax (*sha'atnez*);
4. the obligation to wear *tzitzit*.

Can any link be established between them? In addition to Rashi's link cited above (Part Three), we may see a common denominator in items 1, 2, 3 of prohibitions against particular admixtures or combinations, while the obligation of *tzitzit* provides a contrast to the three prohibitions that precede it: Although mixtures are forbidden in planting, plowing and weaving, an exception is made for *tzitzit*, permitting the use of *sha'atnez* in their manufacture.

A more striking parallel to the prohibition against "mixing" species in planting or weaving would comprise the prohibition against mating two species (Va-Yikra 19:19), rather than harnessing them. This may account for the opinion of some exegetes that an ox and donkey cannot be harnessed together as a hedge against their subsequent mating.

❧ PART FIVE: WEIGHTS, MEASURES AND AMALEK

The last instance of propinquity [*semikhut parashiyot*] in this week's *sidrah* comes at its very end. In 25:13–16, the Torah warns against fraud in commerce, going even so far as to call it an "abomination" (*to'evah*). What follows thereupon (v. 17–19) is the retelling of the attack by Amalek shortly after the exodus from Egypt.

Rashi establishes a connection between these topics by proposing that the latter is a consequence of the former. In his words (actually, the words of the Midrash Tanhuma, which served as the source of many of his comments to this *sidrah*):

> If you cheat in the matter of weights and measures, be concerned about enemy provocation. To wit: "Fraudulent weights are an abomination to God" (Mishlei 11:1), and: "Intentional crime ushers in disgrace" (v. 2).

Note: Does the Tanhuma mean to suggest that the Israelites committed fraud in the desert prior to the Amalekite attack and, therefore, that they deserved it? While the natural inclination is to dismiss the Midrash as categorical (Amalek=any destructive consequence of anti-social behavior) rather than historical, it is nevertheless possible to read such an interpretation into the text of Shemot 16–17.

The attack by Amalek occurs in Refidim, where the Israelites arrived following the incident of the manna, in which weighing and measuring plays a prominent, albeit incongruous role. First of all, even though they effectively collect as much manna as they actually need, Moshe instructs them to procure "an *omer,*" a very precise amount. Second, and perhaps more telling, some of the Israelites "overdo it" (*marbeh*), which can be interpreted as an attempt to procure more than their fair share (v. 17–18), thereby committing fraud.

Ki Tavo'

Rashi and Philosophy

SOME THOUGHTS ON CRIME AND PUNISHMENT

℘ Preface

Following Nehama's habit of closely reading and examining Rashi's reliance upon his sources, we observe that Rashi, unlike the exegetes of medieval Spain and Provence, displays neither sustained nor systematic interest in philosophy. In the few instances in which he evinces such an interest, he generally relies upon Talmudic and Midrashic Aggadah rather than upon a philosophical system, *per se*, and certainly not a system with non-Jewish (i.e., Greek) roots. In this week's *sidrah*, we shall explore some of Rashi's sparse "philosophical" comments.

℘ Part One: Some Early Examples

The Tanakh makes certain absolute claims about and on behalf of God, such as: He is one and indivisible (Devarim 6:4); He is just (Bereishit 18:19; Devarim 32:4); He is omniscient (Daniel 2:22); and He experiences neither remorse nor regret (Bemidbar 23:19). Any verse that appears to contradict one of these – or similar – principles requires interpretation. It is in such cases that Rashi resorts to Midrash.

For an early instance, let us take Bereishit 11:5: "And God descended to view the city and tower [of Babel] built by the mortals." Since an omniscient God does not need to "visit the scene of the crime," so to speak, in order to know what transpired, what prompted God to "descend"?

Citing the Tanhuma, Rashi declares that God's "descent" was not to ascertain information about the incident, but to set a precedent for mortal judges, "not to convict the defendant" (*shelo yarshi'u ha-niddon*) until they had seen all the evidence and had obtained all the information about the case.

Indeed, Rashi handles the similar challenge posed by Bereishit 18:21: "Let me descend [to Sedom] and see," by declaring that it, too, is a precedent for mortal judges "not to render a capital verdict" (*shelo yifseku dinei nefashot*) without eyewitness testimony. (Here, Rashi refers explicitly to his earlier commentary.)

We may ask: Why, in the case of the tower of Babel, does Rashi speak about conviction in general, while in the case of Sedom he speaks more specifically about rendering a capital verdict? The answer, too, comes from the close reading of the context in which each comment appears.

Because the case of the generation of the dispersion (*dor ha-pallagah*) was not a capital case (i.e., unlike the Generation of the Flood, they were not destroyed) while that of Sedom was, God's "descent" – as it were – really comprised going down for a closer look. In the case of *Sedom*, the "cry" of the oppressed made it clear that a crime was being committed; God's "descent" was in the manner of "getting to the bottom" of the matter.

೫ PART TWO: CAN THE SLATE EVER BE WIPED CLEAN?

In the aftermath of the sin of the golden calf, Moshe successfully intercedes with God on behalf of Israel. In a process that bears a striking resemblance to the original theophany (revelation) at Mount Sinai, God passes before Moshe and declares His thirteen attributes of compassion.[1] Curiously, however, the litany of attributes concludes on a note of exacting vengeance: *ve-nakkeh – lo yenakkeh; poked 'avon avot...* (clearing – He will not clear; He takes note of the sin of fathers...).

Rashi (Shemot 34:7) accounts for the apparent contradiction by invoking the *peshat* of the verse, explaining that whereas God will never clear the guilty entirely, He will inflict their punishment incrementally. Then, citing the

---

[1] We are reluctant to translate *rahamim* as "mercy" because "mercy" shares an etymology with "mercenary," signifying something done in expectation of compensation. This is quite the opposite of the Hebrew term, derived from *rehem* (womb), which signifies a maternal feeling that is independent of any recompense. Etymologically speaking, an English equivalent of *rahamim*, i.e., sharing both its signification of a strong emotion as well as its derivation from the womb, would be "hysteria."

Midrash, Rashi also explains that God actually acts contradictorily, clearing the guilty if they repent and not clearing them if they don't, and taking note of the sins of the ancestors [only] when their descendants continue their iniquities.

The Midrashic explanation Rashi proffers sounds familiar; in fact, it is mentioned expressly in the Torah as part of the text of the second "commandment" (cf. Shemot 20:5 and Devarim 5:9). On the other hand, this appears to contradict another explicit verse: "Parents shall not be executed for the sins of children, nor children executed for the sins of parents" (Devarim 24:16).

Rashi's resolution of this contradiction is that children are punished only when they repeat the crimes of their parents. Alternatively, God, the subject of the second commandment, can and will exact punishment from children on account of their parents' deeds. A human court, the subject of Devarim 24:16, however, cannot and will not.

✑ PART THREE: DOES GOD REJOICE IN PUNISHING ISRAEL?

In this week's *sidrah*, we read the *tokhehah*, the divine remonstration with Israel, warning of the dire consequences that will occur should Israel violate the terms of its covenant with God. At one point (28:63), it even goes so far as to say: "Just as God [previously] rejoiced (*sas*) in your benefaction and expansion, so shall He rejoice (*yasis*) in your annihilation and destruction." The question arises automatically: While not denying divine justice its due process, will God actually rejoice in our punishment?

Rashi deals with this anomaly by interpolating the words "your enemies" between "rejoice" and "over you," implying that whereas God will cause our enemies to rejoice in our downfall, He will not, as it were, rejoice Himself.

Note: The text of Rashi's commentary on this verse is complicated. The earliest printed edition (Reggio de Calabria, 1475) contains only the aforementioned interpolation, but other manuscripts and printed editions contain an additional remark that is drawn from the Talmud, *Megillah* 10b:

> But God, Himself, does not rejoice. From this we [derive] that God never rejoices in the downfall of the wicked. The verse does not say *yasus*, but *yasis*; He causes others to rejoice [*mesis*], but He does

not rejoice [*sas*]. He does rejoice, however, in the benefaction of the righteous, to wit: "As God rejoices with you."

These two interpretations are entirely consistent. The verbal form *yasis* appears to be an extensive verb (*hiph'il*) rather than a simple one (*kal*), thus sustaining the Talmudic interpretation on grounds of *peshat*.

ஒ PART FOUR: WHILE WE'RE ON THE SUBJECT...

This week's *sidrah* contains but one of two Torah portions dealing with rebuke, the other coming in Behukotay. Indeed, one aspect of the divine warning appears in both portions, yet with a curious twist. A comparison between Va-Yikra 26:19 and Devarim 28:23 reveals both concurrence and divergence. Although both warn of dire famine, Va-Yikra compares heaven to iron and earth to bronze, while Devarim does the opposite.

Rashi's resolution of the contradiction (Va-Yikra 26:19) is based upon the appreciation of the specific nature of Sefer Devarim as Moshe's first-person narrative.[2] Accordingly, he explains the distinction between the two portions of rebuke as a difference between a threat uttered by God (Va-Yikra) and one delivered by Moshe (Devarim). Of the two, the more severe threat, of course, is that of God. Since iron is less permeable than bronze, an iron sky does not allow any moisture to exude; a bronze sky, however, does.

Once again, we may obtain support for this distinction in the *peshat* of the text. The verse in Va-Yikra is written in the active first person ("I shall make the sky iron"), implying that it is God Himself who is speaking, whereas the verse in Devarim uses the passive voice ("it shall come to pass…").

---

[2] See our unit on Devarim.

NITZAVIM

It's the *Tippehah* That Counts

RASHI AND *TA'AMEI HA-MIKRA*

&_D PREFACE

Nehama was well-versed in the functions of *ta'amei ha-mikra* (trope) and the value of applying them to understanding the Torah. In fact, during several years that her *gilyonot* were issued, she often supplemented them with a *daf* on *ta'amei ha-mikra* that was prepared by Michael Perlman, a member of Kibbutz Yavneh who had compiled a number of handbooks on the subject.

In this week's *sidrah*, we will have an opportunity to see how Rashi treated *ta'amei ha-mikra* as well as how he dealt with words that appear either rarely or in unusual forms, or combinations of words that raise grammatical or syntactical questions.

&_D PART ONE: WHO WILL SWEEP AWAY WHAT?

The entire nation of Israel gathers for Moshe's final exhortation. After reminding them, briefly, of the triumphs that God has engineered on their behalf, he warns them of the continuing presence in their midst of those who are still led astray by idolatry. Even after hearing Moshe's admonition, such people are likely to disregard it, saying: "I will have peace though I walk in the stubbornness of my own heart, with the result that the watered (*ha-ravvah*) will be swept away (*sefot*) along with the parched (*ha-tzemei'ah*)" (Devarim 29:18).

According to the *peshat*, this expression signifies totality, which is often represented literarily by the juxtaposition of extremes.[1] The use of "watered" and "parched," then, would signify that the consequence of stubbornness is total destruction.

Rashi, in contrast, treats the expression as a reference to the cause rather than the effect. According to his interpretation, the words "watered" and "parched" serve here as metaphors for the two principal categories of sin: deliberate/malicious (*meizid*) and inadvertent (*shogeg*). "Parched" signifies someone who sins out of need and desperation. "Watered" signifies one who need not sin, yet does so anyway.

✂ PART TWO: SHOULD IT BE "THIS" TORAH OR "THAT" TORAH?

Rashi's ability to "decode" the text of the Torah is not limited to the definitions of individual words. It included a thorough understanding of the rules of punctuation and the signs by which the Torah's syntax is indicated.

In this week's *sidrah*, the Torah is referred to as *be-sefer ha-torah ha-zeh* (29:20), whereas in last week's *sidrah*, it was referred to as *be-sefer hatorah ha-zot* (28:61). What is the difference between them, and which one is correct?

Actually, both are correct. *ha-zeh* and *ha-zot* are demonstrative adjectives; the former is masculine and modifies *sefer*, and the latter is feminine, modifying *torah*.

Rashi puts it as follows:

> "As written in this book of Torah." Earlier, however, it says: "In the book of this Torah." *ha-zot* is feminine and refers to Torah, while *ha-zeh* is masculine and refers to the book. By means of

---

[1] The juxtaposition of extremes to indicate entirety (e.g., *mi-katon ve-ad gadol*) provides an insight into Bereishit 14:23. In refusing a share in the spoils of Sedom that he had retrieved, Avraham declares that he will not take *mi-hut ve'ad serokh na'al*, usually interpreted as "neither a thread nor a shoelace." If the phraseology of *mi-* (from) *ve-ad* (up to) indicates totality, however, there is not much room between threads and shoelaces.

An alternative interpretation – designed to create a figure of inclusiveness – would take *hut* and *serokh* as threads that can be juxtaposed one to another. Since the *serokh* is used in shoes, the *hut* may well be the cord traditionally used to bind a headdress (such as a *kaffiyeh*) in place. The expression would then be the equivalent of "from head to toe."

punctuation marks (*pissuk ha-te'amim*) they are divided into two forms: In the rebuke (28:61), the *tippehah* appears beneath *ba-sefer,* thereby combining the words "this Torah" together, requiring the [feminine] *ha-zot.* Here (29:20), the *tippehah* appears beneath *torah,* thereby combining the words "Torah book" together, requiring the masculine form (*ha-zeh*) since it is the "book" that is being modified.

❧ PART THREE: MORE ABOUT *TA'AMEI HA-MIKRA*

Whereas our tradition of Torah punctuation goes back to Moshe Rabbeinu, the graphic symbols by which that tradition is represented, known as *ta'amei ha-mikra*, originated in the Middle Ages. Indeed, at one point (ninth–tenth century CE) there were no fewer than three separate systems of punctuation/accentuation in widespread use. One originated in Babylonia, while two originated in the Land of Israel. Eventually, one of the Land of Israel systems – named for the city of Tiberias in which it was developed (by the Ben Asher family) – supplanted the others and became the standard.

To make a complicated story simple, all *te'amim* fall into two categories: disjunctive (separators), called *melakhim* (kings), and conjunctive (connectors), called *meshartim* (servants). The separator with the greatest force is the *silluk* (a.k.a.: *sof pasuk*), the equivalent of a period at the end of a sentence. The next greatest break, called *etnahta*, equivalent, perhaps, to a colon, appears if there is a change within the sentence of either subject or verb. The *tippehah* is a disjunctive of a lower order (as is the *pashta*, which features in the explanation – below – of 31:26).

Two more verses in this (and next) week's *sidrah* feature a Torah book: 30:10 and 31:26. Look at them carefully and try to determine whether their syntax – particularly as indicated by the *ta'amei ha-mikra* – support the interpretation of Rashi that we saw above. [HINT: Look for the location of the *tippehah*!]

1. In 30:10, the *tippehah* beneath the word "Torah" indicates that the demonstrative adjective *ha-zeh* (this) is modifying the combined form "Torah-book."

2. In 31:26, the *pashta* above the word *torah* similarly indicates that it is connected to the previous word, *sefer*, creating, again, the combined form of "Torah-book" (*sefer ha-torah*).

❧ PART FOUR: MORE ABOUT SYNTAX: METONYMY AND ELLIPSIS

In the following three verses, we find an apparent syntactical dissonance similar to that of the Torah-book. Rashi, however, will demonstrate – as before – that there is agreement after all.

1. Shemot 3:5. God instructs Moshe to remove his shoes because the place he is treading upon is holy ground. Ordinarily, ground [*adamah*] is of the feminine gender, yet the verse here uses the masculine pronoun: *admat kodesh hu*.

2. Bereishit 13:9. Lot and Avraham are forced to part company because their combined property is too great for one land to sustain. The word for land [*eretz*] is feminine, yet the verse uses a masculine form of the verb sustain: *velo nasa' otam ha-aretz*.

3. Bereishit 15:17. God forged His covenant with Avraham after sunset. The word for sun [*shemesh*] is feminine, yet in describing its setting the Torah uses both a masculine form: *va-yehi* [and it was] and a feminine one: *ba'ah* [it set].

Rashi restores the syntactical coherence in several ways:

1. Whereas "ground" is feminine, "place" [*makom*] is masculine, and it is the place, not the ground, that is holy.

2. It is not the land, per se, that is capable or incapable of providing sustenance. It is the pasturage [*mir'eh*], which is grammatically masculine, that provides sustenance.

3. The subject of *va-yehi* is not the sun, but – implicitly – the matter that is transpiring, and matter [*davar*] is masculine. The verb *ba'ah* corresponds correctly to the sun in number and gender.

These syntactical adjustments have formal names. In #2, Rashi is using metonymy, a figure of speech consisting of the use of the name of one thing for that of another of which it is an attribute or with which it is associated, like the word "crown" in "land belonging to the crown." In #3, Rashi is using ellipsis, defined as the omission of one or more words that are obviously understood but that must be supplied to make a construction grammatically complete.

Would Rashi have recognized metonymy and ellipsis as formal exegetical devices or was he working intuitively? Metonymy is difficult to determine, but Rashi would have been right at home with ellipsis, which Hazal called either *derekh ketzarah* or *lashon katzer* (or *haser*).[2]

---

[2] On ellipsis, see Va-Yishlah, Part One.

VA-YELEKH

Elementary, My Dear Rashi

DIAGRAMMING A *KAL VA-HOMER*

ೂ PREFACE

The Midrash (*Bereishit Rabba* 92:7) notes that "ten instances of *kal va-homer* appear in the Torah." Rashi, in his commentary, takes particular note of only two: Bereishit 44:8 and Shemot 6:12.[1]

We shall see how Nehama treated the subject of *kal va-homer*, and then move along to her discussion of the word *ra'ah* as it appears in our *sidrah* and as it is treated by Rashi.

ೂ PART ONE: IF A, THEN SURELY B

When Yosef's brothers are arrested on the false charge of theft, they protest their innocence as follows:

> If we returned to you the money we found in our saddlebags on our return from Canaan, surely we would not steal silver or gold from the home of your master (Bereishit 44:8).

In this week's *sidrah*, Moshe employs a *kal va-homer* to chastise the people:

> If during my own lifetime among you, today, you are so rebellious against God, how much more so after my death? (31:27)

---

[1] Although the Midrash utilizes the term "Torah," it cites examples from *Nevi'im* and *Ketuvim* as well. The four actual Torah examples are the two verses noted by Rashi, the verse in our own *sidrah* and Bemidbar 12:14: "If her father had spat in her face...."

Nehama drew the following chart to display the attributes of *kal va-homer* as they appear in that verse and our own.

	Bereishit 44:8	Devarim 31:27
the minor proposition	**The money we found in our saddlebags** (we could have kept it)	**If while I am alive** (and have the opportunity to scold you)
data about minor	(we didn't keep it, rather) **We returned it to you**	**You are so rebellious against God**
the major proposition	**Money or silver belonging to your master** [Yosef] (that only an insolent person would dare touch)	**After my death** (when I can no longer restrain you)
conclusion of major	We **certainly** wouldn't steal it	You **certainly** will continue to rebel

(*Rashi's Commentary on the Torah*, 437)

Note: Using Nehama's chart, plot the *kal va-homer* appearing in Bemidbar 12:14.

✥ PART TWO: A LOGICAL DEDUCTION

In addition to the scriptural examples he notes, Rashi introduces a *kal va-homer* of his own in the text of his commentary on Bemidbar 30:6: "If her father annuls her [vow] on the day he hears of it… God will forgive her, for her father has annulled her."[2] Rashi explains:

---

[2] Whereas a *kal va-homer* may be offered independently, a *gezeirah shavah*, on the other hand, can only be implemented on the basis of a received tradition (cf. *Niddah* 19b). Since the effect of a *gezeirah shavah* is to replace the contextually appropriate meaning of a word with what amounts to a previously unrecognized homonym, if such substitutions could be made arbitrarily nothing short of lexicographical anarchy would ensue.

What [situation] is the verse describing? A woman who took the vows of a *nazir* and was annulled by her husband without her knowledge, who transgressed her vows by drinking wine and being defiled by a corpse. Such a woman requires forgiveness despite having been annulled.

And if those who were annulled still require forgiveness, how much more so those who were not annulled!

In other words, since the Nazirite vows were annulled by the husband according to the prerogative granted him by the Torah, then of what consequence is the woman's subsequent behavior? Retroactively, she has committed no crime, so why does she require forgiveness?

Nehama explains:

The answer comes from the Midrash Halakhah cited by Rashi, namely that we are dealing with a woman who didn't know that her vow had been annulled. Her transgression was intentional; she committed an act that was prohibited in her own eyes. Therefore, she requires forgiveness even if, technically, she didn't sin. "And if those who were annulled still require forgiveness, how much more so those who were not annulled!" A woman who would transgress the terms of a vow that had not been annulled would certainly require forgiveness and atonement (*op. cit.,* 438).

✇ PART THREE: "*RA'AH* IS BEFORE YOUR FACES"

The word *ra'ah* is a homonym. On occasion, it means a sin, while at other times it signifies the catastrophe that comes as punishment for the sin. In this week's *sidrah*, we find both usages.

- And I will surely hide My face on that day on account of all the evil (*ra'ah*) they shall have done (31:18);

- ... and evil (*ra'ah*) will befall you in the end of days (31:29).

Rashi, however, makes singular use of the word *ra'ah* in his commentary on Shemot 10:10. On account of the ambivalence surrounding its appearance in that verse, we shall provide several English translations of it. (Unlike Nehama, however, we are unable to provide the German translation of Buber-Rosenzweig as a contrast.)

In Hebrew, the verse reads: *re'u ki ra'ah neged peneikhem*. The translations [accompanied by the translators' notes] include:

- JPS (1917): See ye that evil is before your face.

- JPS (1962): Clearly, you are bent on mischief.

  [The "evil" is their intention to leave Egypt.]

- Aryeh Kaplan (1981): You must realize that you will be confronted by evil.

- Everett Fox (1983): You see – yes, your faces are set towards ill. [Cf. Abrabanel: Your evil intentions are written on your faces.]

- Robert Alter (2004): For evil is before your faces.

  [The most likely meaning is: You are headed for mischief.]

Rashi comments:

> Follow the Targum [*bisha*=wickedness]. I am acquainted with an Aggadic Midrash that there is a star named *ra'ah*. Pharaoh said to them: I have ascertained astrologically that this star will rise against you in the desert and its sign is blood and death. When Israel sinned with the [golden] calf and God sought their destruction, Moshe prayed, "Why should the Egyptians be able to say that they were taken out by *ra'ah*" (Shemot 32:12). This is what [Pharaoh] intended by: "See that *ra'ah* is before your faces." Immediately, "God had remorse over the evil (*ra'ah*)" and transformed the blood to the blood of circumcision.

૭ PART FOUR: *RA'AH* AND *RA*

Rashi's identification of *ra'ah* as a star, or an astrological sign, opens up another possibility for its identification: the Egyptian god Ra.

Nehama ordinarily eschewed the use of ancient Near Eastern texts in explicating Tanakh. She reasoned that if the Sages and medievals were able to make sense of Tanakh without knowledge of the ancient Near East, then it could not be indispensable to a proper understanding.[3] Nevertheless, her

---

[3] When invited by *Da'at Mikra* to prepare their commentary on Bereishit, Nehama declined. When I asked her why, she replied: Because I don't know the ancient Near East! When I pointed out that she always hastened to eschew ancient Near Eastern

voluminous readings in Bible commentaries of all ages and stripes acquainted her with the possibility. She writes:

> It is interesting to note that not only the Sages [of the Midrash] felt that the phrase "Ra' before your eyes" has accompanying nuances and a connotative significance. Modern scholars, too, have also recognized this and have offered the theory that Ra' and *ra'ah* in the verses cited by Rashi are an allusion to the Egyptian god Re, the sun god and head of the Egyptian pantheon. According to this, Pharaoh was saying to Moshe and Aharon: Know that my god will get you back!
>
> The explanation of the scholars does not contradict the basic meaning of the verse, which is: a catastrophe awaits you. [These] interpretations reveal allusions in the idolatrous king's words to his own spiritual world and echo his pagan outlook: The *ra'ah* he speaks of is neither sin nor its punishment, but a deity who acts arbitrarily or an astrological sign for blood and death (*Rashi's Commentary on the Torah*, 407).

---

texts, she clarified: One can *understand* Bereishit without the ancient Near East, but one cannot write a commentary on Bereishit without it.

HA'AZINU

A Truly "Super" Commentary

KELI YAKAR ON LIFE AND DEATH

ೲ PREFACE

Nehama, as we have noted, had frequent resort to the art of commentary *on* Rashi, known to scholars as "super-commentary."[1] The specific super-commentator we will focus on in this week's *sidrah* is R. Shlomo Ephraim of Lunshitz (1550–1619). R. Lunshitz, a student of the Maharshal (R. Shelomo Luria), served as rabbi and chief of the *beit din* of Prague. However, he was even more renowned as a *darshan* (preacher). Along with collections of his *derashot* (*'Ollelot Ephraim, 'Ir Gibborim*), he wrote a Torah commentary entitled *Keli Yakar,* one of whose facets is an explanation of and elaboration upon Rashi.

ೲ PART ONE: WHO'S WHO?

The *sidrah* begins with an invocation to listen attentively to the speaker. Who is the speaker? God, although throughout most of Devarim the first-person voice we have heard most often has been that of Moshe.[2] That appears to end with 30:1 (the beginning of Va-Yelekh), which, like most of Torah narrative, speaks of Moshe in the third-person. That is the mode with which the Torah continues (see 31:7: Moshe summoned Yehoshua; 31:14: God said to Moshe), concluding with the verse (31:30) that introduces this week's

---

[1] Nehama's aforementioned essay on Rashi's use of Aggadah begins with a list of twenty-three such super-commentaries (see Mikeitz, Part Four).

[2] Indeed, to let you in on a "secret" [*sod*], the third-person nature of the first eight verses of Devarim is so inconsistent with the tenor of the book that Ibn Ezra (Devarim 1:2) hints broadly that someone besides Moshe wrote them!

sidrah. Who is the audience? The intended audience is the Jewish people who have been gathered together by Moshe (29:9 ff.) for the purpose of renewing their covenant with God.

Why are heavens and earth addressed here in an anthropomorphic fashion?[3] In 30:19, God had already informed the Israelites that He was going to call the heavens and earth as witnesses. This speech appears to be what they will be required to testify to.

Why were they chosen as witnesses? Rashi gives two answers. First of all, they were chosen because they are eternal and would be able to testify in perpetuity to what God had said. Moreover [*ve-'od*], Torah law (Devarim 17:7) requires witnesses to take the lead in administering justice to the defendant, and heavens and earth would be instrumental in rewarding or punishing Israel by granting or withholding rain and produce (see Devarim 11:14, 17).

❧ PART TWO: WHAT IN HEAVEN'S NAME IS WRONG WITH THAT?

Keli Yakar is troubled by Rashi's formulation of his response. It is not clear to him whether Rashi is proposing one solution to why they were chosen as witnesses, or two.[4] Since both parts of Rashi's response relate to the function of heavens and earth as witnesses, why does he introduce the latter part with "moreover" as though it were a separate interpretation? In any case, how can heavens and earth testify when they are mute?

Keli Yakar's answer is that heavens and earth need not "speak;" their very existence testifies to the ongoing covenantal relationship between God and Israel. *Keli Yakar* reminds us of an Aggadic theme – introduced by the Talmud (*Shabbat* 68) and alluded to by Rashi – to the effect that creation was conditional on the eventual acceptance and observance of Torah. In that case, the mere existence of heavens and earth offers testimony that Torah is still being observed since otherwise they would have reverted – as God threatened – to the *tohu va-bohu* from which they originally emerged.

---

[3] *Anthropos* is Greek for man; *morphos* is Greek for body. The adjective "anthropomorphic" means to have the properties or qualities of a human body, such as ears and the ability to listen.

[4] It appears from his remarks that some texts of Rashi he consulted contained the word *ve-'od* [moreover] while others may have read [*le-'olam*] *va-'ed* [forever].

Rashi refers to this theme in his commentary on Bereishit 1:31. Noting that the Torah applies the definite article [*ha-*] only to the sixth day, Rashi says it alludes to the sixth day of Sivan, the day on which the Torah was given. Where does God threaten the world with extinction? Yirmiyahu 33:25: "Thus said the Lord: if not for My Torah, by day and by night, I would not have appointed the ordinances of heavens and earth."

Note: I have been consistently using the plural form "heavens" for *shamayim* instead of the singular "heaven" because Biblical Hebrew regards it as a plural noun. In Yesha'ayahu 65:17 (and 66:22), for instance, *shamayim* takes the plural adjective *hadashim* (whereas *eretz*, in both cases, takes the feminine singular *hadashah*), and in Tehillim 19:2, they take the plural verb *mesapperim*.

✌ PART THREE: MAN IN THE MIDDLE?

Keli Yakar continues by asking why the continued existence of heavens and earth should depend on Torah. He explains that celestial and terrestrial bodies are opposites and neither would survive without something mediating between them. That mediator is man, who was created out of a combination of "dirt from the ground" and "a divine breath."

What mediates between the celestial and terrestrial elements in man? Torah. Were it not for his observance of Torah, man would be characterized by his terrestrial (bestial) origins.

✌ PART FOUR: A MATTER OF LIFE AND DEATH

A final contribution from *Keli Yakar* relates to verse 39: "I kill and I make alive." While Rashi offers no commentary, Rashbam interprets it in light of verse 37, in which the other nations questioned God's existence because He seemingly was unable to protect His people. In response, God points to His ability to take life and restore it.

Life and death here can be understood either literally or figuratively.

According to the *peshat* of the verse, the other nations have dismissed God's provenance over the Jewish people because they have been able to kill them, i.e., to defeat them in battle. God's response is to demonstrate His provenance through the reassurance that while that may have been the case in the past, from now on [Hizkuni: *mi-kan va-elakh*] He will defend them and, consequently, guarantee them life.

According to *Keli Yakar,* however, life and death here are metaphors for exile and redemption. He interprets the double use of "I" [*ani ani hu... ani amit...va-ani erpa*] as an allusion to a two-part redemption: physical and spiritual. The physical redemption is the release of the Jewish people from the yoke of foreign sovereignty. The spiritual redemption is their release from the yoke of the evil impulse, which will be nullified in the World to Come. He writes:

> In exile, we are considered as though we were dead. At the time of the redemption, however, God will restore us to life.[5]

---

[5] I have expanded *Keli Yakar's* theme of exile and redemption in my chapter on Ha'azinu in *Hogim ba-parashah* (edited by Naftali Rothenberg; Jerusalem: Yedi'ot Aharonot, 2005), 630–637.

VE-ZOT HA-BERAKHAH

Changing the Lineup

THE ORDER OF BLESSING FOR YAAKOV AND MOSHE

ဢ PREFACE

Nehama observed that:

> In the opening verse, Moses is given a title that has never been accorded him previously in the Torah: ... *the man of God*.
>
> Some commentators consider that this title was accorded him to stress the prophetic origin and force of the words he utters there; that they did not merely proceed from his own mouth, but were endowed with Divine authority. This is the view of Ibn Ezra.
>
> An opposite view is taken by other commentators including Rabbi S.R. Hirsch. The title implies, on the contrary, that that these were Moses's own words... (*Studies in the Weekly Sidrah*, first series, 48).

Whichever view we adopt, this observation prompts us to consider the contrast between the sequence in which Moshe blesses the people (ostensibly, his own choice) and the sequence in which the Torah relates their blessings by Yaakov (ostensibly, on "Divine authority").

Whenever we are required to put a list of people "in order," the question arises: In which order? Do we arrange them by age or by size? Do we start with the youngest or oldest, with the largest or smallest?[1] Throughout the Torah, the twelve tribes are listed several times, with their order changing according to the circumstances. (See, *inter alia*, Bereishit 35:23 ff., 46:8 ff.; Shemot 1:2ff.) In this unit, we shall examine some of those appearances.

---

[1] See our discussion of the daughters of Tzelafhad in the units on Noah and Mas'ei.

Note: Their birth order was: Reuven, Shim'on, Levi, Yehudah (Leah); Dan, Naftali (Bilhah); Gad, Asher (Zilpah); Yissakhar, Zevulun (Leah); Yosef, Binyamin (Rahel).

✂ PART ONE: IN WHAT ORDER DO THE TRIBES LINE UP BEFORE YAAKOV?

Let us begin with the order in which Yaakov "blesses" his sons.[2] Yaakov first blesses his grandsons, Efraim and Menasheh – inverting their birth order – before turning to his own sons.

a) He reverts to Reuven, the firstborn, and continues, in order, through Yehudah;

b) Then he blesses Zevulun and Yissakhar out of turn, as well as inverting their own birth order;

c) Dan, Gad, Asher and Naftali are next, with Naftali out of birth sequence;

d) Finally, Yosef and Binyamin.

Let us now attempt to provide a rationale for his actions:

a) The precedence given to Efraim and Menasheh is due to the fact that Yosef brought them along on his visit to his ailing father. As long as they were there, albeit coincidentally, he blessed them first. The inversion of their birth order is explained by Yaakov himself (and is reminiscent of similar inversions of siblings starting with Kayyin and Hevel).

b) The formal blessings, however, begin with the firstborn, Reuven, and by continuing through Yehudah they give the impression that Yaakov intends to follow the birth order all the way through.

c) The interruption of the birth order by Yissakhar and Zevulun, however, suggests that what Yaakov really had in mind was to sort his sons by birth-mothers. The precedence of Zevulun over Yissakhar, though, has no apparent reason.

---

[2] See our study on Va-Yehi, where we dealt with the misnomer "blessing" in this context.

d) The postponement of Naftali until after Gad and Asher has no apparent reason.

e) The blessings conclude, appropriately, with the last two sons born.

ಶ PART TWO: IN WHAT ORDER DO THE TRIBES LINE UP BEFORE MOSHE?

Rather than following Yaakov's precedent, Moshe bestows his blessings upon them in an entirely different sequence:

a) He begins with Reuven, skips Shim'on, and inverts Levi and Yehudah;

b) Binyamin and Yosef follow, in that order;

c) Zevulun and Yissakhar are inverted;

d) Gad, Dan, Naftali, Asher preserves the correct order of the two in the middle, at the expense of the first and last.

A possible rationale for Moshe's actions is:

a) Beginning with Reuven, the firstborn, seems to be S.O.P. The elimination of Shim'on is without obvious reason (although the behavior of Zimri is suggestive, cf. Ibn Ezra Devarim 33:6), and the inversion of Yehudah and Levi may be Moshe's attempt not to show favoritism to his own tribe.

b) The interpolation of Yosef and Binyamin could be an attempt to distribute the blessings on a more equitable basis, based upon matrilineal relationships.

c) The interpolation of Yissakhar and Zevulun may also be matrilineally inspired – an attempt to group together the children of Leah and Rachel in the beginning with the children of Bilhah and Zilpah grouped together at the end. The precedence of Zevulun over Yissakhar, again (!), has no apparent reason.

d) Neither is there an apparent reason for the precedence of Gad over Dan and Naftali, nor for Gad's separation from his brother, Asher.

℘ PART THREE: RASHI ATTEMPTS TO ACCOUNT FOR THE CHANGES

Of all the aberrations we have cited above, Rashi addresses a single one – albeit the only one that is common to both Yaakov and Moshe – namely, the inversion of Zevulun and Yissakhar. Rashi's explanation is that Zevulun's precedence over Yissakhar is on account of an arrangement imputed to them by the Aggadah. Since it was Zevulun's commercial activity that made Yissakhar's Torah study possible, Zevulun deserves to be mentioned first.

Equally curious, however, is the fact that Rashi addresses this inversion only in Devarim. Why does he not offer this explanation in Bereishit, too? In fact, Rashi, in Bereishit, does not address any of our questions and does not appear concerned with the sequence of the blessings at all! If that is the case, why does he bother with the inversion in Devarim? Perhaps because of the use, here, of the conjunction *ve-Yissakhar*, implying that their inversion is due, somehow, to the nature of their relationship.

Note: In Devarim, Rashi also deals with the elimination of Shim'on and the out-of-sequence appearance of Yehudah, explaining (33:7) that Moshe deliberately left Shim'on out on account of the episode with the Midianite women at Shittim and then grouped Yehudah with Reuven because they were the ones who admitted their guilt in (similar) questionable moral actions.

℘ PART FOUR: OTHER PARSHANIM

Whereas Rashi, as noted, makes no attempt to account systematically for all the changes, other medieval *parshanim* (exegetes) do.

Ibn Ezra

In Bereishit (49:13), Ibn Ezra explains that Yaakov's blessing places Yissakhar between Zevulun and Dan because that is where his apportioned territory lay geographically. (In Devarim, in contrast, Ibn Ezra offers no comment at all.)[3]

---

[3] Hizkuni gives the same explanation in Bereishit as Ibn Ezra. While we have a tendency to view the approach of French exegetes, such as Hizkuni (R. Manoah ben Hizkiyah, thirteenth century), as incompatible with that of Ibn Ezra, this is a generalization often belied by the facts on the ground.

Ramban

In Devarim 33:6, Ramban deals at considerable length with the question of the sequence, subjecting both Rashi's and Ibn Ezra's interpretations to cross-examination. His conclusion, based on that of Ibn Ezra, is that the sequence here is determined by the eventual apportionment of land (see Yehoshua 13:15 ff.).

a) Reuven received his allocation first (in Trans-Jordan), hence he is cited first.

b) Yehudah was the first tribe to receive its allocation on the West Bank, hence he is cited second.

c) He is followed by Levi, whose principal allocation was Yerushalayim, which was in the precinct of Yehudah.

d) Next is Binyamin, whose allocation was also adjacent to Yehudah, included part of Yerushalayim, and was also heavily populated by *leviyyim*.

e) Yosef is next because he was adjacent to Binyamin geographically.

f) Zevulun precedes Yissakhar because he received his allocation first (Yehoshua 19:10, 17).

g) Gad precedes the other sons of the *shefahot* (Bilhah and Zilpah) because his allocation came with that of Reuven (in Trans-Jordan).

The most striking instance of "fraternization" between Ibn Ezra and the French exegetes of the school of Rashi (i.e., the *ba'alei ha-tosafot*) concerns the likelihood of an actual encounter between the Spanish sage and Rashbam. See Norman Golb, *History of the Jews in Rouen in the Middle Ages* (Hebrew; Tel Aviv: 1976).

∾ An Afterword

Nehama's observation about the phrase "man of God," with which we began this final *sidrah,* is matched by a similar observation she makes in its continuation. It merits specific mention here because what she has to say about Moshe Rabbeinu is fitting to serve as her own epitaph.

> However, he is accorded yet another title in the very last action associated with him, a title that had previously been employed by the Almighty when He rebuked Miriam and Aaron for speaking ill of Moses and comparing themselves with him.
>
> There, God called him "My servant Moses" (Bemidbar 12:7), which is, no doubt, the highest honor that could be paid him.
>
> "So Moses the servant of the Lord died there" (Devarim 34:5) (*op. cit.*).

It behooves us to close here with an encomium to Nehama's lifetime of selfless service: to her family, her students, and, above all, to God. Small wonder, then, that her actual epitaph, at her own insistence, reads simply *"Morah"* – teacher. She would have declined the comparison with Moshe Rabbeinu categorically and adamantly, but, as we noted in our Introduction, Nehama's innate modesty was yet another trait they shared.

יהי זכרה ברוך.

May our recollections of her, and of the Torah she
taught us, continue to be a blessing.

Rabbi Dr. Moshe Sokolow is the Fanya Gottesfeld Heller Professor of Jewish Education at the Azrieli Graduate School of Jewish Education and Administration of Yeshiva University. He studied with Nehama Leibowitz (1905–1997) and translated and edited *Nehama Leibowitz: On Teaching Tanakh* (New York: 1987), *Nehama Leibowitz: Active Learning in the Teaching of Jewish History* (New York: 1989), and *Mafteah ha-Gilyonot: An Index to Nehama Leibowitz's Weekly Parshah Sheets* (New York: 1993). Rabbi Professor Sokolow is the author of numerous scholarly and popular articles on Bible and has conducted a weekly class on the *sidrah* at Lincoln Square Synagogue in New York City for more than twenty years.